ELUSIVE CHILDHOOD

ELUSIVE
CHILDHOOD

Impossible Representations
in Modern Fiction

Susan Honeyman

THE OHIO STATE UNIVERSITY PRESS

Columbus

Library of Congress Cataloging-in-Publication Data

Honeyman, Susan.
  Elusive childhood : impossible representations in modern fiction / Susan Honeyman.
      p. cm.
  Includes bibliographical references (p.   ) and index.
  ISBN 0-8142-1004-X (cloth : alk. paper) − ISBN 0-8142-9082-5 (cd-rom)
  1. American fiction−20th century−History and criticism. 2. Children in literature.
  I. Title.
  PS374.C45H66 2005
  813'.5093523−dc22
                              2005006677

Cover design by Janna Thompson-Chordas.
Text design and typesetting by Jennifer Shoffey Forsythe.
Type set in Adobe Caslon.
Printed by Thomson-Shore, Inc.

The paper used in this publication meets the minimum requirements of the American
National Standard for Information Sciences−Permanence of Paper for Printed Library
Materials. ANSI Z39.48-1992.

9 8 7 6 5 4 3 2 1

contents

⫷ acknowledgments ⫸

*T*his book began as my dissertation at Wayne State University under the guidance of Ross Pudaloff, John Reed, and Barrett Watten, to whom I am grateful for their individual expertise, breadth, and willingness to try something new. I am also indebted to several scholars who gave me, a complete stranger, crucial advice that led to this publication: Beverly Lyon Clark, Karen Coats, Richard Flynn, and James Kincaid. Thanks to my editor Heather Lee Miller for being available (even when on leave) and defending my work; also thanks to the Research Services Council at the University of Nebraska at Kearney for a grant aiding completion, to Justin Sevenker for the index, and to artist Joseph P. Ascherl for generously sharing his *Moby-Dick* map. My appreciation for permission to reprint previously published excerpts from *Mosaic* 34.2:117–32 (2001), *The Henry James Review* (courtesy of The Johns Hopkins University Press), and *Children's Literature in Education* 35.4:347–66 (2004), and many thanks to all comrades and acquaintances (too many to name all here) who led me to new and exciting sources: Tina Zawacki, Heidi Eichbauer, Marguerite Tassi, Shaun Padgett, Nanne Olds, and Mary Pickering.

William Avilés has shared his love, insight, and collectable comics. To pool partner and drinking buddy Peter Zeiler, thank you for your unflagging humor and support throughout grad school. And to my beloved friend Anne Turner, who would tell me I was brilliant even when I couldn't remember things like the main character's name in *Billy Budd*, my deepest gratitude.

Thanks to my mother, Mary Honeyman, whose respect for children, I hope, resonates here. Thanks to my nieces, Ashley, Jamie, and Becca Honeyman, who serve as refreshing reminders that children aren't just inscrutable, they are fascinating people.

Finally, I would like to dedicate this book to the family (and memory) of Anne Turner, who died from cancer less than a month after I defended my dissertation. Her brother, Jay, told this story at her memorial:

> It all started when my parents discovered teeth marks on the top corner of their dresser. I couldn't really explain to you now why I happened to chew on that corner. It just seemed like the thing to do at the time and it seemed to satisfy my appetite for destruction. I was the first of the usual suspects my parents rounded up and was subjected to their standard interrogation procedure. During the questioning, I calmly stated that I was unaware of how the marks got there but that I would certainly look into the matter.
>
> Left with only one other possible suspect, my parents confronted Anne, believing that they had apprehended the guilty party. After all, the corner of the dresser came up to the level of Anne's mouth, not mine, never once considering that I had stood tiptoe at that corner. During the interrogation my parents informed Anne that they knew that one of us had committed this infraction. In one of her earliest feats of dizzying logic and self-assurance, Anne replied, "How do we know that one of you didn't do it?"

This question should resonate throughout my book, culminating in the final chapter. The retort, "How do I know?" is not childish preamble to elusive legalese—it protests that truth is not the issue in such conversations, authority is. And kids seem to understand that the power imbalance (where knowledge and age have the potential to override intuition, and sometimes even the truth) can relegate whatever they do know to inconsequentiality when measured against adult interests. According to this anecdote, Anne and Jay Turner weren't innocent—they hid the truth—but Anne's question cuts to the point that innocence or guilt doesn't necessarily matter. What matters is that parents have the power to decide, if they choose, because they "say so." And kids might resist by questioning their say.

⇥ introduction ⇥

"INTERPRETATION IS NOTHING BUT THE
POSSIBILITY OF ERROR."
—Paul de Man (*Blindness and Insight*, 141)

*A*t the beginning of Alice Childress's *A Hero Ain't Nothin' but a Sandwich* (1973), 13-year-old Benjie Johnson explains, "Don't nobody wanta be no chile cause, for some reason, it just hold you back in a lotta ways" (9). He complains of alienation in his family and school system, as well as his unmet need for recognition and freedom: "bein a chile is bein a slave" (76). From this position he easily exposes the unknowing rhetorical level on which well-meaning adults, like his teacher Bernard Cohen, fail to fully respect those his age: "He say, 'You can be somebody if you want.' How the shit he don't know I'm somebody right now?" (89). Benjie's (and Childress's) point cannot be taken lightly. Though focusing intently on Benjie's identity, the fact that his teacher's rhetoric places that identity outside of his present experience rejects Benjie's existing selfhood. We imply the same dismissal through common rituals like asking children, "What do you want to be when you grow up?" In fact, the more common the phrase, the more automatically and guiltlessly we overlook the exclusionary ideology it can implicitly carry. This is particularly true of adult discourse with children, who might be at a linguistic disadvantage and so more silenced by our words than we realize. We need to pay closer attention to the silencing effects of our rhetoric and recognize (and encourage) the potential resistance imposed silences can harbor.

What Althusser has said of ideology is still a common premise for post-structuralists, post-modernists, constructivists, and devotees of deconstruction: "It is indeed a peculiarity of ideology that it imposes obviousnesses as obviousnesses, which we cannot *fail to recognize*" (161). That which is obvious requires no further proof; so, pre-scripted ideological "truths" enable us to accept unquestioningly, with the unfortunate consequence of muting other perspectives. In modern Western culture, the obviousnesses of childhood have been: children are helpless; children should be protected; and if children do wrong, it is because they do not know any better. And yet, if we actually look at individual experiences, examining those whom we have discursively set apart as children, we are likely to note only exceptions that unravel the parameters of that definition, unless, that is, we persist on seeing what we want to see. Either way, we are interpreting children in reference to an arbitrary and narrow standard and trying to pass off our interpretations as "truths." But interpreting is selective and involves a narrowing of perspective that, in Althusser's terms, *denegates* other possible interpretations when we read manifestations of culture—social roles, shared public expectations, and stereotypes. This denegation and the large perceptual blind spot it creates remain largely uncontradicted where children are concerned, because the very ideologies that shape our perceptions of them pre-determine that we view them as not having agency or consequence in ideology—they are helpless, they are innocent, they are too ignorant to represent themselves. This might seem an overstatement, which is true. Western discourse generalizes about children with such unchecked confidence that it is difficult to address the issue without sweeping absolutes. But, as Paul de Man explains, "What we call ideology is precisely the confusion of linguistic with natural reality" (*Resistance* 11). The linguistic "truths" in adult discourse on childhood only appear "obvious" because we accept them for natural reality—they are pre-totalized for us and restrict our comprehension beyond.[1]

In this book I attempt to deconstruct the flawed interpretive process as it has pertained to the concept of childhood—in literature, developmental theory, and popular discourse. I seek to demonstrate the great but underestimated extent to which we impose "childhood" on those we define as children according to biased standards of adult nostalgia and desire. These standards and impositions reveal a slow backlash from the Age of Reason embedded in both romantic and modern notions of childhood: a need to escape the burden of rationalist epistemologies, their demands for hyperliterate knowledge, and the responsibilities of power. The concept of childhood serves as a *tabula rasa* for adult constructions, which seem all the more legitimate for their lack of opposition, as discursive boundaries already exclude possible counter-expressions from unspeaking or illiterate young still in the process of achieving the socialized means to power in adult ideologies—mastery of literate language. My goal is to illustrate our pervasive silencing of those we call children, show the inconsistent imposition entailed in that labeling, raise awareness of how we deny this impos-

ing process and our complicity in it, and, most importantly, expose overlooked opportunities for subversion fostered by these imposed silences.

To do so I will need to focus primarily on childhood discourse itself
(not the actual persons subject to it) and the embedded biases of those who
produce it. Whether out of resentment toward the responsibilities of
adulthood, desire for youthfulness, or hopes for an escape from the trappings of logic and language grown rusty and inflexible with use, adults
construct childhood based on biases that are personal, constantly changing, and often contradictory.

There is no irrefutable or universal meaning of "child." Experience and
basic human individuality make it impossible to generalize a definition, yet
we often try, like Humbert Humbert, to "fix" childhood. In the West adults
have generally insisted that childhood is innocent (or ignorant in the Puri-
tan tradition), pre-sexual, irrational, and unschooled, but without verifica-
tion from persons so defined, all that these definitions can really tell us is
that we construct childhood as such in order to protest that adulthood is
experienced, sexual, rational, and schooled.

The modern concept of childhood evolved with and in contrast to the
Enlightenment ideal of rational adulthood, in response to a chain of events
that followed the advent of printing: increased literacy, public education,
and the defining of developmental stages toward a goal of maturity. Neil
Postman argues that

> Almost all of the characteristics we associate with adulthood are those that
> are (and were) either generated or amplified by the requirements of a fully
> literate culture: the capacity for self-restraint, a tolerance for delayed grat-
> ification, a sophisticated ability to think conceptually and sequentially, a
> preoccupation with both continuity and the future, a high valuation of rea-
> son and hierarchical order. (99)

Literacy has produced rationalist adults. We are trained to impose linearity and analytical framing on our perceptions, even when they can only be
validated by relativistic rhetoric.

The novelist is no exception. To represent creatively requires models as
common frames of reference for author and reader. Models, always generalizing (thus, essentializing), appeal to an adult rationalist's tendency to
categorize, explain, and pin truths. For the novelist, whose task depends
upon language entirely; whose narrative mode, no matter how experimental in terms of chronology, depends upon linearity for its execution; whose
genre, no matter how dramatic and "objective" in point of view, springs

from and inspires interpretive thought; these essentializing tendencies emerge. At the same time, the impulse to flatly stereotype identity is frustrated by a commitment to truthfully represent others, real or imagined. Dorrit Cohn has pointed out that "Narrative fiction is the only literary genre, as well as the only kind of narrative, in which the unspoken thoughts, feelings, perceptions of a person other than the speaker can be portrayed" (*Transparent Minds* 7). When the novelist tries to bridge subjectivities to convincingly "get into the mind" of and create a character, he/she has to rely on speculation. Yet, as Cohn states, "the special life-likeness of narrative fiction—as compared to dramatic and cinematic fictions—depends on what writers and readers *know least in life:* how another mind thinks, another body feels" (my italics, 5–6). No matter how empathetic, we are limited by our differing socialization and experience in our abilities to understand, let alone represent, others.

In fictively and academically representing the social, subjective position of those we call children, even the illusion of an inter-subjective link between adult writer and child is impossible. As James Kincaid explains in *Erotic Innocence,* the essentialist notion of "the child" evolved as "everything the sophisticated adult was not, everything the rational man of the Enlightenment was not" (15). Thus, the concept of childhood has been defined by adult discourse as that which cannot engage adult discourse. There is a language gap, an inherent inaccessibility, between the concept of "child" and the adult minds that create it. The position of childhood is typically constructed as prelapsarian, relatively preverbal, outside empowered discourse, unsophisticated, unknowing, irrational—the very opposite of (though constantly shifting to foil) "adulthood." Childhood is whatever adults have lost and maybe never had. How can any adult writer convincingly represent such an inconsistent and imaginary position with any sense of authority? The first chapters of my book ponder the impossibility of such representations, especially in fiction, and the ways in which some writers have dealt with the resulting challenge.

Western scholarship has not satisfactorily dealt with it yet. The inaccessibility of those we call children has been glossed over or carefully explained away by psychoanalysts and developmental psychologists (at best circumvented through play therapy) for a century. The gap in understanding caused by adult language and socialization demands mediation but allows no means. Tim Morris writes, "Childhood is a form of Otherness, possibly its archetypal form" (9), yet the necessity of an ethnographic approach to the subject of childhood is frequently overlooked because we imagine children are accessible and essentially definable. Jay Mechling has explained the difficulty of overcoming this presumption, even within cultural anthropology and folklore: "The white, male folklorist recognizes that he will never really know what it means to be a black woman, but we all think we know what it means to be a child" (91). If our only link to re-experiencing what it is like to be treated as a child[2] is through our admittedly unreliable, selective, and highly suggestive memories, we do not really know. All we know is a composite stereotype we create and impose upon young people who (can be made to seem to) fit it.

Childhood, then, is not an essentially definable position but a cultural construct. This is not to say that younger and older persons are indistinct, or that perceptible differences should be denied, or even that we have imagined our own childhoods (that is, those of us who grew up in cultures and families that could afford such a luxury for their young). It is to say, however, that one cannot generalize based on those differences—the cultural relativity of child-identification must at all times be acknowledged lest we blindly disregard a young person's individuality, potential, and basic human rights.

Illustrating the difficulty of rigorous contructivist reevaluations in the face of stubborn essentializing, Jean Baudrillard uses childhood as his example: "If, going against every assumption, you maintain the little utopian fact that childhood does not exist and that the child is perhaps the only one to know it, then everything blows up in your face" (*Baudrillard Live*, 112). With post-structuralist approaches to subjectivity and difference, this is precisely what has happened. In 1960 Philippe Ariès declared that childhood is a relatively recent "invention" of Western culture—a social construct rather than a biological fact. Though he has since been refuted as an empirically applicable historian, his premise has informed subsequent studies of childhood, and most current scholars heed his warning that "we must never forget to what extent [the] representation of childhood remains relative" (32). As we question the assumptions made in adult constructions of childhood, illusions of defining such a position break down. In most literature and academia, except for the fields of folklore and cultural anthropology, the voices of those we label children have been excluded from empowered discourse (or heavily mediated within it). Consequently, we are left with the realization that our discourse defines children from adult points of view without authorizing our representations through those represented. I have chosen to investigate literary attempts to represent the position of childhood despite (and in light of) this fact.

Writers often utilize childhood as a ludic space through which to criticize the adult world. In doing so, they mimic social constructions of childhood, exposing the very constructedness of such representations, decentering the adult discourse that created them. In modern American fiction, there is a tendency to stage or spatialize the position we call childhood—avoiding impossible interior "glimpses" into the minds of child figures by focusing on the spaces they might inhabit. This technique reflects an increasing belief in the social construction of identity, but also a self-consciousness regarding the challenge that childhood poses in terms of representation, as there is no accessible referent to study. I will concentrate on techniques that authors have used to depict childhood in spite of their awareness of the impossibility of verifying their accuracy. These include externally focalizing narratives (decreasing the otherwise necessary illusions of agency and presence), depicting childhood as a mappable but uninhabitable space (reflecting that childhood is a socially determined and culturally isolated position), reversing the fundamental narrative on which modern constructions of childhood depend (namely, that of development), and attacking the authority of discourse itself (in this sense defining childhood as that which lies outside of it). All of these techniques, in attempting to forge *alternatives to constructing* "the child," can in fact only pose *alternative constructions*. In my analysis I argue that these reconstructions reflect adult desires for resistance to our rationalist upbringings and longings for an impossible escape from discursive power in all its dependence and insistence upon linear, analytical, and paradigmatic thought.

chapter 1

A CHILDHOOD STUDIES PRIMER

*L*iterary childhood studies has emerged from traditional children's literature criticism under the influence of the identity politics of cultural studies, to reevaluate the dubious definition of its genre by "intended audience." This reevaluation has already allowed for an expanded focus and interchange within the otherwise "adult" canon, from which cultural critics feel freer to sample "children's texts." It should also encourage critics traditionally restricted to the child-canon to reconsider (more radically) the boundaries and agendas of that canon.

From its inception, the study of children's literature as a separate genre has posed problems. Many children's literature critics have been restrained by the limits of the field, as defining the field's genre by audience (i.e., "for children") runs counter to the professed aims of many children's literature authors and critics. P. L. Travers, creator of Mary Poppins, has said, "There is no such thing as a *children's* book. There are simply books of many kinds and some of them children read. I would deny, however, that [they were] written *for* children" (my italics, qtd. in Haviland 155). My impression is that many writers with a supposed age-defined audience agree with Travers. To name only the first few that come to mind, Russell Hoban, Roald Dahl, Chris Van Allsburg, Robert Cormier, and J. K. Rowling have made similar admissions. We will further discuss the impossibility of defining a juvenile audience, but Travers makes a good starting point: to read any work as exclusive to an age group discredits its artistry and reach.

American literary criticism has traditionally upheld the isolation of "children's literature" and has suffered for it. Although during the 1970s and 1980s the formerly white, male canon democratically expanded, Tim

Morris points out that "restructuring the canon to include texts by women and nonwhite writers did not extend to an inclusion of texts for children" (3). The introduction of identity politics to the literary curriculum failed to bring attention to the factor of age. When literature for children gained scholarly attention outside of children's literature criticism, it was generally marginalized as "popular culture," indicating a "low-brow" niche in literary academia.[1]

From the grown-up side of the canon's age-divide, Reinhard Kuhn's *Corruption in Paradise* (1982), a keen study of the figuration of children, comprehensively surveys modern Western literature without consulting "children's" books (except the predictable crossover *Alice* books, which he insists on attributing to the mathematician Charles Dodgson, not his nonsense-persona Lewis Carroll, as if to distance himself and the two). The age segregation attributed to audience has been kept so constant in literary criticism that comprehensive single-author studies often entirely overlook crossover titles. Even now it is difficult to find scholarly discussion of an author's crossover text, because it is lost in the divide. Many artists in the adult canon (Langston Hughes, James Baldwin, Donald Barthelme, Gwendolyn Brooks, Toni Morrison, John Updike, James Thurber, and Kurt Vonnegut, to name a few) have written picture books that remain relatively untreated by scholars because they are held apart as (academically liminal) irrelevant diversions. By merging canons, or simply breaking such outmoded barriers, scholars (especially those interested in childhood as a subject) will have a broader and more realistically complex range for contextualization as well as more comprehensive discursive evidence for analysis.

Even more troubling to the field of children's literature is the condescension implicit in its prescriptive classification. Though the term "women's reading" was widely understood to indicate socially permissible reading for women in the nineteenth century, such marginalization of readings and readers is no longer acceptable. In fact, curricula for "women's literature" and "African-American literature" reflect the chosen or perceived identity of the authors, not the supposed identity of suitable readers. If this were true of "children's literature," the canon would be reduced to a negligible number of titles. The only two "classics" I can think of that would fit are nine-year-old Daisy Ashford's *The Young Visiters* (1919) and thirteen-year-old Anne Frank's *Diary of a Young Girl* (1947), neither of which, ironically, fits common standards of reading *for* children.[2]

Maria Tatar does not exaggerate the extent to which young people are excluded from the definition and production of literature that hails them:

"Adults not only have almost exclusive control over the public production of words and images for children, they also have virtually exclusive rights when it comes to the task of interpretation" (276). Parents and educators dominate the market, at least exercising veto power, which often directly results in censorship. Although book reviews and pick lists written by children can be found on the Internet, the bulk of purchasing choices are already limited by adult decisions in publishing. In this light, justifications for an audience-based genre become murky and politically suspect at best. Children's books are not texts for children *by children*—they are books written *by adults*, chosen *by other adults* to be published and recommended /given/assigned to children *by adults*.

The first widely recognized attempt to investigate this double standard and the ageist canon (for those in literary childhood studies, at least) came in Jacqueline Rose's *The Case of Peter Pan, or the Impossibility of Children's Fiction* (1984). In it Rose argues:

> Children's fiction rests on the idea that there is a child who is simply there to be addressed and that speaking to it might be simple. [. . .] [It] sets up a world in which the adult comes first (author, maker, giver) and the child comes after (reader, product, receiver), but where neither of them enter the space in between. [. . .] If children's fiction builds an image of the child inside the book, it does so in order to get at the child who is outside of the book, the one who does not come so easily within its grasp. (1–2)

Rose insists that the only children existing in adult culture are figurations of adult desire. Thus, she exposes the impossibility of defining an academic field that exclusively limits its definition of genre to works supposedly written for an audience that is undefinable itself.

Though the importance of Rose's text has been acknowledged in children's literature criticism, almost twenty years later I see only superficial changes made there in light of the "impossibilities" of the field's vocabularies and methodologies. It would appear that critics have given Rose's thesis lip service without internalizing the subsequent logic of her argument, which dismantles both genre and field—if one cannot "grasp" children, one cannot define them as an audience or define a literature as "age-appropriate" for that audience. Certainly one can *interpret* an implied audience in any given work but not a singularly defined implied audience for an entire genre. Further, to enforce the exclusion of other readers and/or readings based on such an interpretation would be ludicrous. Yet these are the presumptions of age-appropriateness.

Along with Ariès's constructivist premise, Rose's influence has opened up the field for something akin to a Foucauldian (discursive) analysis of childhood, yet it has taken decades to clearly redefine the genres and fields associated with *both* children and literature. Only a handful of scholars have successfully reevaluated their methods or vigilantly curbed efforts to generalize and speak for children. This is a seemingly impossible and sometimes maddening task, and there has been much unsuccessful hair-splitting in the effort to find a common vocabulary that resists essentializing. Take, for example, two works in the field that seem to attempt what Mary Galbraith has called "emancipatory childhood studies": Ellen Pifer's *Demon or Doll: Images of the Child in Contemporary Writing and Culture* (2000) and Joseph L. Zornado's *Inventing the Child: Culture, Ideology, and the Story of Childhood* (2001). The former study, like mine, follows the focus of Reinhard Kuhn's (on figuration) while updating methodology in consideration of today's identity politics. Pifer states, "I neither assume the child's essential nature nor seek to uncover the naked truth about real children allegedly reflected in their fictional counterparts" (6). The second work claims, though according to many critics fails,[3] to recognize and encourage subversive potential by exposing the one-sided power and authority of adults. In either case, however, I have trouble getting past the titles and tables of contents, which definitively repeat the phrase "*the* child" so often that it seems to undermine the authors' progressive intentions.

To study "the child" is to limit one's focus to a child-figure, indicating awareness of social constructedness. One cannot doubt from Pifer's stated plan and the execution of her work, for example, that she is committed to limiting her focus to representations in order to avoid essentializing. Very likely this was the reasoning behind using the phrase in titles by pioneers Coveney and Kuhn, and to note more recent authors cited in this book, Goodenough et al., Hurst, Iskander, Levander, Macleod, and even Jo-Ann Wallace, whose own argument critiques adult constructing. Though their titles identify "the child" (a figure) as their focus, the choice of definite article implies a universal or stereotype, revealing a deeper obstacle: in recognizing that we are presumptuous in our construction of childhood, we seem to excuse ourselves from the need to radically alter our rhetoric and thought. Abstraction hides prejudice, enabling us to overlook the near bigotry revealed in readings of "the child," when it would be plenty obvious, not to mention offensive, if we constantly generalized representations of "*the* woman," "*the* black," or "*the* Hispanic" and in doing so dared to speak for all. As a case in point, Dorothy Broderick's *Images of the Black in Children's Fiction* (1973) would clearly not be so titled if written a decade later.

Methodologically, acceptance of Rose's thesis demands shifting the focus of our analysis from a supposed audience ("children") to authors (almost always adults), so that all child-focused writings can be read as constructing children (whether as characters, test subjects, or readers/listeners). Thus, we accept the impossibility of penetrating children's minds to represent them fairly and attempt reparation by looking more critically at our motives for constructing them as we do. For many, the first departure from the boundaries of traditional criticism has been to consider children's literature and *children in literature* together as reflections of adult perceptions, as the distinguishing trait between them, the audience, cannot be defined in any consistent manner.

We must also develop a vocabulary that reflects this new awareness and be vigilantly reminded of the abstract limits of our study. Even the social sciences have to curb temptations to essentialize the least accessible of subjects, as Ben Bradley points out: "Because infants and animals are not able to base their actions upon linguistic descriptions, they cannot be deemed to intend in the same way as adults do. When scientists and others ascribe intentions to nonverbal creatures, this shows more about how adults like to use (or over-extend) a particular linguistic form than it reveals about the subjective lives of infants" (152). Likewise, in the humanities, when we discuss "children," we must always do so with an ear/eye to what we are really saying about ourselves, so that we can make an effort to filter it out.

With the imperative move away from essentializing subjects, in this case children, comes the need to dismantle the discourse we have built around them. This is the primary aim of childhood studies.[4] Along with constructivist sociology and postcolonial studies, childhood studies results from the increasing awareness of culturally relative identities that compelled the new methodologies of cultural studies. My vocabulary will reflect the shared aims of these fields somewhat eclectically to indicate the larger political context of my argument; however, I hope others are more successful in developing less jargoned means of expressing these theoretical imperatives.

Some of the fairest efforts to study childhood began in the soft sciences, some of which, like literary childhood studies, analyze social construction through cultural narratives. In their broadly relevant text of childhood constructivist sociology, *Constructing and Reconstructing Childhood*, Allison James and Alan Prout point out that the focus of adult discourse on childhood "has been development, and three themes predominate in relation to it: 'rationality,' 'naturalness,' and 'universality.' [. . .] The concept of 'development' inextricably links the biological facts of immaturity, such as dependence, to the social aspects of childhood" (10).[5] The popular conflation of nature and nurture narratives, inherited from developmentalism, has made it difficult to recognize the extent to which we impose "childhood" on children based solely on our interpretations of physical or behavioral signifiers.

Every time we say "she's going through a phase" or "he's too young to understand," we essentialize children temporally—as if individual development proceeds in a universally consistent, chronologically determined and measurable manner. We have learned to recognize that biology is not destiny—sex does not necessarily determine gender or orientation, nor do fictitious absolutes like blood ratios measure ethnocultural identity—yet we still overlook the equally variable factor of age in constructing and sometimes limiting identity. We must recognize and constantly remind ourselves that young identities are too complex and individual to categorize by biology or chronological age. In fact, we should be weary of categorizing altogether by now.

Patrizia Lombardo writes, "We would be blind or ideologically conservative if we believed in a universal nature of childhood [. . .]. The child is a cultural object, and is culturally and historically determined, like everything else, even our body" (2). Pressing for this recognition, childhood studies tend toward inter-disciplinary methods for studying age/maturity as a central factor of socialized difference (following already highly theorized considerations of race, class, gender, and sexual orientation). There is much promise of exposure in this more general arena of methodologies through readers like *The Children's Culture Reader* (Jenkins, 1998), *Childhood in America* (Fass & Mason, 2000), and *The American Child: A Cultural Studies Reader* (Levander and Singley, 2003), not to mention many excellent contributions still disciplinarily entrenched in fields like history and sociology.

In the meantime, new approaches have been stirring within children's literature criticism in response to Jacqueline Rose and constructivist theory. From this side of the outdated audience age-divide, scholars have wondered if the expansion of the canon has been too one-sided. Richard Flynn has described this lasting challenge: "The relative invisibility of children's literature and culture from the field of cultural studies and the mere handful of books examining the construction of childhood in 'adult' literary texts suggest that new tactics are called for if an exploration of childhood is to be recognized as central" (144). Flynn, whose article appeared in *Children's Literature Association Quarterly*, is not the first there to take issue with the boundaries of the field; he is, however, the first there (that I know of) to declare his field as "Childhood Studies," creating a niche between literary and cultural studies for his work. He provides a sort of mission statement, characterizing the field as one that

> 1. Examines the representation of children and childhood throughout literature and culture; 2. Analyzes the impact of the concept of "childhood" on the life and experience of children past and present; 3. Investigates childhood as a temporal state that is often experienced more in memory than in actuality; 4. Explores childhood as a discursive category whose language may provide a potentially useful perspective from which to describe the human person and to understand subjectivity. (144)

These literary agendas match those of constructivist sociology, though we tread on shaky ground with the fourth premise and must vigilantly qualify our "perspectives"—after all, how can one "describe the human person" or "understand subjectivity," once it is agreed that any such construction is yet another imposition? Children's literature scholars often admit to personal interest in (re)constructing childhood, yet our interest is politically precarious according to the constructivist enlightenment. In the last few years, the confusion has mounted, as many are criticized for "essentializing the child" when it is the precise act we are trying, perhaps impossibly, to avoid. Likewise, there is a passionate backlash of good old-fashioned essentializing.

When Karín Lesnik-Oberstein declared, in *Children's Literature: Criticism and the Fictional Child* (1994), that "the child does not exist," Margaret Meek, writing on "The Constructedness of Children," responded as if personally attacked: "As a teacher and therefore compromised, in Lesnik-Oberstein's terms, by my studies of what and how children read, I simply cannot imagine how I can *not* learn about children from children, for all her assertions to the contrary" (11). Meek has such an earnest concern for children that she has overlooked the limits of theoretical applicability to her personal experience with individuals, assuming that her generalizations are authorized through them. Both positions reveal the rift that constructivism has brought about in the study of childhood culture, demonstrating the "impossibility of children's literature" not simply as a genre but as a field.

Karen Coats, in her contribution to the debate, has identified this rift in terms of discipline and methodology, arguing that social scientists are too likely to essentialize children, and literary critics are too likely to completely dissociate their study from real children. Comparing ours to other identity-focused literary fields, she comes to the conclusion that "While excluding either way of conceiving the focus of study is limited, I think Children's Studies is the more inclusive term. After all, Women's Studies is never called 'Womanhood Studies' or 'Woman Studies' [. . .] womanhood is not an ideal, nor is woman a singular entity" ("Keepin' It Plural" 140). But real women can write for, teach, and attend classes in women's studies—the study is not only *of* them and *for* them but also *by* them (or at least generally authenticated/verified *by* them). Real children rarely enter the academy or the classes we call "children's literature," and even if their voices do, they are eventually mediated by adults in dissemination. Coats would understandably characterize my approach as limited, but any literary study of children is limited to the *idea* of childhood according to the discursive nature of our specialization.

Confusing the concept of childhood with the (albeit undefinable) subject position as it may truly exist in the experiences of certain youth, many critics have glossed over the distinction between studying discourse and studying its subjects. On this point, I disagree with Coats's phrasing above: "womanhood" *has* been an ideal in the past and still is—the study of that idealization has been the means of many literary efforts to dispel restrictive and impossible expectations put on women as a result. Likewise, childhood is an abstraction created within discourse, an ideal which few young persons are likely to fit perfectly if at all. Ideal childhood is constructed as a luxury of prolonged dependence and sanctioned irresponsibility, as well as a perceived right to protection that relatively few people throughout the world and history have afforded. And for those who have, childhood could equally seem a stifling imposition of obedience to undeserved authority, selectively preserved ignorance, and caged vulnerability. We can verify neither interpretation, however, but merely consider the possibilities and try to act with a heightened awareness of their multiplicity in spite of our simplifying biases.

Literary critics, especially those of us influenced by cultural studies, are often accused of trying to get away with amateur social science in our otherwise text-based analyses. From the position of literary study, we must be careful to recognize the discursive level of our expertise and respect the discursive limitations of our study. Far from being restrictive, this approach levels literary, scientific, and historical sources, opening up the possibility for all to be read as discourse, provided that we approach them as texts, not testimonies that provide us with authoritative access to "real children." This temptation, as Coats points out, is the danger of our merging methodologies and one against which we are constantly negotiating boundaries.

Take, for example, Gillian Adams's progress in establishing medieval children's literature in the field. She is understandably defensive about the now-famous Ariès hypothesis of childhood constructedness, which she calls "logically absurd" (3), because he positions childhood as an Enlightenment phenomenon by claiming that "there was no place for childhood in the medieval world" (Ariès 33). But her defense blurs the distinction between real medieval children, who she argues indeed existed and were loved by parents, and the idea of childhood (or a family épistémè) that Ariès investigates. Her counterpoints obscure the mutually exclusive applicabilities of their arguments. To my understanding, both would agree that there were cherished medieval young persons we might call children today—Ariès simply reminds us that surviving representations suggest that such a distinction came with very different rights and limitations then, and it is necessary to study those conditions carefully to understand how changed and historically relative our expectations are today.

We need to remain clear about the difference between childhood as we individually define it at present and the varied experience of young persons in the past. Too often we extend generalized notions of childhood experience to the point of isolating ourselves in our present cultural perspectives. One can, however, ask questions aimed at thinking outside of one's current ideological biases for more socially relativistic study by considering the layers of historical difference implicit. Biases become especially clear while investigating the censorship or editing of material for children (e.g., how and why did Joel Chandler Harris, and later, Disney, alter the mythology of Brer Rabbit?). To reach further into the past, it helps to look at oral tales from traceless generations as transmitted through one point in history with a "child audience" in mind. The editing of the Brothers Grimm proves an effective example.

Reading not simply our present responses but the different standards they imply, we might ask, for example, "Why, when editing collected tales to be more appropriate for children in their 1819 edition, did the Brothers Grimm omit 'Puss in Boots' but retain such harsh tales as 'The Maiden Without Hands'?" Tales such as "Puss in Boots" and "Bluebeard" with French roots did not suit the Grimms' interest in demonstrating a common German source of folklore, but clearly violence (or at least a little tidy maiming) was not considered inappropriate subject matter to their notion of childhood, that is, at least when its presence encouraged the audience to obey and forgive their parents. Here we have a simple set of contrasts that illustrates how relative, indeed, are historic/cultural expectations for childhood. The difference highlighted here would be the apparent prioritizing of politics and obedience in the 1819 tales, and today's higher priority of (or louder lip service to) protection.[6]

The above example also demonstrates a methodology suggested by Rose's argument that children's books construct children: in fully imagining the implied audience of selected Grimm tales, we have a composite construction of childhood via the Grimms (or, to keep biases we know explicit, definitions of childhood according to two early-nineteenth-century, middle-class, well-educated, pro-unification, German males). If we investigate the above agendas further in order to understand the evolution of concepts of childhood, we can see in the tales, too, women storytellers' concerns and hopes for their offspring (complete with subversive feminist advice) co-existing, contrasting the Grimms' patriarchal biases, enriching our impressions of the composite construction. Such range helps us to further understand the constructing context, rather than inserting our present stereotypes of childhood where they do not even have a chance of fitting.

This approach allows us to see as if from a distance that our constructions are, likewise, deeply rooted, over-simplified stereotypes. This happens frequently in my classes when we discuss European and Middle Eastern folklore. Someone will object to the "gruesome violence" in the tales, but after considering the reality of violence in the United States and its cultural productions, we wonder why we react so—how can we maintain such an oblivious but absolute disconnection between what we conceptualize and defend as appropriate childhood experience and the reality young people experience and witness? Because our essentializing abstractions cloud our ability to fairly comprehend those we essentialize as children.

Awareness of the blind spot that obstructs even our sincerest efforts at understanding those we "diagnose" as children should serve as a constant reminder of the automatic self-invalidation we enact in our questioning. Any adult study of childhood is precariously hypothetical due to the "lost" childhood-subjectivity of adult scholars biased and favored by ideologies that are unavoidably adult-serving. Mounting ideological resistance on behalf of those we deem outside of ideology is impossible, yet we who are empowered by ageist essentializing (adults) are the very subjects who must alter our ways of thinking, meaning that constant reevaluations (made at the necessary risk of simply "reconstructing") are necessary steps in deconstructing our own solipsistic power. Gayatri Chakravorty Spivak calls this process "strategic essentializing," explaining that "In deconstructive critical practice, you have to be aware that you are going to essentialize anyway. So then strategically you can look at essentialisms, not as descriptions of the way things are, but as something that one must adopt to produce a critique of anything" ("The Problem" 51). What we can produce with such "looking" is a better view, though primarily of our own gaze, and one that will refuse, ultimately, like anything real, to come fully into focus.

By focusing on the spaces and words that adults cast around children, keeping representations distinct from any supposed authentic referents, I hope to avoid the false confidence of unreflective essentializing and get a better view of how and why we do it. My method is to approach childhood as portraiture in relief, reading adult desire in the "empty spaces" created for hypothetical children in discourse. I will also look at childhood itself represented as a space, an empty one—the *tabula rasa* on which the author plays with notions of what it must be like to inhabit that ideally constructed position ("again"), furnishing the space with qualities that are lacking in his/her own social position.

James Kincaid's groundbreaking text, *Child-Loving: The Erotic Child and Victorian Culture* (1992), bares the discursive framework by which we essentialize children: "The child is that which we are not but almost are, that which we yearn for so fiercely we almost resent it, that which we thought we saw in the mirror and almost wanted to possess yet feared we might. The child is the embodiment of desire and also its negation" (7). Impossible to validate through this perpetually deferred otherness, childhood is a freely imaginable concept because it is a representation of everything that can be imagined but never grasped. Desire begets repetition. Kincaid writes: "We seem to take pleasure in constructing the other not simply as an absence but as a seductive inexplicableness" (32). Childhood in literature is an inviting, uninhabited space, void of the agency that is already an unquestioned right of adulthood. It is always marked by lack— a lack that is frequently cast in a positive light. In its inaccessibility and emptiness childhood poses a representational challenge yet enables unlimited signification.[7] Reading this signification, I find the most frequent desire revealed in fictional childhood spaces is to escape dependence upon linear thought and language (the narrative writer's most urgent skills).

Method and Sample Reading

I have found American literature to be more neglected than British from this angle, and so to show the wide prevalence of the biases I deconstruct, and some variations unique to this country, my literary examples favor American sources. But children's literature thrived and set precedents in England, and European tales have been transported via Hollywood to such an extent that any investigation of Anglophone childhood discourse is best focused somewhat transatlantically. Applications of theory will be even more geographically flexible, their influence being untraceably boundless and deep. Methodologically, I aim to inform close readings with a continuous deconstruction of ageist biases, so, as in cultural studies and Foucauldian discourse analysis, fiction and nonfiction will constitute "primary" texts.

Applying my training in both cultural studies and literature has proven more difficult than I had anticipated, and I am still seeking solutions. When I began this project the only methodological model I found was James Kincaid's *Erotic Innocence* (1998), which successfully levels film and news media discursively by studying each as specific manifestations of a more general and pervasive narrative—in his case that of pedophilia (and pedophilia-phobia). I, too, am following narratives on various levels of discourse constructing childhood: romanticism, developmentalism, and anti-rationalism. My sources include film, picture books, comic books, psychology, sociology, geography, and post-structuralist theory, but primarily fiction. Though still leaning heavily on close literary reading, the following chapters draw from increasingly diverse sources, as the logic of my argument, not literary genres or timelines, propels the structure and analysis of evidence. Roderick McGillis explains the necessity of such a method as part of the "political emancipation" of children and discourse. He writes that we can raise consciousness and set new discursive patterns "only by taking a trajectory that passes through formal features of textuality and heads directly toward that spot where the literary and the social intersect" (204). I attempt this by reading literature on the same level as social and scientific discourse, but also by applying literary methods of analysis to nonliterary texts.

In this spirit, I will illustrate the premise of elusive childhood with a reading of Sigmund Freud's "Analysis of a Phobia in a Five-Year-Old Boy" (1909),[8] which was Freud's only analysis of an actual child (in contrast to retrospective readings of adults' "inner children," as with Dora and the Wolf Man). This study is especially fascinating because the exchanges between Freud and his patient are almost entirely carried out by mail, mediated completely by the boy's father, Max Graf, a follower of Freud's. Hans (Freud's fictional name for Herbert Graf), whose problem is an extreme phobia of horses that eventually intensifies to include vehicles and the street, is "cured" through a series of sessions in which his father interviews him (very suggestively), analyzes the interview, awaits Freud's comments on his analysis, and responds according to the synthesis of both their conclusions.

Freud was aware of the unscientific method of the study: "The case history is not, strictly speaking, derived from my own observation. It is true that I laid down the general lines of the treatment, and that on one single occasion, when I had a conversation with the boy, I took a direct share in it" (5). This disclaimer suggests early on that Freud was hesitant in trusting the representation of a child to his father, or any adult. However, despite this, and his awareness of transference and suggestibility, Freud took up the case. Allowing the father's interference, he faithfully quotes preliminary analyses along with mediated observations, authorizing them as he progresses: "[The dream] was the first dream of his that was made unrecognizable by distortion. His father's penetration, however, succeeded in clearing it up" (19). What follows is more like a case study in suggestion, as Graf repeatedly provides his son with convenient symbolic interpretations and explanations. In response, Freud admits that

> a child, it will be said, is necessarily highly suggestible, and in regard to no one, perhaps, more than his own father; he will allow anything to be forced upon him, out of gratitude to his father for taking so much notice of him. [. . .] The whole thing is simply 'suggestion'—the only difference being that in the case of a child it can be unmasked much more easily than in that of an adult. (102)

Freud, ever constructing children as essentially honest, justifies suggestion with his own generalizing, essentializing representation of Herbert as Hans. More important for my point here is that in the interviews' extreme suggestibility something more universal is exposed: that Graf runs rhetorical circles around his son, wrapped up in his own (and Freudian) discourse, unaware of his inability to "read" the boy. In his sincere and tireless efforts to unfold the mystery of his son's fear, he is doing little more than imposing conclusions, most of which appear to be useless or uninteresting to the boy described in his letters.

Almost a century later, the interviews can seem comically misguided, but they anticipate discourse that surrounds, targets, and hails children still today. Graf theorizes the cause of "Hans's" phobia, allegedly originating in a traumatic scene in which he witnessed a large horse fall and struggle to stand. Often out of the blue, he bombards his son with Freudian suggestions, hoping one will fit. He reports the talks to Freud:

> I: "When the horse fell down, did you think of your daddy?"
> HANS: "Perhaps. Yes. It's possible." (51)

[...]
April 9th. This morning Hans came in to me while I was washing and
   bare to the waist.
HANS: "Daddy, you *are* lovely! You're so white."
I: "Yes. Like a white horse." (53)
   [...]
HANS: "A loud row sounds as though you were doing lumf. A big row
   reminds me of lumf, and a little one of widdle."
I: "I say, wasn't the bus-horse the same colour as a lumf?"
HANS: *(very much struck):* "Yes." (64)

But the boy generally avoids confirming his father's hypotheses, at times
even disrupting the process of analysis. Responding to the dishonest and
conflicting accounts of how his sister ("Hanna") was born, Hans takes up
the dialogue and turns his father's meddlesome discourse into a game. He
begins to instruct his father with his own "stork" story. In his version,
Hanna was carried in a box before she was born and stored in the attic.

HANS: "Then Hanna got out."
I: "Why, she couldn't walk at all then."
HANS: "Well then, we lifted her down."
I: "But how could she have sat on the horse? She couldn't even sit up at
   all last year."
HANS: "Oh yes, she sat up all right, and called out 'Gee-up,' and whipped
   her whip [...] I'm not joking, you know, Daddy." (70)

Freud interprets Hans's "parody" as revenge against his father's dishon-
esty in sex education. Yet it can also be seen as an echo of his father's rule
of discourse—"because I say so, it's true." This sort of disruption can challenge the very authority of discursive centers, exposing that Hans's father
usually falls back upon his identity (age/size in particular) to make his narrative the correct one.

   At the center of yet excluded from and powerless within this discursive
practice, Hans can only mimic his father and be interpreted. A play theo-
rist might argue that his actions dramatize a child's lack of power, especially
when he mimics (mocks?) authority. Hans becomes so inconsistent in his
version of Hanna's birth that it is impossible to follow: "'Just you write it
down,'" he commands his father, who only laughs (76). Continuing, he tells
his baffled father, "'I say, what I'm telling you isn't a bit true'" (77). (Notice
the use of his father's phrase, "I say.") Freud again interprets this rebellion

as Hans giving his father a taste of his own medicine, but he is also resist-ing his father's inadequate explanation of procreation *and* the imposition it represents. Whether or not Hans has the agency to consciously resist is unknowable but beside the point here; his imitation of his father reveals to the adult reader that the father's discourse dominates the boy's space and that an accurate analysis is impossible because of its one-sidedness. The Hans case perfectly exemplifies Rose's hypothesis of discursive construc-tion and Kincaid's premise that childhood is centerless. The representation of this child is prejudicially mediated, apparently unrelated to his interests, and those who represent him seem unaware of the extent of their inability to read him. Here we are witness to construction in progress, where the real boy is, at best, a disregarded target. In short, Freud's Hans is as hypothet-ical as Huck Finn.

I hope to remain clear about this issue—the constructions of childhood that make the subject of my study are by that definition *hypothetical.* It is the *hypothesis* of childhood itself I seek to locate and investigate. I will not be *applying* theory to *the real* in my analysis but following narrative lines that infiltrate both it and more popular discourse.

The project of this book is to investigate various means of negotiating the inaccessibility of childhood in literary representations by writers self-conscious of the "impossibility" of the task. It follows in two parts: first, a demonstration of techniques that authors have used in attempting to over-come the obstacle of representing the absent "child"; second, analyses of thematic reversals that authors use to decenter traditional constructions of childhood (often only to recenter them, replacing one hypothesis for a seemingly fairer one), ultimately to throw the entire authority of adult dis-course into question.

Chapter 2, "Refocusing Representations," and chapter 3, "Childhood Bound," focus on technical issues of representation, showing a general pro-gression in modern literature toward representing inaccessible subjects more spatially and externally, reflecting a growing reception of construc-tivist interpretations of subjectivity. Henry James provides a groundwork case, as his innovative narrative techniques already aimed at producing fic-tional subjects as "ironic centres" who could only be seen from ambivalent points of view. James recognized defining gaps in communication and power between children and adults, and he identified differences in lan-guage proficiency as the cause of these inequities. I chose to use a single-author study here to allow the close focus necessary to fully illuminate the depths of this language barrier and how it operates, as it is consistent throughout both oppressive and subversive constructions and will become the pivotal premise for the argument culminating in my final chapter. Like Hans, conscientiously rendered literary children are less accessible than adults through language, the tool upon which the writer depends. Childhood in adult discourse might be seen accordingly as a silent space in which children are linguistically and discursively beyond reach. This inaccessibility calls the whole process of representation into doubt.

In *What Maisie Knew* (1897), James brings the problem of accessibility, and thus representation, to the foreground—as the title suggests, the novel asks the question, "What *does* Maisie know?" This child, the center of the narrative's events and our lens into James's fictional reality, is impenetrable, empty, functioning only as a reflector for the adult players. James draws our attention to the fact that this ironic representation is the closest we can get to Maisie, whose "infant mind would at best leave great gaps and voids" (10). Thus, to James, a literary child is technically and fictively an empty glass—practically invisible to those who construct her, thus limitless in what she can reflect. *What Maisie Knew* leaves us aware of the impossibility of knowing what Maisie knows, exposing adult curiosity.

As we have seen with the case of "little Hans," and will see demonstrated throughout the following chapters, the adult-centeredness of legitimated discourse could potentially alienate those who are still acquiring language. The writer who tries to represent the muted position of childhood is up to a great challenge; James met it with a method that would become useful for many other writers I discuss, especially Harper Lee, Alison Lurie, and Toni Morrison. I focus primarily on James first, however, because he was so transparently troubled by the challenge children present to realist representation, and he foregrounded his method as a means of exposing and confronting that challenge through his externalized focalizations.

Externalizing focalization curtails the otherwise necessary illusions of presence and agency, restricts mediation, refocuses the spotlight on adult culture (as adults make up the stage that surrounds a child character, or ironic center), and, ultimately, leaves the reader in an ambivalent state, forced to fill in his/her own conclusions, possibly leading to a self-awareness of the imposition involved in this process. This method is particularly useful to writers representing a discursively inaccessible position. It is not surprising, then, that externalized focalization is common in texts dealing with childhood.

Another method of externalizing the focus on children is to spatialize fictive realities, focusing not *in* the minds of children but *on* their hypothetical worlds. One can witness this technique in *Peter Pan* (1911), where J. M. Barrie describes mapping a child's mind, doing so in spatial and social terms:

> Doctors sometimes draw maps of [. . .] you, and your own map can
> become intensely interesting, but catch them trying to draw a map of a
> child's mind, which is not only confused, but keeps going round all the
> time. There are zigzag lines on it, just like your temperature on a card, and
> these are probably roads in the island; for the Neverland is always more or
> less an island. [. . .] It would be an easy map if that were all; but there is
> also first day at school, religion, fathers, verbs that take the dative, choco-
> late pudding day [. . .] and either these are part of the island or they are
> another map showing through, and it is still all rather confusing, especially
> as nothing will stand still. (5–6)

Barrie suggests that mapping a child's mind is like reading a palimpsest
that defies linear comprehension. Childhood becomes a region as difficult
to map as it is to fix by language, and perhaps for that reason, it is all the
more desirable to imagine. In my third chapter, "Childhood Bound," I
consider the popularity of spatializing and mapping in childhood literature, and I posit that these techniques reflect attempts to fantasize an
impossibly accessible childhood while evading the temporality and linearity of written narrative. Not only are adults childhood bound, in terms of
a fantasy destination, but such desire necessitates binding childhood spatially in order to provide the illusion of its graspability.

Peter Hunt suggests that maps are used in fiction to "stabilize the fantasy" (11). As in *Moby-Dick* (1851), a map can be used to authenticate a
fictional reality—in fact, the skeletal plot of *Moby-Dick* is given away in
the map by Joseph P. Ascherl (figure 1), included in many editions (which
shows the Pequod going down in the South Pacific) before one even begins
the narrative, as if what follows is merely a document recounting actual
events. The maps in books by Robert Louis Stevenson, A. A. Milne, L.
Frank Baum, J. R. R. Tolkien, Ruth Stiles Gannett, and Avi have done the
same with fantasy spaces. They can validate the unreal, but they also play
against the limitations of reality. Barrie's written map expresses a common
desire in constructing childhood—nostalgia for impressionistic, systemless
thought.

Important American exemplars for this tradition are the Oz books,
which negotiate the impassable boundaries of adult-imagined childhood
through a heavy reliance on territorial marking, with carefully delineated
borders and gratuitous hints of access. Full of maps, direction markers,
and visual sectioning (especially color-coded territories), L. Frank Baum's

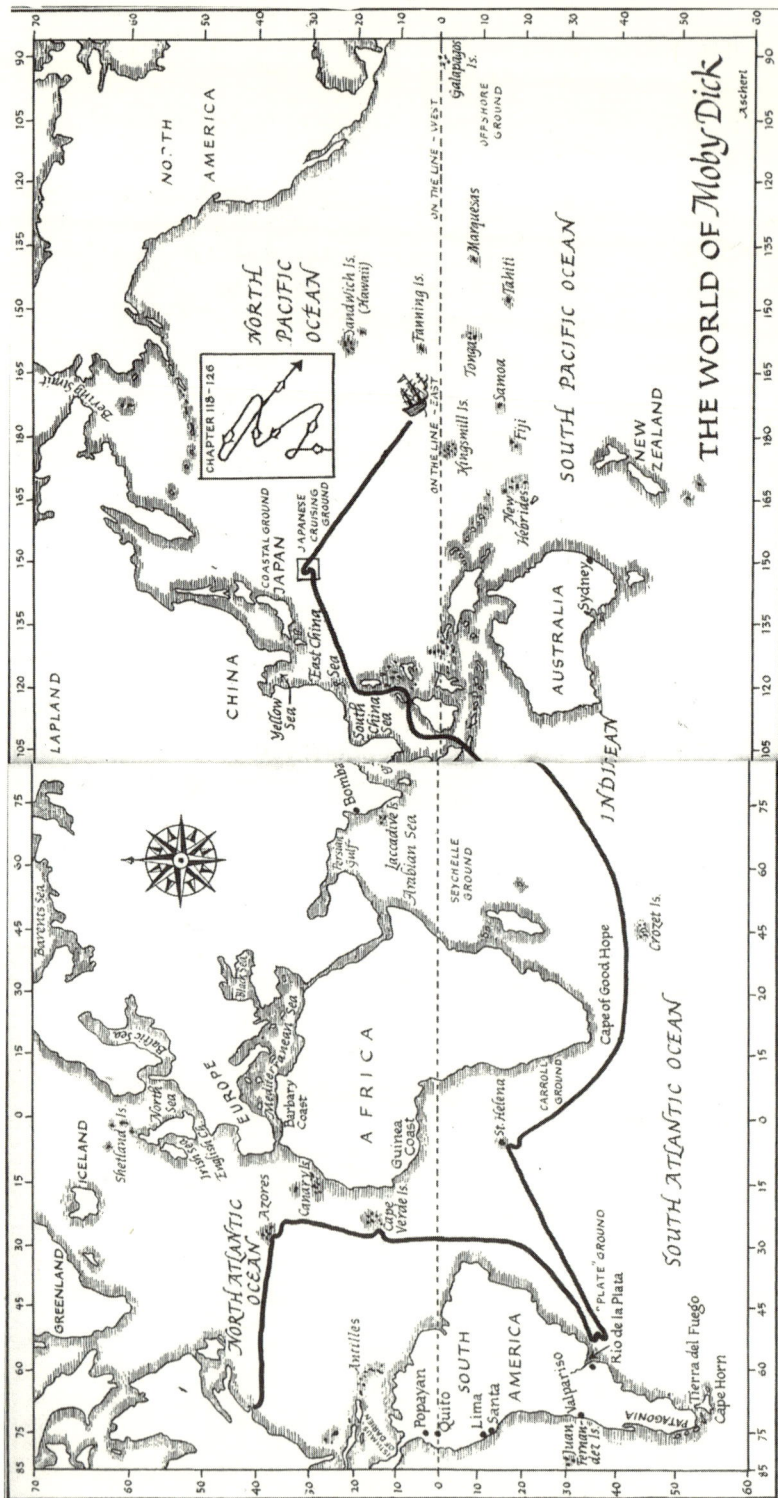

Figure 1. (From *Moby-Dick* by Herman Melville, Macmillan Publishing Company, 1985, courtesy of Joseph P. Ascherl)

make-believe world authenticates itself. Grappling with a popular theme in children's literature, ontological uncertainty, Baum's Oz could be seen as a map that precedes its territory (to put a spin on Baudrillard). Baum attempts to fix the imaginary Oz and establish a textual certitude (map) of childhood, since the concept (territory) itself is a floating discourse. But he also destabilizes the rationalist demand for certitude (noncontradiction) by pressing for acceptance of simultaneous contradiction. "Childhood Bound" explores this technique in visual and verbal illustration to wordless storytelling that posits childhood (spaces) as a challenge to linear, absolutist thinking.

In chapter 4, "Reversing Development," I investigate the pervasive narrative of development—the fundamental model for childhood discourse that stretches its genealogical roots back into misapplications of Darwinian theory—from recapitulation to developmental psychology. I begin with concrete demonstrations of recapitulatory tropes from two British experiments in brutal honesty—William Golding's *The Lord of the Flies* (1954) and Richard Hughes's *A High Wind in Jamaica* (1929). Through exaggeration, these novels expose the pervasive yet masked rationalist bias of developmental discourse.

Writers representing childhood must contend with developmental presuppositions, which cast childhood as a definable phase in a temporally measured progression from irrational dependence to abstractly reasoning adulthood. In direct contrast, some delight in what Kincaid calls the "seductive inexplicableness" of childhood by holding it up as a position of infinite potential, resistance, and idyllic wisdom. Budding in the poetry of William Wordsworth and consequent romantics, this tradition attempts to make sense of adult shortcomings by locating seemingly inaccessible ideals, like natural creativity, free spontaneity, and innocent intuition, in a personal past called childhood. Inaccessibility then becomes explained by the irrevocable decline of age. Constructing childhood as a position of limitless possibility snuffed by growth, such writers envision a reversal of the development narrative. With socialization poised as the detriment of idealized childhood, this romantic reversal was easily reconciled with increasing modern interests in social construction. I illustrate American uses of this theme in canonical texts like *The Adventures of Huckleberry Finn* as well as science fiction by Henry Kuttner, Theodore Sturgeon, and Virginia Hamilton.

The reversal of development replaces patronizing constructions of childhood with an idealized position that is "beyond us" because it is irretrievable. From this perspective, adults are handicapped by schooling and accumulated knowledge, only hoping for glimpses of "childish" intuition.

This is a common sentiment—even Jacques Lacan's and Louis Althusser's conceptions of *méconnaissance* suggest that the more indoctrinated a social subject is, the more misknowing and removed from the real he/she becomes (and, it would follow, adults are). This reversal legitimizes the adult writer's (and reader's) own sense of misknowing and unreality through contrast.

Ultimately, the romantic view simply inverts the temporal pattern of development, reversing the direction of a supposedly fixed and still lineated process. The discourse remains uncentered, as children are still inaccessible, yet the shift exposes an adult desire to escape intellectual authority. After all, if childhood is inaccessible due to adult inadequacies, rationalist adults can hardly be expected to try harder to understand those socially defined by the concept.

The space, lacking fixed signification, between adult discourse and the negation it names childhood allows much play in meaning. Nonsense writers are not the only ones to exploit this territory (although, we will find in science fiction and comic books, Lewis Carroll greatly influenced exploration of the theme)—many writers expose the language barrier as a way of heightening readers' awareness of the limitations of their own language and logic. Oskar Negt and Alexander Kluge explain this as an alienation effect: "One of the most effective ways of exposing the true nature of any public sphere is when it is interrupted, in a kind of alienation effect, by children. [. . .] [T]he fact that the public sphere is always that of adults, immediately become[s] apparent" (283). In chapter 5, "Disrupting Discourse," I investigate scenes in which children's questioning of authority demonstrates the extent to which they are excluded from the discourse that defines and holds power over them. Such scenes suggest that adult-centered discourse needs disruption by a child in order for us to recognize its ageist exclusivity.

Depicting children as capable of indirectly (often unknowingly) disrupting discourse is perhaps the most consistent ideal in child-focused American fiction. This is often accomplished through a child's questioning: "The propensity of children to ask questions is noticeable throughout American fiction and [. . .] heuristic speech seems to dominate fictional children's linguistic output"[9] (Hurst 60). Literary children use indirect means to disrupt discourse when they are prohibited from directly engaging it. A question enables passive resistance and redress at the same time, soothing adult egos with a child's assumed unknowing while drawing attention to what is debatable or flawed in adult logic.

For example, like Hans, Harriet Welsch disrupts the practice of her psychologist in Louise Fitzhugh's *Harriet the Spy* (1964):

> Harriet could see all sorts of games, dolls, doll houses, and trucks. She tried
> to be nice about it, but she was curious. "Do you sit here all day playing
> with all those things?" Wait till her mother got a load of this.
>
> He looked at her archly, "Do you think I sit here all day playing with
> these toys?"
>
> "How do I know? You got a whole closet full of 'em."
>
> "Don't you have toys at home?"
>
> This was too much. "Yes," she shouted, "but I'm eleven." (254)

Regardless of whether we interpret simple honesty or rebellion as her
motivation, Harriet's question, "How do *I* know?" reflects an awareness
that the doctor is in control of their discourse—that she is not expected to
know answers, and that even if she does, as an adult he will have the final
say. Such samples also prove, however, that an outsider can disrupt the discourse that defines and excludes her.

Jean Baudrillard has called this disruptive ability a "double strategy,"
because, he argues, children "do not just have subject-consciousness, they
have a kind of objective ironic presentiment that the category into which
they have been placed does not exist" (*Baudrillard Live* 112). Such a construction is reminiscent of what W. E. B. DuBois called "double-
consciousness," which would also suggest that any marginalized subject
has a critical edge because, out of the spotlight, he/she can see unseen, subversively hiding in the cloak of unrecognized otherness. In illustrating the
use of this subversive technique in modern fiction and film, I draw from
many of the sources that are central to preceding chapters in order to
demonstrate its predominance and usefulness in the persistent deconstruction of adult discourse.

That writers indulge in the play of representing childhood, especially
as nonlinear and outside of legitimated discourse, reflects a desire for
something antithetical to their own art, their labor, and their intellectual
world—childhood becomes an escape from rationalist adulthood.

In the opening of the film *American Beauty*, the main character and
narrator, Lester Burnham, tells us that his wife and daughter think he's a
"loser," that he *has* "lost something" in approaching his midlife, but "it's
never too late to get it back." This is the impossible work we make youth
do for us. Lester thinks a budding high-school girl (nestled in rose petals
not so unlike the baby in Anne Geddes's *Cheesecake*) will bring him back,
as he is "already dead." Death, in his sense of the word, was the full-time

job, family car, heeding mortality, obeying rules. Innocence, in his view, is the out-of-reach but always hoped for escape. It is an attempt to undo the learning that brought about the loss of that ineffable "something" he wants back. James Kincaid explains the logic of this impossible desire: "Memory is constructed from observation; the powers of observation are never so strong as when we are young; though most adults lose such powers, they can cast back into childhood and perhaps regain contact with them; thus, we can remember childhood only by asking the child to do the remembering for us" (*Child-Loving* 230).

As a function of our shared cultural imagination, childhood undoes experience. It is a canvas for writers frustrated with their medium, where its creators can imagine a past without writer's block, miscommunication, the limitations of language, and demands for linear coherence. All of the techniques discussed in this book—externalized focalization, (re)territorialization, reversing and subverting age-centered discourse—reflect a growing awareness of the impossibility of representing childhood, and at the same time a unique intellectual nostalgia, which through contrast, validates the struggle involved in the writer's own labor.

REFOCUSING
REPRESENTATIONS

*A*t the end of the nineteenth century, Americans saw birthrates drop, life expectancies rise, and a new minority group emerge: children.[1] On one hand, this meant that children were more likely to afford prolonged dependence, cherishing, and protection. It also meant that children came under closer scrutiny and adult control. Exploitation and high mortality rates gave way to increasingly institutionalized obedience. The lucky children were starting to grow up under idolatrous surveillance. Some provided evidence for study after study anxiously trying to define the nature of childhood, map human development, or discover keys to adult psychology.

Psychological novels of the time reflect this fascination. Muriel Shine even correlates the interest in children to the development of the genre: "An outstanding characteristic differentiating the modern novel from that of the nineteenth century is the shift in emphasis from concern with external phenomena to preoccupation with inner experience [. . .] . The simplistic view of the child yielded to the probing analytical impulse of the writer and the child became a vessel of consciousness to be explored in depth" (18).

With the modern "inward turn" toward investigating psychological processes, novelists began to favor narrative techniques that provide an illusion of mental access. Popular modes, such as the omniscient narrator, gave way to figural narration (fixed, or limited third person). But as Wallace Martin points out, "figural narration has certain limitations. When representing actions, the narrator can substitute present-tense dialogue for past-tense summary easily enough; but how can the same shift be effected when conveying thoughts and feelings?" (134). With this representational dilemma Martin explains the modernist preference for self-narration (first person), yet his formula disregards another response to the challenge—a concurrent movement away from "conveying thoughts and feelings" by making figural narration increasingly experimental, a trend that continued and still exists in post-modernist fiction.

Though first-person narratives can offer a convincing illusion of accessing the minds of characters, "Infancy and death point up the most obvious limitation imposed on self-narration by the figural identity of hero and historian" because they are inaccessible positions (*Transparent Minds* 144). Even so, more authors have approached the former than the latter in the frequent figuration of children (who appear more convincingly accessible than infants do). But for Henry James, to whom authentic characterization was key, children posed a further challenge to credible representation, as he was intent on avoiding trespasses into unknowable subjectivities. James's fictional children exemplify the complex challenge that children pose for fiction writers, and James openly admits they are ever elusive, both representationally and narratively, even while seeming to legitimately represent them in his narrative. His unique combination of externalized characterization and focalization anticipates post-structuralist approaches to social subjects and draws attention to the one-sided and unchecked power of adult discourse when constructing children. He, as an adult, would not presume to represent a child through self-narration, a method toward which he was already disinclined.

In his preface to *The Ambassadors*, James explains that, despite the importance of his characters' subjective states, he would not use first-person narration in his effort to represent them convincingly:

> It may be asked why, if one so keeps to one's hero, one shouldn't make a single mouthful of "method," shouldn't throw the reins on his neck and [. . .] equip him with the double privilege of subject and object—a course that has at least the merit of brushing away questions at a sweep. The answer to which is, I think, that one makes that surrender only if one is prepared not to make certain precious discriminations. (371)

Though James expounds no further, the evidence of his craft hints that the "precious discriminations" one overlooks in using first-person narration are the unverifiable gaps between subjectivities rendered unverifiable by any author's subjective isolation.

Perhaps his awareness of these "discriminations" drew James to the challenge that child characters presented. In his "Art of Fiction," James criticized Edmond de Goncourt's *Chérie*, "which strikes me as having failed deplorably in what it attempts—that is in tracing the development of the moral consciousness of a child" (180). Though he gives no explanation, his choice of this novel as an example in his discussion of verisimilitude (and writing from experience vs. impressions) seems significant. It reveals that he was already associating children with the various imaginative leaps, or, as he calls them, "impressions," upon which even the realist must depend. He compares representing a child to describing an unseen land—the *terra incognita* no adult can explore.

In *The Fictional Children of Henry James*, Muriel Shine traces James's career in terms of an increasingly realistic portrayal of children. Her argument is that his work gradually eschews the convention of sentimental figuration for more probing and believable portraits, and she credits James with the introduction of child figures into the psychological novel: "Twentieth-century novelists owe a debt of gratitude to Henry James for his active role in the movement to sweep away outmoded convention and prejudice and to establish the child in literature as a worthy object of complete and honest investigation" (174–75). Marcia Jacobson depicts the importance of this contextual contrast by providing a brief history of the sentimental tradition in *Henry James and the Mass Market*, concluding that although "many writers in the [1890s] indulged themselves in an imagined return to the apparent simplicity of childhood [. . .] [i]t is apparent that James fought against the regressive tendencies of his genre even while he indulged himself in it" (104).

Beverly Lyon Clark describes the changing literary and critical culture in which James wrote as one very biased against the young, even though much of the national literature still popular sentimentalized youth: "If nineteenth-century America was pervaded by the metaphor of America as child, then America's emergence as a world power in the twentieth century was marked by a desire to put away childish things" ("Kiddie Lit in Academe" 150). In her later expansion on this issue, in *Kiddie Lit: The Cultural Construction of Children's Literature in America*, she reveals that James's criticism, likewise, reflects "disdain" for perceived juvenility, but an increasing awareness of "otherness" in youth also drew him to that perceived social position as a subject: "If the novel is to be associated with that which is Other, perhaps it's not completely surprising that even as James was disparaging children in his criticism, he was turning to children to redeem his fiction" (38). It is because of his unique historical vantage point, at a neurotic intersection of extreme child worship and child scrutiny, that James has become the central exemplar in modern American figuration of children. The aim of my analysis is to highlight James's meta-mimetic running commentary, show his foreshadowing awareness of post-structuralist subjectivity in his characterization, and consider the implications of ageist identity politics on such representing, especially as it concerns our faulty dependence upon language.

Most critics, like Shine, interpret James's investigations of child figuration as breaking with sentimentality and setting a new standard by introducing children into modernized realism; however, his experiments with child characters were not simply mimetic successes. As James states in "The Art of Fiction," "The characters [. . .] which strike one as real will be those that touch and interest one most, but the measure of reality is difficult to fix" (171). Aware of the relativity inherent in the act of representation, his attempts to delineate children realistically helped him to recognize the impossibility of the task and to exploit it. The inaccessibility of childhood provided him with an ironic center for his trademark ambiguity. In this respect, Maisie is his crowning achievement.

In his preface to *What Maisie Knew* (1897), James wrote, "Small children have many more perceptions than they have terms to translate them; their vision is at any moment much richer, their apprehension even constantly stronger, than their prompt, their at all producible, vocabulary" (10). Locating the obstacle to representation in the inequitable language gap between adults (writers) and children (subjects), James plays off of the inaccessibility of childhood to create an ironic center. Though Maisie is the central figure of the novel's development, James never lets the reader forget that she is mentally inscrutable because there is inadequate common language through which to gain access to her mind. Maisie, we are told, "had ever of course in her mind fewer names than conceptions" (163). But James constructs her as not wanting words: "there were a sense and a sound in everything to which words had nothing to add" (180). He gingerly avoids putting words into her mind. When a thought is revealed the narrator reports it only through a veil of distancing qualifications like, "it then fell into its place in her general, her habitual view of the particular phenomenon that, had she felt the need of words for it, she might have called her personal relation to her knowledge" (204).

Hypothesizing Maisie's view at so many removes draws attention directly to her inaccessibility rather than creating an illusion of access. Mary Galbraith points out that when "a character's experience is represented propositionally in sentences containing a verb characterizing this experience ('she thought she was crazy': 'she felt sad') [. . .] , this narrative technique does not purport to be faithful to the words a character might use" ("What Everybody Knew" 205). James gives an impression of Maisie's situation "without implying her verbal participation in their expression" to avoid, literally, putting words in her mouth (207). For much of the novel, Maisie is constructed as a preverbal child-figure who exists mentally outside of the discourse surrounding her.

James does not presume to give a "faithful" representation of Maisie's inexpressible thought. In fact, his frequent use of indirect discourse ensures that the reader remains constantly aware of Maisie's inaccessibility. In *Story and Discourse*, Seymour Chatman writes, "only direct forms cite the speaker's exact words; indirect forms give no such guarantee. [. . .] The indirect form in narratives implies a shade more intervention by a narrator, since we cannot be sure that the words in the report clause are precisely those spoken by the quoted speaker" (200). James avoids imposing interpreted cognition on the child-figure and prevents his reader's probing by foregrounding his narrator's mediation.

Despite her apparent lack of concern for language, all Maisie appears to do is listen to the adults around her, and in doing so, she is bombarded with language used opaquely and manipulatively. Forced to "read the unspoken into the spoken" (205) words of her parents and caretakers, she often behaves as if she misunderstands their intent. Using dramatic irony and a common technique of children's writers, hyperliteralism, James draws attention to the exclusive, yet arbitrary, nature of sophisticated language (i.e., adult discourse). Rather than following on the suggestion that Sir Claude is an idle womanizer, "Maisie wept on Mrs. Wix's bosom after hearing that [he] was a butterfly" (89). "'He leans on me,'" Mrs. Wix dramatically boasts of being in Sir Claude's confidence, "and she was more surprised than amused when, later on, she accidentally found she had given her pupil the impression of a support literally supplied by her person" (95). In such passages, James highlights Maisie's incomplete socialization and linguistic estrangement—he stages the drama to spotlight her discursive separateness.

The text even technographically reproduces Maisie's isolation by relating only a fragment of dramatic dialogue. Maisie hears Sir Claude's outburst at her mother as "'You damned old b—!'" and later reports the missing word as "brute," yet the reader is left aware that the original utterance was a more potent (though unfamiliar to Maisie) term (126). Despite her implied ignorance of more unpleasant adult behaviors, the process of her education reveals much about the adult social selves around her, in such a way as to heighten the reader's curiosity about just what she can understand.

Figure 2. (From *WHAT MAISIE KNEW* (JACKET COVER) by Henry James, copyright. Used by permission of Doubleday, a division of Random House, Inc.)

Maisie provides the only eyes and ears through which the reader perceives James's fictive reality, yet writer and reader alike are barred access to her conscious thought. We see what Maisie sees, but we cannot know what Maisie knows. Galbraith has said, "The absence of Maisie's epistemology [. . .] suggests that her subjectivity is not perceptible or describable within the [...] socially constructed webs of meaning which comprise the worlds of 'high society,' public opinion, or the courts" ("What Everybody Knew" 201–2). James brings attention not to Maisie's innocence (despite many critics' insistence on interpreting her so) but to her exclusion from adult society and discourse. Without sufficient linguistic and social experience for conveyance, her mind can only be represented as an unknowable void that reflects not only the fictive adults' desires but also James's and the reader's as well.

James remains especially ambiguous about Maisie's ability to understand matters of sexuality, and just here, her perception is less important than our own that she is actively excluded from knowing those things that seem to make up the bulk of any plot that intrigues adult readers. While her parents, governess, and stepfather interact in a complex and unpredictable love-hate quartet, Maisie stands as the lens through which the reader discerns clandestine courtships and deception. Yet, after even blatant flirtations and sexual innuendo, we are told simply that she perceives "that something beyond her knowledge had taken place in the house" (90). In fact, her governess has become her father's lover, but there are no indications that this penetrates Maisie's consciousness. Her parents and their lovers use her as a pawn for their own espionage and wrath, only to heighten our awareness of the girl's lack of involvement. As everyone speaks over and around her, she is excluded from the adults' discourse to the extent of seeming absent: "Maisie had a greater sense than ever in her life before of not being personally noticed" (124). Edward Gorey brilliantly conveys this in the jacket cover (figure 2) he illustrated for Anchor Books in 1954. Maisie silently sits sketched as a mouthless white blank at a distance from whispering adults; the rest of the picture is colored in.

Not only is Maisie excluded from certain knowledge, but the reader is constantly reminded of her discursive isolation, lack of voice, lack of power. When Miss Overmore marries Beale and quickly becomes disillusioned, she freely conveys to Maisie that her parents are "vile" and "wretched," yet presumes to protect her at the same time:

> Well, if no one had been squared it was because everyone had been vile. No one and everyone were of course Beale and Ida, the extent of whose power to be nasty was a thing that, to a little girl, Mrs. Beale simply couldn't give chapter and verse for. Therefore it was that to keep going at all, as she said, [she] had to make, as she also said, another arrangement—the arrangement in which Maisie was included only to the point of knowing that it existed and wondering wistfully what it was. (136)

The repetition of "she said," "she also said," emphasizes the one-sided authority and focus of adult-child communications reminiscent of Hans's father. Mrs. Beale knows that Maisie's parents are vile, because she says so.

Like Miss Beale, the only time Ida speaks "lucid words" and "almost converses" with her daughter, she is trying to relinquish all parental duty by pawning Maisie off on her stepfather (169, 172). Though she has never sheltered Maisie from her affairs and arguments, she, too, pretends to play a protective role: "'There have been things between us—Sir Claude and me—which I needn't go into, you little nuisance, because you wouldn't understand them'" (173). Here, she actively excludes Maisie from knowing what she has never cared to shelter her from, conveniently falling back on the stereotype of innocent childhood when it suits her rhetorical purpose. And as the narrator cannot report Maisie's understanding, the reader is left guessing what she might think of the situation. In this way, James sets the spotlight on his adult players. Through Maisie's (unknowing?) eyes, the reader gains a removed and inquisitive view of adult folly.

To justifiably and convincingly keep the unknowable Maisie at the center of the novel without representing her consciousness, James limited its focalization to a relatively dramatic point of view, often shifting into indirect discourse (as opposed to free indirect discourse) to foreground the narrator's mediation, and only offering critical interjections through the safe distance of irony. In *Narrative Discourse: An Essay in Method*, Gérard Genette uses *What Maisie Knew* for his defining example of fixed focalization, emphasizing that our window to James's fictive reality is restricted to her view. But more specifically, our view is restricted to what she sees, hears, and says in dialogue with other characters, not what she thinks, or as the title taunts, what she knows. Genette's definition of external focalization from *Fiction and Diction* seems more fitting: "abstaining from *any* intrusion into the character's subjectivity, reporting only their acts and gestures as seen from the outside with no attempt at explanation" (66). Though, strictly, there are some intrusions, to most usefully apply Genette's established terminology, *Maisie* utilizes a modified version of externalized and fixed focalization.

The inaccessible subject challenges even experimental methods in representing point of view. In "Characters and Narrators: Filter, Center, Slant, and Interest-Focus," Seymour Chatman explains that the factor of cognition complicates established approaches that seem to take access for granted: "Genette has always seemed to mean more by *focalisation* than the mere power of sight. He obviously refers to the whole spectrum of perception: hearing, tasting, smelling, and so on. What is not so clear is the extent to which he means it to reflect other mental activity, like cognition" (192). James's technique is to laboriously obscure Maisie's cognition, and this is of such significance to his overall method that it is important to recognize focalization as more than a matter of angle but also of opacity.

Chatman provides a new rubric for discriminating degrees of cognitive disclosure—a factor that becomes increasingly important to consider in the representation of elusive childhood. Using Oliver Twist as an example of a child-center whose misfortunes the reader knows as observed by an omniscient narrator, he writes,

> We immediately infer that for the new-born babe, from his "point of view" (for it makes perfect sense to speak of it as such), it is a matter of concern that he was born in a certain workhouse. [. . .] Since he is too small to see or understand or to have an attitude about such matters, this concern cannot be a matter of filter or slant. We need another name to describe this narrative effect, and I propose "interest-focus." ("Characters and Narrators" 197)

Whereas "filter" and "slant" imply that a focalizing character's consciousness shades our view, "interest-focus" refers to the character on which our interest is focused, thus highlighting that our inference, more so than a narrator's, imposes interpretations of the character's thoughts and feelings. Chatman's terms are effective here because they take opacity into account and suggest the influence that narrative method has on interpretation. Representation is not simply an act of writing, but one of reading as well.

These discrepancies are crucial to understanding a work of fiction in which we are reminded of our inability to access another's consciousness: "'Interest' is of particular importance in narrative-media like film, where a strong sense of identification with one character is built up in the audience, though we have no more access to the character's mind than what we can deduce from what he or she says" ("Characters and Narrators" 190). It should be no surprise that James, whose technique has often been seen as exemplifying a dramatic point of view, shares qualities with filmic (and dramatic) representation in lacking the very thing that Cohn identified as unique to fiction—direct reports of the character's thoughts and feelings. James shows, rather than tells, Maisie's story, leaving us to "construct" her in our own minds the best we can.

James strove for illustration in lieu of exposition, which could be one reason for his frequent comparisons of fiction to painting. In "The Art of Fiction" he praises George Eliot's realism for taking "direct personal

impression" and "convert[ing] these ideas into a concrete image" to "produce a reality" (172). In his notebooks his plans for depicting Maisie and
the events around her reflect his quest for the image, for visual objectivity.
Limiting the novel's focalization to what Maisie sees (gleaning partial
explanations from the gossipy Mrs. Wix) "facilitates [his] making the child
witness the phenomenon in question—prepares the mirror, the plate, on
which it is represented as reflected" (150).

Maisie is described in the preface as a "register of impressions," and she
serves as a canvas throughout the novel: "she found in her mind a collec-
tion of images and echoes to which meanings were attachable—images
and echoes kept for her in the childish dusk, the dim closet, the high drawers, like games she wasn't yet big enough to play" (24, 41). Her function is
a triple task, serving herself, the narration, and the reader: she completes a
picture for herself, providing the canvas of a fictional world for the reader,
who can then piece together a picture of her in turn.

Chatman's specific meaning of "interest-focus" is sharply demonstrated
in such images, where James makes us aware of the visual necessities in
reading narrative. Dorrit Cohn points out, in *The Distinction of Fiction*,
that realists have been fond of highlighting visual mediums as part of the
convention of transparency:

> The assumption of transparency [. . .] has a highly respectable ancestry in
> the paratextual discourse of novelists with a realist orientation, where it
> inspires such images as house of glass (Zola), windows (James), and glass
> pane (Sartre). Conversely, for modernists and postmodernists "trans-
> parency" figures as a crucially denigrating term in their critique of realist
> fiction, signifying the benighted ignorance of the impact of presentational
> conventions on presented content (discourse on story), the illusion that the
> linguistic sign immediately and invisibly gives access to the world as it is.
> (173–74)

Transparency, however, is not a safe assumption in *Maisie*. Cohn's contrast
obscures a continuum in fiction where foregrounding the pane or frame
through which we see a constructed fictional world makes us aware of the
fact that it is constructed—that transparency is a conventional illusion that
is part of fiction. Or, to use Chatman's filmic analogies, a lens can vary in
degrees of transparency—the more opaque, the more we are aware of its
presence. In calling attention to the convention's conventionality, allowing
focus on the medium and the frame, this self-reflexive focus negates the
possible illusion of access (transparency). Just as recognizing transparency

as a fictional convention leads to narrative opacity, in recognizing social constructedness, identity becomes opaque. Where the social subject is concerned, James thus remained remotely respectful. Fictions become explicitly fictive and characters become explicitly constructed.

In *Imagining the Penitentiary*, John Bender points out that "modern novelistic realism in general is marked by its self-representation as a transparent medium, a mode of writing that one sees through rather than a form one looks at" (67). However, realists and modernists have varied in the extent to which they rely on or recognize transparency as a convention. Some rely on a "paradoxical modern conception of a self at once isolated and transparent to view" (201), yet some highlight this paradox. James was such a transitional exemplar—a realist in his quest for accurate representation, a modernist in his use of transparency, but like post-modernists as well, in exposing transparency as a conventional illusion. As Maisie's two governesses quarrel over her and the impropriety of Miss Overmore's affair with Maisie's father, she has a "sharpened sense of spectatorship. [. . .] It gave her often an odd air of being present at her history in as separate a manner as if she could only get at experience by flattening her nose against a pane of glass" (101). James could be describing the reader's experience as well here, and no doubt he recognized the ironic implications of the "pane of glass" imagery.

In his *World-Games*, Christopher Nash calls such images "frame-objects" and identifies them as characteristic to "anti-realist" fiction (perhaps James's example alone proves this a misnomer—Nash uses it to refine the term "post-modernist"): "the mirror now becomes its own counter-reflection—the sign of inadequacy of mimesis itself" (183). Surely the misty pane that obstinately remains between the reader and Maisie also reflects the barrier that James experienced as her creator—the limitations of psychological mining and representation. The fact that he foregrounded these limitations through an externalized, ironic point of view is enough to convince me of his concerns with the "inadequacy of mimesis"—more likely because of a frustrated commitment to realism than anti-realism. James reminds us that one should not forget the frame in looking through it. We should heed this point in our close readings of fiction, as well as in critical discourse that attempts to treat fairly those who are by definition outside of that discourse.

Knowing that his tendencies toward psychological investigation would only lead to futile impositions, James redirected his skills to present Maisie as a lens through which he could stage his narrative dramatically. Later he would articulate this technique theoretically for his preface to *The Awkward*

Age, which he "constructed as a play" (311). He writes, "The divine distinction of the act of a play—and a greater than any other it easily succeeds in arriving at—was, I reasoned, in its special, its guarded objectivity. This objectivity, in turn, when achieving its ideal, came from the imposed absence of that 'going behind,' to compass explanations and amplifications" (309).[2] Drama served as a model for representing the character through external expressions and situations rather than "going behind" the social persona to an inaccessible recess of personal information.

Child characters especially necessitated this "guarded objectivity." Reinhard Kuhn also explains this as a result of a language barrier:

> The writer dares not dwell too long on the child himself, because at best he can recapture only the disappearing echo of his faint voice. [. . .] Faced with this elusive language, the writer is forced to focus his attention not directly on the child but on the reaction to him, and that is why we must resign ourselves to being satisfied with the adult perception of the child without giving up the hope of some day gaining insight into his reality, or an approximation thereof. (61)

By dramatizing social situations rather than developing a speculative inner narrative for Maisie, James keeps the reader aware that an "approximation" of understanding is the closest we can get to the subject position called childhood.

James uses dramatic irony to convey the barrier between adult discourse and those defined by and excluded from it as children. When discussing one of her father's mistresses, "the Countess," Mrs. Wix reveals that Beale has become a kept man of sorts: "'She pays him!'" But Maisie's ironic response accentuates the rift in communication between them: "'Oh *does* she?' At this the child's countenance fell: it seemed to give a reason for papa's behaviour and place it in a more favourable light" (208). To Maisie, who simply disliked "the Countess" based on racist first impressions, the exchange of money is evidence of the woman's generosity, if not her father's prudence. To Mrs. Wix and the implied reader, pay scandalizes the affair even more, but Maisie's response is equally logical, only unsocialized, accenting her exclusion from the complex and culturally relative codes that revolve around sex but exist through language.

Through dramatic irony James can mock adult culture without "amplifying" Maisie's reasoning. Early in the events of the novel, Mrs. Wix shows Maisie a photo of her new stepfather, Sir Claude. Maisie, not recognizing that the photo is a cherished possession to her governess, asks to keep it.

Mrs. Wix replies: "'Keep the pretty picture, by all means, precious. [. . .] Sir Claude will be happy himself, I daresay, to give me one with a kind inscription.'" Again dramatic irony is employed to suggest Maisie's exclusion from the significance of the exchange: "The pathetic quaver of this brave boast was not lost on Maisie, who threw herself [. . .] gratefully on the speaker's neck" (65). In fact, the pathos that Maisie takes as an outpouring of generous reassurance is a revelation of Mrs. Wix's infatuation with Sir Claude. The point seems to be that the point *is lost* on Maisie.

James uses dramatic irony to reveal the construction of "the child" through adult desire because it keeps the focus away from his main character's comprehension, which cannot be fathomed, and places it on the manner in which she is used by the others. He sets the stage for his adult players to cast Maisie in whatever role suits them at the moment, while she absorbs and responds to their expectations in whatever manner she can make sense of them. Mrs. Wix, who early on confides in Maisie about the death of her own child, constructs Maisie as a surrogate: "She's your little dead sister" (49). Ida (Maisie's mother) sees Maisie as a horrible burden that she must bear, serving her self-image of martyr. Miss Beale finds Maisie a useful tool in her courtship with Sir Claude, as Maisie provides a pretext for their meetings, keeping them "perfectly proper" (58). The arbitrary and self-serving nature of such adult constructions is exposed by the rapidity with which they shift.

In the climactic scene when the abandoned Maisie must decide whether to live with Sir Claude and Miss Beale or Mrs. Wix, Miss Beale calls her an "angel" when she thinks she has been chosen, but an "abominable little horror" when she has not (261, 264). Only Sir Claude is consistent in his construction of Maisie—as an honest girl: "'I know when people lie—and that's what I've loved in you, that *you* never do'" (108). Yet he has made her an (unwitting?) accomplice in his own lies, just as all the other adults do. Even the narrator falls back a bit on the traditional construction of child as truthful innocent. Maisie's reporting of her parents' harsh language is described as passive and unknowing: "Then it was that she found the words spoken by her beastly papa to be, after all, in her little bewildered ears, from which, at her mother's appeal, they passed, in her clear shrill voice, straight to her innocent lips" (42). Again, however, the emphasis (seen in the exaggerated diction) is on the parents' manipulation of Maisie as a go-between informant. The harsh words "pass" through "bewildered," not hurt or understanding, ears "straight to her innocent lips" apparently without stopping to register on the way. She is a medium, not a player, in the drama.

Fiona Björling describes the common device of figuring child innocence to function as a medium: "The Romantic and realist writers
approached the child from without, as an object, the redeemer or the victim of a corrupt social order [...] . From the end of the eighteenth and
through the nineteenth centuries, children represented a measuring rod by
which to establish patterns of right and wrong" (6). Following a tradition
of literary child-figuration (like that of Dickens and Twain) that held "the
child" up as an innocent reflector of social ills, James's Maisie is a satiric
mirror. But she is an empty mirror, and James generally takes care to foreground rather than legitimate traditional constructions (of purity and
ignorance) in his representation. Maisie figures the "imposed absence" of
psychological exploration—she is a model for his method. She does not
simply reflect social ills; she reflects the process of adults constructing children, and in doing so she reflects James's own grappling with realist representation. After all, what is representation but self-conscious social
construction?

For those who disregard as imposing and essentializing any cognitive
models that standardize the figuration of child personalities, the fictional
representation of children is limited. But at least the process of learning
can be speculated more convincingly than its starting point. As a result,
Björling writes, "The modernist artist is interested in the transition from
ignorance to knowledge, from the pre-verbal to the verbal state of mind. A
paradox consists in the fact that the artist can only feign access to the
child's pre-verbal state of mind to which he would give expression" (6).
James was aware of the relativity inherent in social subjectivity, and even
more so, of the adult-child language barrier that limits articulation of
resulting differences.

A central theme of *Maisie* is the transition from "ignorance to knowledge," and James continually foregrounds the constructedness of knowledge through Maisie's development. Her impressions of others form in
terms of how Maisie observes them being defined by each other. James
illustrates how her perceptions are socially prescribed. Her initially negative reactions to the Countess are implicitly due to the woman's dark skin
and some vague racism she has been exposed to, but Maisie is mostly troubled by the unexpected need to redefine her father according to others'
perceptions of his association with her: "all in a moment she had had to
accept her father as liking someone whom she was sure neither her mother,
nor Mrs. Beale, nor Mrs. Wix, nor Sir Claude, nor the Captain, nor even
Mr. Perriam and Lord Eric could have possibly liked" (158–59). Based on
a composite of the public views she discerns, Maisie's mind simply reflects

the prejudice of those around her. Likewise, her impressions of Mrs. Wix are based on how she sees others seeing her: "At first she had looked cross and almost cruel; but this impression passed away with the child's increased perception of her being in the eyes of the world a figure mainly to laugh at" (49–50). At a surprisingly brutal moment, Maisie seems to have accepted this socialized view of her mentor when she tells Mrs. Wix, "'Oh you're nobody!'" (231).

A more theoretically direct example of James's attention to the process of socialization comes when Maisie considers the concepts of youth and age. Reflecting the various contextual meanings of "youth," a term that she clearly recognizes as one socially applied to herself, she wades through the apparent inconsistencies of adult discourse:

> The only mystification [. . .] was the imposing time of life that her elders spoke of as youth. For Sir Claude then Mrs. Beale was "young," just as for Mrs. Wix Sir Claude was [. . .] . What therefore was Maisie herself, and, in another relation to the matter, what therefore was mamma? It took her some time to puzzle out with the aid of an experiment or two that it wouldn't do to talk about mamma's youth [. . .] . Yet if she wasn't young then she was old and this threw an odd light on her having a husband of a different generation. [. . .] [T]hese persons, it appeared, were not of the age they ought to be. (84–85)

In one of the rare illusive indulgences into Maisie's thought, James establishes that "youth" and "age" are relative and constantly shifting concepts, which brings into question Maisie's own status as "a child." Clearly youth is not simply, as Maisie considers, a definable "time of life" but a socially constructed idea that changes with and serves adult agendas. In this passage James not only reminds the reader that "youth" is a cultural construct, but he foregrounds his (and our) own act of constructing.

By creating an interest-focus with limited cognitive disclosure, James draws his reader's attention to his method and theory as much as to character or plot. As Sonja Bâsíc has said, "Point of view for James served both these ends: a passionate recreating of the sense of life and a detached awareness of the process of constituting it in literary form" (205). Every time he denies access to Maisie's thought, he reminds us of his diplomatic epistemology. *Maisie* is a case study in the inaccessibility of child minds and the impossibility of realist representation in light of relative subjectivities. James wrote in his preface, "The effort really to see and really to represent is no idle business in the face of the *constant* force that makes for muddlement" (30). In embracing the challenge, he reveals his commitment to psychological realism while jumping directly into questions typical of modernist epistemology, even technically prefiguring some postmodernist answers.

"Recreating the sense of life" in *Maisie* is difficult to achieve without some interruptions on the part of the narrator, who even admits to the difficulty: "I so despair of courting her noiseless mental footsteps here that I must crudely give you my word" (212). But for the most part, James turns the impossibility of representation into an opportunity for self-reflective irony. He teases, "What she knew, what she *could* know is by this time no secret to us" (184). In fact, the reader knows what Maisie is exposed to and might comprehend, but the very secret that taunts us is the unanswerable question of what she does know. By foregrounding his own struggle in representing a child, he draws our attention to the impossibility of fairly comprehending one and heightens our awareness of the adult construction of children and the relativistic speculation inherent in psychological realism.

In his introduction to the novel, Paul Theroux points out that James turned to writing about children "at a harrowing time in his career (his play had been a humiliating failure late in 1895)" (8). This topical shift, apparently, is not uncommon (for example, William Faulkner and Toni Morrison did the same under similar pressures). Björling might offer an explanation in her analysis:

> The artist attempts to channel despair into creation and turns to the child [. . .] as a source of inspiration. The creativity of the child consists in the fact that he passes from a state of complete ignorance at birth to a state of knowledge. It is the actual moment of transition from ignorance to knowledge which bears witness to creativity; knowledge once obtained becomes automatic and loses its value. (6)

The above perspectives might suggest that James is projecting through Maisie, but there are theoretical reasons for his choices. The inaccessible child allowed him to investigate the process of acquiring language and crossing boundaries of cultural knowledge. It also gave him the opportunity to demonstrate his narrative control despite an awareness of the limitations of his craft, and to encourage sensitivity to social difference. In *Narrative Discourse Revisited*, Genette wrote, of James's shift from first-person to third-person narrative and even dramatic point of view, that the reasons behind "James's conversions for *Maisie* and *The Ambassadors* are vouched for only by the later testimony of the prefaces. The difficulty

James evoked for Maisie is clear enough (the little girl's limited vocabulary) but not very convincing (Maisie could have told the story many years
later)" (111). To the contrary, I think James's explanation for the shift is
more than sufficient, because it is the very difficulty of representing a child
that keeps the novel so interesting. His choice to focus on the younger
Maisie suggests an interest in the inter-subjective void created by her "limited vocabulary." Genette's point, however, draws one's attention to the
fact that the limits of (child) representation, even more than narrative
technique, were his primary consideration.

In light of this reasoning, one might argue that James reverted to first
person in *The Turn of the Screw* (1898) to get even more removed from the
minds of his focal child characters. The novella certainly continues his
investigation of adult attitudes toward children implemented in *Maisie*.
Robin Hoople points out that the focal characters in each work "share in
the functions of illustrating James's exposure of social corruption represented in the abandonment of the child, and they are strongly parallel in
their being exploited by adults whose sexual impulses are stronger than
their sense of responsibility to the children who rely on them" (285). Both
works isolate children in order to sharpen a more critical view of the culture that surrounds them; however, I would replace Hoople's term "corruption" with "construction." We can never know whether Maisie, Miles,
or Flora is effectively corrupted by the influences that surround them—
James suggests that we cannot know their minds. Shine writes, "At no
point in the story does James have Flora or Miles do anything that might
not be construed as perfectly normal behavior for children of their class
and obvious intelligence. The reader can never, with any degree of certainty, say what the children really are, only what they could possibly be"
(138). By resisting stock child characterization and distancing us from the
children through a narrator with understandably narrow but empowered
biases, James denies us any illusion of certainty about the children's
cognition.

If we recognize that we cannot access children's minds but only the
constructions we have created around the young persons who seem to fit
those ever-changing definitions, an investigation of childhood demands
that we look more closely at adult desire for the reasons behind the constructions. *The Turn of the Screw* forces just this sort of reflection. James
distances the reader even more from his interest-focus (the children) by
shifting the narrative control to an adult, emphasizing the void and lack of
verbal representation for children in adult discourse. In this way, the reader
is encouraged to look critically at adults' perceptions even while dependent

upon them. Millicent Bell points out that James's use of first person achieves this by confining "us to the subjectivity of a single observer who can never know everything, and who must be acknowledged to have no final vision" (14). Though limited to the governess's view, we are likely to question it because it cannot be validated. Bell argues that this critical awareness can be expected: "the reader finds himself unable to trust [the narrator's self-] validation. A modernist illusion of reality is more likely to be based on the feeling that life is *not* a determined-upon narrative in the head of the author-God. *Our* sense of reality includes the recognition of randomness and irrelevance" (14). If the reader of *The Turn of the Screw* is aware that multiple perspectives are necessarily silenced through first-person narration and that the fictive reality is shaped only by what she sees and comprehends, the story becomes a case study of her perceptions and the act of interpretation itself.

Most criticism of *The Turn of the Screw* has debated whether the children are truly possessed or if the governess is going mad. But James leaves this question unanswerable. The answerable question the work provokes is "Can we know?" Clearly not. Centering the conflict (and interest-focus) on two children who cannot engage adult discourse (if only for lack of an adult who can hear them without prejudice) yet narrating from that alienating, adult-biased position, he leaves his fictive reality impossible to validate. As Bell puts it, "the first-person narrative imprisons us in indeterminacy" (202). That indeterminacy hopefully inspires the critical reflection necessary to question our own power and bias as adults.

It is through James's rendering of the governess constructing the children that he effectively raises questions about the possibility of doing so with fairness or certainty, with the resulting demonstration that imposing simple interpretations upon ambiguous reality is dangerous. Bell writes that James's "occasional sorties into the first-person mode are open demonstrations that absolute truth is inaccessible to the reader" (15). In this case, the "truth" readers want, namely to know whether the children are deceiving and malicious, is inaccessible—even the fictive illusion of a discernible reality is destabilized by a recognition of the dominance of adult desire.

The story could be seen as a cautionary tale against imposing definitions (especially that of innocence) upon children. Reinhard Kuhn writes, "The enterprise of defending what is doomed by fate is ineffectual and can be as disastrous as simple submission to an ineluctable destiny. This is the bitter lesson which the governess [. . .] seems incapable of learning. When she arrives at Bly, the estate is to her eyes the perfect childhood paradise as envisioned by adults" (145). According to this interpretation the governess imagines a fairy-tale world that cannot exist, insisting upon the children's cooperation in the staging of it, failing to recognize that she has unrealistically imposed it herself. James Kincaid portrays this as a typical adult misunderstanding: "no child can ever live up to our imaginative and nostalgic demands. The child can never fulfill our desire for it, a desire based on a void within us so vast as to be measureless" (*Erotic Innocence* 144).

Whether or not we interpret the children as possessed, their dialogue and actions suggest the ill-fitting simplicity of adult expectations for them. As no human being's complexity fits narrow definitions, Miles often deviates from expectations of unquestioning obedience and sweetness, which draws attention to his inscrutability. When he wanders out at night (with the help of Flora's diversion), the governess asks, "'You must tell me now. [. . .] What did you go out for?'" And his response challenges the simplicity of her constructing: "'just exactly in order that you should do this. [. . .] Think me—for a change—*bad!* '" (46).

The inscrutability of the children provides the conflict of the fiction. The governess has very little evidence to help her assess the motives and safety of her wards. Because she has no access to what Miles thinks, she often interprets/projects adult motives in lieu of accepting simply not knowing. When Miles demonstrates scholastic ability, she writes, "the impression I might have got, if I had dared to work it out, [was] that he was under some influence operating in his small intellectual life" (38). Rather than crediting his own intellect, she attributes his performance to an influence, not surprisingly, an adult's (Quint). His cognitive inaccessibility defies her attempts to classify so that she can only justify her conclusions by characterizing deviations as unchildlike.[3] Toward the end she says that he "appear[ed] as accessible as an older person [. . .] almost as an intellectual equal" (62). However, his mind remains unyielding to her, especially because she cannot see him as a complex person but a stereotype.

Millicent Bell writes of the narrator, "In crafting her story she is like the writer in her efforts; she is also like the reader, who seeks, by interpretation, to organize the impressions of her and of what she perceives into a continuous narrative with a single meaning" (228). Though many readers accept the governess's "single" interpretation of events, James hints that such a reading is dangerously simple: "as regards a presentation of things so fantastic as in that wanton little tale, I can only rather blush to see real substance read into them" (*Letters* 297). In his preface to *The Aspern Papers*, James discusses *The Turn of the Screw* and makes his meaning clearer:

There is for such a case no eligible *absolute* of the wrong; it remains to fifty other elements, a matter of appreciation, speculation, imagination—these things moreover quite exactly in the light of the spectator's, the critic's, the reader's experience. Only make the reader's general vision of evil intense enough [. . .] and his own experience, his own imagination, his own sympathy (with the children) and horror (of their false friends) will supply him quite sufficiently with all the particulars. (101)

Does James include the governess among the children's "false friends"? He curiously does not mention the possibility that the true source of horror could be the children themselves—a possibility brilliantly exploited, yet kept ambiguous, in the 1961 film adaptation, *The Innocents*. But in the text, he leaves this possibility open. The "particulars" that the reader can supply in speculation are impossible to validate. That is the point: child subjectivity is as inscrutable as the text. The "reader's experience" shapes the reading—leaving us only with "particulars" that we supply ourselves. Ellen Pifer notes irony in this: "each reader participates in creating the novel's meaning by building on the elusive and ambiguous image of childhood. That is why, in surveying the voluminous criticism on this novella, one can learn as much about a critic's construction of childhood as about the governess's" (52–53). The reflections in James's opaque glass never seem to end.

Ellis Hanson adds spin to this insight: "There are no innocent readers of this text, it has often been pointed out, but we are infantilized by our very belief in innocence" (369). The tendency of critics to read Miles and Flora as victimized either by ghosts or the governess, but not as possible agents of harm themselves, reflects how the stereotyping of young persons as children not only confines them to discomfort or dissembling but limits us to denial and hypocrisy: "The erotic innocence of children is founded on the presumption that they cannot possibly understand or experience sexual desire except as trauma" (374). Limiting possible interpretations to adult struggles for the children's souls negates the possibility of their sexuality (however defined) and, more importantly, their agency. Our constructions are complicit in this negation. We, as readers of *Turn of the Screw*, find the evidence in the governess of our own impositions on children, revealing the self-serving nature of our sentimentality toward children. We insist on their simplicity for our own comfort.

James robs us of the security that comes from the fictive illusion of a discernible reality, and he does so with the insistence that there are no absolute truths, no matter what we reason ourselves into accepting. Through his work child-characters became a device through which to investigate margins of subjectivity. Whereas earlier nineteenth-century writers (Dickens, Twain, Stowe, Hawthorne) may have recognized the power of child figures to represent stock attributes (vulnerability, naturalness, purity, original sin), James's work represents a shift in thinking about the unsocialized subject—from flatly knowable agent to complexly inaccessible outsider. As a result, his fictive worlds narrativize children into the periphery, allowing them to become irreducibly complex focal points of interest. Through James we take a watchful, diplomatic step back from the subject position carved out through discourse as "childhood," if only to see its discursive nature and our own motivations a little more clearly.

Referring to James's indirect treatment of children (the inaccessibility of them), Leslie Fiedler asks, "why have our writers welcomed so indirect an evocation of the child's passage from innocence to experience? In a way, it seems the last genteel reticence; a refusal to portray the child as an actual sinner, though it is no longer possible to postulate his innocence as absolute" ("Eye of Innocence" 500–501). I would argue that James resisted this "genteel" impulse in order to heighten awareness of the dangerous self-deception and harmful intrusion that results from "postulating innocence as absolute." He evokes the "child's passage" indirectly to avoid any further imposition of unverifiable subjectivities.

Capitalizing on the unique challenge that child characters present to the conscientious social observer, he further developed his own theme on the limitations of language in creating inter-subjectivity. Reinhard Kuhn writes that the enigmatic child figure "is the forever undecodable signifier" whose "universe represents a self-enclosed non-referential system. [. . .] [C]ommunication between the child and adult is virtually impossible" (20, 60). Recognizing the obstacles that language and ideology create in bridging subjectivities, James found in child-figures a vehicle for representing the void between them. As "self-enclosed" language users, his child-figures evade the rationalist grasp of the psychological novelist, and his treatment of them allowed him to work through some questions that became fundamental to twentieth-century thinkers. Björling asks,

> Does language communicate something which exists independently, or is that which is communicated actually created in language? Central to modernist literature concerned with the child is a preoccupation with the question of the child and language. The poet draws an implicit analogy between his own creativity and the child on the lines that the poet searching for the word which will bring reality to life is like the child who comprehends reality in learning to name it. (6)

James anticipates contemporary approaches to discourse that would answer Björling's question with the latter. "Reality," subjectivity, and "childhood," for the purpose of literature and discourse, are all "created in language." If only in "learning to name" reality it is real, and yet still a function and construction of discourse, then children (defined/excluded by an inability to represent themselves according to legitimated standards of linguistic sophistication) cannot enter social "reality" without entering discourse. And the reverse follows: if children cannot enter into discourse (for lack of vocabulary and capable adult listeners), they are inaccessible to adults, who are trapped in their own socialized realities. As I will show in chapter 5, James and many others who focus on the inaccessibility of children are not so fatalistic about children's exclusion from discourse as Kuhn would suggest. But in James subjective inaccessibility is concretely dramatized, and from his precedent we can fully appreciate twentieth-century efforts to represent that social space we call childhood without trespassing.

CHILDHOOD BOUND

*P*eter Pan has Neverland; Mary Lennox, her secret garden; Laura Ingalls, her "magic circle";[1] Fern Arable, the barnyard; Harriet Welsch, her imaginary "town"; and Dorothy Gale has the Land of Oz. Fictional children (even Laura Ingalls is "constructed" through the memory of Laura Ingalls Wilder) often have a magical place to visit, inhabit, explore, or even rule. All of these friendly spaces, of course, were dreamt up by adult authors—the tradition of creating such spaces is so pervasive as to be untraceable.[2] The most popular landscapes are the garden and remote island, but all of these childhood spaces share one quality—they are clearly bound and inaccessible to adults. Peter Pan's Neverland bars parents, Mary's garden is walled and locked, Fern's barnyard is exclusive in that only she can talk with the animals, Harriet's "town" is her creative alternative to the adult spaces she spies on, and Dorothy's Land of Oz is surrounded by an "impassable desert." Yet these spaces invite us, as Tim Morris has put it: "In each case, the text is an appropriation by an adult of a territory that is supposed to belong to a child. Each text proposes a place that belongs to children alone—the Garden, Neverland [. . .] and adults who take an unseemly interest in invading it" (89). Adults imagine such inaccessible spaces in order to be the exception to the rule—the adult who has access.

Rather than settling for the impossible illusion of accessing child-minds, we spatialize childhood to receive us by creating escapist fantasy worlds. Such spaces reflect an increased awareness of the inaccessibility of that inner identity we call childhood. In the case of pastoral literature, these spaces surrogate our own inaccessible pasts through nostalgia; in literature about children, they provide the illusion of vicarious accessibility to the current childhoods of others. To sustain the illusion of (im)possible accessibility, writers who spatialize childhood must enable a private fantasy that the space is uniquely friendly to the reader, and for the reader to suspend disbelief that such spaces exist without visible proof they must be clearly isolated and bound.

Pastoralism and the spatialization of childhood draw from similar adult desires and are often fused (as in edenic myth, which spatializes the concept of innocence that enables the concept of childhood). The romantic association of children with the pastoral was articulated by Rousseau, through whom childhood became idealized in simplified contrasts to adult experience: natural vs. civilized, unknown vs. knowable, irrational vs. rational. Frances Hodgson Burnett, who wrote of her childhood England during her adulthood in the United States, created one of the most famous pastoral landscapes for children in *The Secret Garden* (1911). Burnett envisions the worlds of child and adult as distinctly separate by spatializing Rousseauistic oppositions. In "Digging Up *The Secret Garden:* Noble Innocents or Little Savages?" Christine Wilkie describes Burnett's division of spaces: "The narrative events take place between the house and garden, which respectively carry all the negative and positive connotations embedded in primitive thought: the artifice of Civilization versus the Wild" (79).

It is only natural that adults would dream up protective spaces for fictional children and their readers, but surely the civilized world is safer for children than true wilderness. In fact, this idealized (and enclosed) wilderness is more likely an adult's refuge—escape from the "artifice of civilization" that includes routine, responsibility, public activity, and abstraction.

Burdens of adult experience define childhood through contrast. Take, for example, a bias in popular thought (inherited from developmental psychology) that abstract thought is unique to adults. This assumption seems to be wrapped up with the definition of children as irrational but also comes from a long history of measuring adult status by literacy. Thus, Mary rejuvenates Colin's health by getting him to put down books and be active. In fact, Colin could easily represent an adult trying to recapture youth through a rejection of civilized constraints and abstract thought. Henry Nash Smith has defined the pastoral as an escape from abstraction: "The central meaning of the pastoral is the rejection of the aspiring mind [. . .] [T]rue content is to be found in this renunciation" (10). Colin's rejuvenation requires that he move from his bookish and unhealthy interior to the outdoors to get simple, hands-on experience in the garden—as believably an adult fantasy as a child's.

Likewise, popular adventure narratives, often featuring islands with buried treasure or isolated from adult society, indulge adult fantasies of fortune and escape as much as child fantasies of empowerment. For example, in Scott O'Dell's *Island of the Blue Dolphins* (1960), one can easily pick up feminist and child-positive messages of self-reliance as Karana teaches herself the necessary skills (weapon-making, home-building, hunting/fishing) for surviving alone on the island. But the novel's idealization of social isolation serves a double purpose. Ellen E. Seiter describes one of them: "In presenting challenges to the human will and spirit, survival tales have enormous appeal. They speak to the fantasy of living in a state of complete independence, alone with nature and free of all social responsibilities. For children, this fantasy is particularly powerful because of the dependent and subordinate [*sic*] nature of children's relationships to parents and teachers" (183). Surely, however, adults are as burdened by social responsibilities. This is escape for them as well.

Adults fantasize a *locus amoenus* (friendly place) for child-characters, through whom we can vicariously enter as well. Even in a historical novel such as *Island of the Blue Dolphins* this pattern is suggested. Beverly Lyon Clark has pointed out that the "historical Lost Woman of San Nicolas was a woman. She was left behind on the island not because she'd returned for her brother, as in O'Dell's novel, but because she'd returned for her child" (letter to the editor, January 16, 2004). O'Dell's reasons for lowering her age seem significant to fulfilling the fantasy. Just as fantasy spaces are often accessible to child-characters through special means—Dorothy's silver shoes, a magic clock in *Tom's Midnight Garden,* a secret door in *The Secret Garden,* platform 9¾ at King's Cross in the *Harry Potter* books—the child-character becomes the vicarious means to accessing such spaces for adult writers, consumers, and (dual) readers. Regardless of genre—pastoral, fantasy, or "children's"—such spaces serve and are shaped by adult desires. They comprise adult fantasies of and for childhood.

Vladimir Nabokov's *Lolita* (1955) could be said to best make this point, and brutally. This dark parody of romantic child-worship exposes the ugly underside of adult idealizations and possessiveness toward childhood—demonstrating how we silence individual thought by imposing rigid and needy expectations of innocence/ignorance. In *Lolita,* the blind adult desire behind such constructions is exaggerated to pedophilic envy. But Nabokov, through his ever-layered, ironic narrator, makes it clear that this novel is not about sexual perversion, it is about the hypocritical, nonsensical, and damaging ways we construct youth in the name of nostalgia, enabled to do so *ad infinitum* because the very thing we seek is inaccessible to us.

Humbert Humbert writes, "I am not concerned with 'sex' at all. [. . .] A greater endeavor lures me on: to fix once and for all the perilous magic of nymphets" (134). In *Reading Lolita in Tehran*, Azar Nafisi explains this more straightforwardly: "The desperate truth of Lolita's story is *not* the rape of a twelve-year-old by a dirty old man but *the confiscation of one individual's life by another*" (33).

Only toward the end of his confessional narrative, when listening to "the concord" of some children laughing, does H. H. recognize the impossibility of "fixing" youth and the cruelty that results from his attempts: "then I knew that the hopelessly poignant thing was not Lolita's absence from my side, but the absence of her voice from that concord" (308). His statement reveals a dawning awareness that Lolita has not been allowed a voice in any context in which he listens. In their travels, H. H. had only absolutes (inherited from romantic literature, like Poe's "Annabel Lee") with which to imagine Lolita's mind, and when he comes closest to deconstructing these absolutes, he automatically reconstructs her along pastoral lines: "it struck me [. . .] that I simply did not know a thing about my darling's mind and that quite possibly, behind the awful juvenile clichés, there was in her a garden and a twilight, and a palace gate—dim and adorable regions which happened to be lucidly and absolutely forbidden to me" (284). Even Humbert Humbert recognizes that the nymphet-identity he imposes and his own inability to listen bar him from truly accessing and "fixing" a child-mind, which he, too, resorts to spatializing.

In *The Poetics of Childhood*, Roni Natov claims that *Lolita* exemplifies the "anti-pastoral"—I disagree. Nabokov's novel engages the pastoral in a meta-discourse on romanticism. In it he shows how our cherished romantic attitudes toward children, illustrated in the above pastoral imaging of Lolita's mindscape, are complicit in simplifying, manipulating, and appropriating experiences of supposed children. Perhaps Natov has overlooked this point because her approach is still partially invested in nostalgic reterritorializing, as revealed in such statements as "Behind the fractured adult a child hides, estranged from his or her own history" (2) and "Through language, the adult can recapture in part what can never fully be reclaimed" (6). But this is probably a matter of mincing methodologies. More pertinent to my reading is Natov's succinct expression of Nabokov's theme as a "convoluted perversion of a search for newness" (171). Humbert Humbert's ennui is that of an aged aesthete, like Des Esseintes in J. K. Huysmans's *Against the Grain* (1884)—someone who has courted so much indulgence that nothing can seem refreshingly new.[3] It is this modern need for novelty, exemplified to an extreme by the decadents, that can create yet seem sated by nostalgia, which, ironically, makes the old seem new again.

Childhood landscapes, which are defined in contrast to and as an escape from known adult spaces, can appear simply in Western literature as the untamed, unknown—particularly because they take on a characteristic of newness. Joseph Conrad's Marlow in *Heart of Darkness* (1902) associates unmapped territories with the fascination of his youth: "when I was a little chap I had a passion for maps [...] . At that time there were many blank spaces on the earth" (5). Steinbeck's Jody in *The Red Pony* (1945) also expresses the most fascination with a place he has never been—the mountains he can see from home: "Jody knew something was there, something very wonderful because it wasn't known" (41). The association of childhood with geographical exploration hints at the adult's colonizing grasp,[4] but more so, it reveals adult envy of the greater opportunities for novelty that younger and less experienced persons must possess, and adult feelings of entrapment in an increasingly industrialized and developed territory. Sylvia Patterson Iskander points out that "the first great age of writing for children took place in the United States in the 1870s, when [...] many Americans turned to the business of economic and geographic expansion. This great shift in the national culture, away from a largely rural and agricultural way of life, led inevitably to a kind of nostalgia for the past" (257). The past, that is, made new again by constructing "children" as an audience and lens.

For modern American writers the pastoral is often modified into rural/agricultural settings, as in Baum's *Wizard of Oz* (1900). Though sometimes frightening, the rural areas of Oz are mostly depicted as safe and charming. Some critics might object—for example, Virginia Wolf assumes the opposite in "The Linear Image": "The road and the city are beautiful; civilization is better than nature" (42). However, such an interpretation overlooks Baum's direct criticisms of urban culture. Civilization, though it appears beautiful in Oz, is deceptive. This is especially evident in the green lenses the citizens unquestioningly wear. Oz is not really green, but the surrounding, uncivilized areas are full of color.[5] Oz offers an ironic confirmation of Natov's description: "the green world in the literature of childhood is a response to the worldliness of the world. Whether it represents a retreat from the world's injustices—parental or the extended social world—it offers a natural critique of civilization and stands in contradistinction to the 'unnatural'—machines, laws, and customs" (91).

The Land of Oz is a magical place because of its lack of "civilizing" and industrializing influences. Glinda contrasts it with Kansas by explaining: "In the civilized countries I believe there are no witches left; nor wizards, nor sorceresses, nor magicians. But, you see, the Land of Oz has never been civilized, for we are cut off from all the rest of the world" (*Wizard of Oz* 14). That she fails to mention the city of Oz as civilized might suggest a way to interpret Baum's construction of this varied world. Oz is not so much civilized as it is a parody of civilization as Baum knew it in America. Most notable of its features (and relevant to the Gilded Age in which Baum was writing) is its artifice. Its inhabitants are willing to wear green glasses and believe that all they see is splendid emerald. Baum is dramatizing what Lacan and, especially, Althusser would call *méconnaissance*—the inevitable "misknowing" that comes from linguistic or ideological indoctrination. Just as we are limited by means of our socialization from thinking outside of it, the people of Oz "misrecognize" their city's true colors in order to adhere to the ideology that defines their community—love of wealth, glamour, and artifice. This subversive view of the city debunks their "enlightened consumerism"[6] of all things emerald and increases our appreciation for the surrounding countryside (blue, yellow, purple, and red).

Dorothy escapes from her home in gray, economically depressed Kansas to a pastoral refuge. Though both are rural spaces, only the fantasy one is truly safe because Dorothy is empowered there. The parallel focus on rural space allows a familiar escape and yet at the same time serves as neutral territory for thinking through conflicts back home (the latter theme/device is emphasized more in the film than in the books). As Iskander puts it, childhood offers a fictional space in which adult pressures are worked out: "the tremendous social conflict of urban and industrial America is transmuted into generational conflict between irrepressible children and authoritarian adults, and that conflict in turn is tamed through recourse to the land" (258).

Usually, as Natov has pointed out, greenspace in pastoral literature is straightforwardly peaceful and regenerative. In *The Secret Garden*, images of green growth suggest a positive development for children: "the secret garden was coming alive and two children were coming alive with it" (295). This theme is appropriated for adult readers in Alison Lurie's *Only Children* (1979), where the adult characters and children experience a pastoral escape, though from perspectives carefully kept separate. The Hubbards and Zimmerns spend a weekend at the rustic farm of Anna King, their girls' "magical" and liberal-minded teacher. Here Lurie uses the pastoral setting to release the adults from their urbane lifestyles and responsibilities, some regressing to "childish antics," others demonstrating adult corruptness. Lurie associates Anna and her farmhouse with childhood spaces via the pastoral. A child visitor there, Lolly Zimmern, personifies the Virginia creeper that adds magical green to the surroundings in her imagination: "Virginia loving Anna's house, surrounding it holding it hugging it safe forever" (41). Her friend, Mary Ann, observes her parents' relaxation as a response to the safe space: "Suppose there was a sort of magic spell on Anna's house that made everybody who visited her slowly turn into children, if they weren't already" (201).

In *White Mule* (1937), pediatrician poet William Carlos Williams suggests a deeper motive behind adult nostalgia for pastoral childhood spaces. Two urban parents want a pastoral escape for their child, Flossie. Gurlie, her mother, also associates greenspace with the baby's healthy development, urging her husband to move to the country, or at least the suburbs where they can have a garden: "I tell you we've got to move. [. . .] Or else the baby will die. It can't live here. [. . .] It has no air, it's dying from these rooms" (58). Yet in the following sentence she reveals that she's projecting her own desire to escape the city: "I'm dying. We're all dying here" (58). As an immigrant from the "old world," she evokes a nostalgic image of the countryside that reveals a bias many urban adults share: "It's because there's no tradition here, no peasants that love the land. There is no feeling of . . . of reality" (138). Her sense of disconnectedness has become the impetus behind so much nostalgia for the past and its symbolic American equivalent, the countryside.

That the pastoral has so easily conflated with narratives of childhood reveals between them a common adult desire to reinhabit their own pasts (ideally remembered). Iskander explains the conflation of personal memory with a rural past in expansionist American literature: "Conceived of as a vacant continent, the land for white Americans was not simply the source of raw materials and economic abundance but was linked inextricably with their own selfhood. To move into supposedly vacant land was equivalent to occupying the inner landscape" (258). Deleuze and Guattari point out that reminiscing expresses the impossible adult desire for such revisitations: "Memory brings about a reterritorialization of childhood" (78). If you build it, your inner child will come.

However, when Gurlie visits the country, she realizes that the adults who live there have the same concerns and strains as those in the city. Her nostalgia gives way to a more balanced view of rural life. Nevertheless, *White Mule* ends with an image of the pastoral child, Flossie (not insignificantly named for Flora), who, unlike Gurlie, finds communion with nature in the final scene, "the baby's face, smeared with berry juice, her hands sooty, quite part of it all" (291).

Though the child-focus of the novel becomes "part of" the pastoral setting, Gurlie's complaint draws attention to the difficulty of such communions. The disconnectedness she feels is a result of becoming an experienced socialized subject. In his preface to *The Garden and the Map: Schizophrenia in Twentieth-Century Literature and Culture,* John Vernon argues that socialization (which is inescapably hegemonic) can trap us in misknowing: "A culture is the most pervading organization of experience for each of us; it is what, after childhood, makes the perceptions of a few accessible to the many, and also what enslaves us to those perceptions" (x). Though once absorbed into a culture and its ideologies we might believe in shared perceptions, a sense of a knowable, shared reality is dependent upon some amount of perceptual entrapment. As Louis Althusser has pointed out (and Paul de Man in my introduction), we are generally unaware of the ideological nature of the ideologies to which we subscribe—what we have taken on faith limits our perceptions more than we realize. Yet experience exposes us to social differences and relativity, both of which belie the myth of inter-subjectivity, especially when they reveal our own misperceptions. What Frederic Jameson has written of post-modern experience applies here (as it does in much literature on childhood, perhaps because of a shared focus on ontological uncertainty). With an increasing awareness of "a gap between phenomenological perception and a reality that transcends all individual thinking or experience" comes "the incapacity to map socially" (353). When we begin to recognize that "reality" is subjective rather than "inter-subjective," the result is, as in Gurlie's case, a sense of fragmentation and isolation. Thus, cognitively mapping a social totality in which the self is centered and connected to others becomes impossible. Jameson's use of the term "cognitive mapping" is significant here, as his response to fragmentation and social isolation highlights the need for envisioning a totalizing space. Writers who turn to spatializing childhood are responding to the same impossible need—to bridge a gap between child and adult subjectivities. Behind this need lies the assumption that childhood offers totalizing spaces, if only we could regain access to them.

Roger Hart, a geographer who studied a small group of children in the 1970s, expressed this sentiment in *Children's Experience of Place.* To his thinking, socialization aids in a gradual mapping and naming of one's environment that leads to a sense of inter-subjective belonging: "Places and objects carry meaning for each of us because we were given a name for them which we could then use to differentiate the place or object from the totally perceived environment. Through this process we each come to live in an inter-subjective landscape where there is a consensuality over what meaning these places and objects have" (342). Like Jameson, Hart is equating the ability to cognitively map with totalization. His analysis suggests that childhood spaces, because they are smaller and more clearly bound (the home, a backyard, school, and playground) can be totalizing: "understanding the extent and diversity of the world is an important part of any child's developing conception of his or her own existence in the universe. The large amount of time spent by children deeply involved in modelling the environment in micro-scale is one demonstration of their desire to give order and meaning to the larger environment" (340). As adults, we may yearn for the apparent control, order, and simplicity of cognitively mapping smaller spaces, expressing envy for what we perceive as a lesser challenge in orientation. This also explains the tendency toward constructing literary childhood spaces as limited, small, and mappable. Hart concludes, "There may be a basic urge for each of us to surround ourselves with *a known,* and hence, safe space to which we can retreat in times of danger or difficulty" (my italics, 340).

In his study of child spatializing ability, Alexander W. Siegel explains, "Like any type of learning, the construction of cognitive maps is not a process of accumulating facts, but rather a process of becoming unconfused" (25). But the larger our own cognitive maps become, as we grow and experience the world, the more potential for confusion. It is not surprising, then, that adults seek consolation in the comfortable imaginary confines of nostalgic spaces. That we locate such places in childhood reflects our longing for the kind of rootedness those of us fortunate enough are granted in childhood—a static sense of home, belonging, and safety, or what E. Relph calls "an irreplaceable centre of significance" (39).

Exile-in-hiding Salman Rushdie experienced just how irreplaceable such centeredness is after being condemned to death by Ayatollah Khomeini, and he brings his unique perspective to light on MGM's *Wizard of Oz* (1939),which emphasizes the importance of home far more than Baum's book. Taking the British holiday tradition of viewing the film to heart, he has written, "I've done a good deal of thinking, these past three years, about the advantages of a good pair of ruby slippers" (19). He explains that a nostalgic space embodies a relative concept of "home," which, for most of us, is never as simplistically, cognitively manageable and small as we retrospectively believe it was in our youth. Thus, the communal function of the filmic Oz for grown-ups: "Oz finally *became* home; the imagined world became the actual world, as it does for us all, because the truth is that once we have left our childhood places and started out to make up our lives [. . .] we understand that the real secret of the ruby slippers is not that 'there's no place like home,' but rather that there is no longer any such place *as* home" (57). What Rushdie has experienced seems to me an extreme but useful analogy to the alienation most adults feel as they grow into accepting relative subjectivities and the difficulty of bridging them. Perhaps growing up means learning that there is no such place as totalization.

Geographer John K. Wright wrote of the importance of imaginary spaces as surrogates: "If we look closely enough—if, in other words, the cartographical scale of our examination be sufficiently large—the entire earth appears as an immense patchwork of miniature *terrae incognitae*" (3). He promotes a closer relationship between geography and the humanities, what he calls "aesthetic geosophy," to convert "personal *terrae incognitae* into personal *terrae cognitae*" (4). This is what we attempt in creating and reterritorializing friendly childhood spaces—to convince ourselves (and "child" readers) that the unknown is knowable.

In *The Power of Maps*, Denis Wood distinguishes between the abstract and concrete as known versus sensed, clarifying the gap between them that maps elide: "every map facilitates some living by virtue of its ability to grapple with what is *known* instead of what is merely seen, what is *understood* rather than what is no more than sensed" (7). Maps, then, enable us to take a rationalist leap of faith, trusting reason over that which we can see. But they could also be said to destabilize singular reasoning when they insist upon the existence of something we "know" to be nonexistent: "the map presents us with the reality we know as differentiated from the reality we see and feel and hear" (6). With maps, we can "know" the hypothetical self-reflective of its hypotheticality—to open our unknowing minds to unknowability while satisfying our need for visual security.

Strangely enough, what we comfortably define as known is generally identified and articulated through learned abstraction—labels or associations that give them meaning—but the "process of becoming unconfused" necessary for cognitive mapping is one that depends not on learning ("accumulating facts") but orientation, a capability not measurable in abstract terms. For this reason, children are often envied for their presumed flexibility as spatial thinkers. A recent study of children's orientation on playgrounds begins with the mandatory awareness that "while children may be as competent as adults in constructing environmental meanings, often different methods are required to elucidate their knowledge" (Loukaitou-Sideris 132). Usually the language barrier is circumvented in such studies, as in play therapy, by having children draw visualizations rather than articulating them verbally. Regardless, we know that children's understandings of their environments are ultimately inaccessible to us as adults, and we maintain the illusion of accessibility by retreating to visualizations of small-scale, knowable spaces.

The only refuge in which to believably create such an impossible space is in the imagination. Thus, adults recast their personal memory in terms of an irretrievable and isolated friendly space. When Ishmael considers his loss of innocence, in *Moby-Dick* (1851), he conjures such an image: "In the soul of man there lies one insular Tahiti, full of peace and joy, but encompassed by all the horrors of the half known life. God keep thee! Push not off from that isle, thou canst never return!" (364). Bound by irretraversable borders, the presumed paradise of childhood (this time a combination of the edenic garden and island) is separate and protected from hasty inhabitants, so the impossible return is a necessary device in literary reterritorialization. In children's books and movies, it is often modified for the audience as "you can play here, but you can't stay." Thus Fern Arable and Wendy Darling grow up, losing access to a totalizing space; Alice awakens from her dream with only memories.

Because childhood is inaccessible phenomenologically and geographically, the writer who maps childhood must enclose it carefully in order to be convincing. Reinhard Kuhn writes that the literary child "moves in a realm whose nature has tantalized many writers. [. . .] Yet the cartographers of these fictional countries are of necessity adults, and thus there is always a residue of doubt in the reader's mind concerning the authenticity of their geographies" (65). Created to soothe adult anxiety about the inaccessibility of childhood, such geographies must be isolated in order to maintain the fiction that they exist.

Maps can accomplish this while seemingly authenticating fictions, at the same time keeping them remote, bordered, static, and abstract. *Moby-Dick* and other crossover adventure stories like *Gulliver's Travels* (1726) and *Treasure Island* (1883) may have started this trend with their attempts at making the fictional events seem real through mapping. Interest in literary maps, however, can surpass interest in the books they are meant to supplement. Such maps captivate the imagination on their own, which is probably why Mitsumasa Anno extracted the one from *Treasure Island* for his *Anno's Alphabet: An Adventure in Imagination* (1974) under the letter M for map, not I for island, drawing attention to the image rather than the object in it. Mapping provides more than verisimilitude; it gives the imagination free space and a cartographer's authority; it brings fictional worlds closer while drawing believable borders.

That maps are especially popular in books marketed for children reflects the obvious tradition of illustration in this genre as well as assumptions about its audience beyond a simple dependence upon illustration. It is generally assumed that a young reader is engaged in the gradual

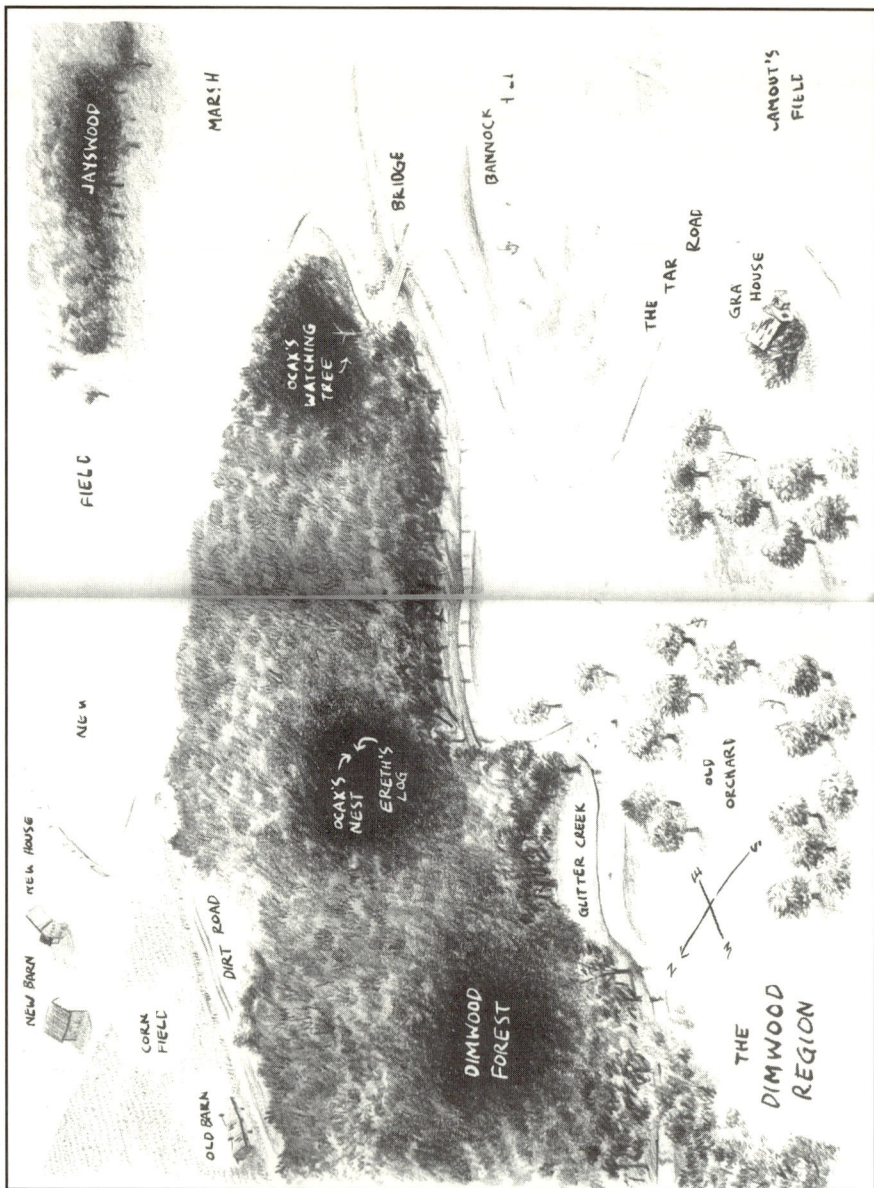

Figure 3. (Map by Brian Floca from *POPPY* by Avi. Published by Orchard Books, an imprint of Scholastic Inc. Illustration copyright © 1995 by Brian Floca. Reprinted by permission.)

cognitive mapping of his/her surroundings. Peter Hunt says of *Winnie-the-Pooh*, "the Shepard map shows the 100 acre wood as within the child's grasp" (13). Some territory-focused children's books dramatize the cognitive mapping process through journey narratives. For example, in Laura Ingalls Wilder's *Little House in the Big Woods* (1932), the setting is first described as immense and unknown: "As far as a man could go to the north in a day, or a week, or a whole month, there was nothing but woods" (1). It is only much later, when Laura goes to town, that we find this has been an exaggeration in (probably) her child-mind: "It was seven miles to town" (164)—a leisurely day trip by horse and wagon. Her cognitive world is growing as she sees it to name it.

Young characters are shown, likewise, growing into the spaces they are capable of comprehending. In Avi's *Poppy* (1995), the title character, a young mouse, plans her journey to New House by calmly consulting a map (figure 3) and reasoning out a frightening but ultimately less dangerous route through the forest (69). When she gets to the real forest, "she gazed at it in awe. [. . .] [S]he'd never imagined it so vast, so dense, so dark. The sight made her feel immensely isolated and small. Feeling small made her feel a part of all she saw. Being part of it made her feel immense" (85). Like *White Mule*'s Flossie, Poppy becomes "part of all." Cognitively mapping enables her to know the space in part and whole simultaneously (what better description of our impossible demands for totalization?). Afterward, the care-paced journey she had planned and cautiously executed is easily retread in two sentences, indicating her confident mastery of space. Again, this sense is achieved through a combination of abstract understanding and concrete experience—an ideal combination of macro- and micro-scaling.

Mapping may provide a sense of empowerment and control to young audiences, but it also reterritorializes childhood for the adult author and reader. What adult does not want to feel small (unburdened) and immense (belonging), like Poppy, at once? By applying the worldly method of cartographers to small and namable spaces, illustrators like Brian Floca (*Poppy*), Shepard, and Ruth Chrisman Gannett (*My Father's Dragon*) have seemingly legitimated impossible, inviting, isolated spaces full of adventure but safely contained. The combination of abstraction (macro-scaling) with the concrete (micro-scaling) draws together methods associated with both adults and children but also creates a visual sense of totalization similar to Poppy's unburdened belonging. This technique might explain, for example, the popularity of superimposing images of state products on U.S. maps, famous buildings to mark and represent their cities, or flowers and birds in each state. It is a quick, comforting, and totalizing way of communicating ideology and telling the map reader "you are here" on multiple levels.

Textual orientation is as much a function of modernity as adulthood itself. Valerie Krips points out that in the modern épistémè, with its increasing empowerment of literacy and information, memory is less exercised and less valued: "Modernity's response is to create archives and records, to replace or even erase memory, the faculty upon which, until a few centuries ago, we mostly relied for our knowledge of the past" (45–46). We rely more on displaced memory—representations, which "offer the promise of re-connection to the past" (46). A dependence upon "archives and records" can be seen in the nostalgic attempt to capture the past and imaginary places. In early modern publishing, cartographers often included "Paradise" on world maps, likely as an effort to indulge nostalgia amidst increasing secularization (Eisenstein 78). In the same spirit modern writers attempt to map an idealized childhood. The map provides a comforting verisimilitude, and "re-connection" seems easier the less an imagined space is bound by the restrictions of authentic geography. W. F. H. Nicolaisen points out that "the more imaginary a landscape becomes the more mappable it becomes or the more it demands a map to prove its existence" (57).

The most mapped fantasy territory in American literature must be Oz, which was first mapped by Baum and later by sequel writers. Judy Pike supplemented these maps further in 1971 with her new map of "the Wonder City of Oz" in the *Baum Bugle*. In 1979 James Haff and Dick Martin created a comprehensive map for the International Wizard of Oz club, "The Marvelous Land of Oz" (which was published in some paperback editions). That Baum fans and scholars were digging for cartographic clues so long after publication reflects a deep interest in authenticating the nostalgic childhood space.

According to Peter Hunt, maps are popular in children's literature because they "stabilize the fantasy, while releasing greater imaginative potential—and, it might be said, they also symbolize the tension that exists for the writer between the real landscape and the fantasy which inhabits it" (11). This tension creates the need to map realistically yet keep the "real world" fenced off. One solution is to keep the scope of the fantasy landscape small. Hart imagines that childhood spaces are exclusive because adults simply cannot appreciate children's micro-scaling because their sphere of experience is so much larger:

A child's degree of differentiation is remarkable; simple backgardens described by their adult owners as "lawn," "vegetable plot," "apple tree" and "ditch" will commonly have dozens of highly minute niches for different activities. These places are a part of child-culture which is not shared with adults unless the adults make a special effort. They have barely been studied, although certain adult writers such as A. A. Milne have tapped them. (342)

The map for *Winnie-the-Pooh* (1926) depicts all the dwellings and play spaces associated with its characters and names them by their private functions and significance to each member of the micro-community ("where Roo plays," "where the Woozle wasn't"). Yet the North Pole (which Pooh supposedly found by picking up a pole) is off the map, with only the direction indicated. Lest a reader confuse Pooh's stick with the real North Pole, illustrator Ernest H. Shepard kept the scope of the map comfortably limited to the small, personal world of the characters' experience.

Creators of childhood refuges must keep the "reality" barrier clear yet authenticate the space at the same time. To maintain this balance, L. Frank Baum gradually made Oz less accessible in his series. In the first sequel, *The Marvelous Land of Oz* (1904), his characters know of Dorothy as being "from Kansas, a place in the big, outside world" (23). At one point the Gump (their transportation) overshoots the Palace of Glinda "entirely out of the Land of Oz and over the sandy deserts and into the terrible outside world" (141). That his characters fly over the "real world" (only to retreat back into Oz) connects them geographically, yet they never land.

In *The Emerald City of Oz* (1910), Dorothy brings Aunt Em and Uncle Henry away from the "terrible outside world," with its agricultural struggle and threats of farm repossession, with her to Oz for good (passively, though, through Glinda's magic). Once this nostalgia for escape is vicariously sated, however, the borders are closed. The Nome King and his troops have broken through only to drink from the "Water of Oblivion," which, consistent with adult nostalgia, makes "the great warriors [. . .] like little children" who forget how they got there or even their visit, further enabling the impossible taunt of ungraspable accessibility (286). How do we know we have not been there ourselves if one is made to forget? The fantasy of reterritorialization is complete when Glinda applies the same amnesiac to all who may access the land but simply will not see it: "those who fly through the air over our country will look down and see nothing at all" (296). Her magic renders the Wizard's plan unnecessary: "I'm working

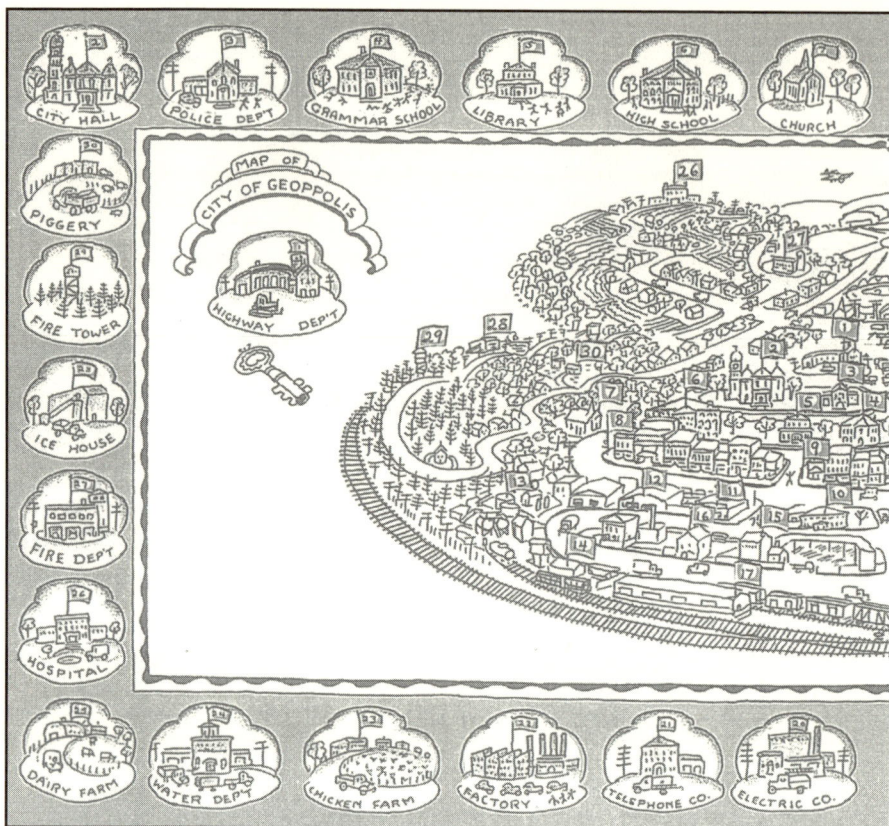

Figure 4. ("Map of City of Geoppolis" from *KATY AND THE BIG SNOW* by Virginia Lee
Burton. Copyright 1943 by Virginia Lee Demetrios; copyright © renewed 1971 by George
Demetrios. Reprinted by permission of Houghton Mifflin Company. All rights reserved.)

out a magic recipe to fuddle men's brains, so they'll never make an airship
that will go where they want it to go" (231). His plan, however, reveals a
deeper motive behind the sealing off of Oz: to legitimate the notion that
fantasy lands can exist outside of the scientific power to prove or disprove
them, thus releasing adults from the rationalist need to verify the real or
reject the ideal.

In his prologue to *The Patchwork Girl of Oz* (1913) Baum explains that
Oz had "been rendered invisible to all who lived outside its borders" and
"shut off from all the rest of the world" (15). Yet he plays the "Royal His-
torian of Oz" and stabilizes the fiction of its existence by claiming that
Dorothy has reported to him by telegraph. Jack Zipes, who sees in the
Land of Oz a populist, suffragist utopia, explains its eventual invisibility as

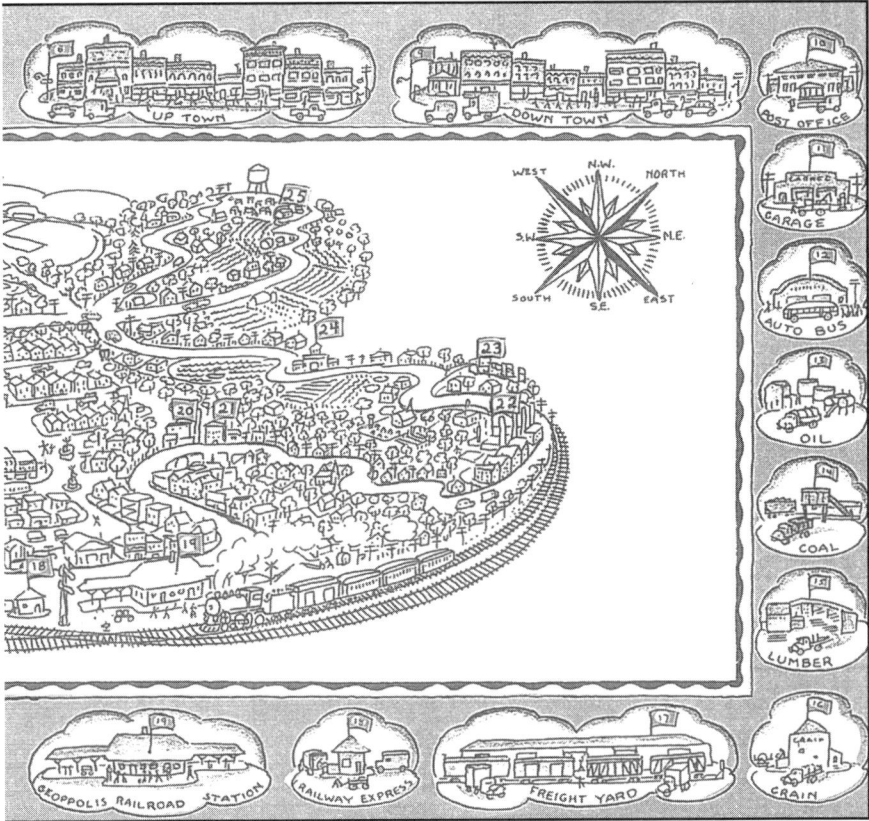

Figure 4 continued.

a reflection of Baum's growing skepticism: "he grasped that technology in the hands of capitalist entrepreneurs would mean the doom of utopian developments like Oz. By making this land invisible, Baum was saying that the chances for the realization of utopia in America had been cancelled and forfeited" (130). This skepticism, like Gurlie's in *White Mule,* reflects the industrialized modern era's nostalgia for an idealized agrarian past. But like the Wizard's technological sabotage above, it suggests a rejection of the economic and modernizing conditions Baum witnessed. Baum's fictional retreat (of Dorothy) into Oz simply reflects his preference, and the sealing off of Oz suggests that, although the utopia might be too ideal for "developed," capitalist nations, it can be protected from them and at least preserved for nostalgic purposes.

A less skeptical cartographer of modern pastoral spaces for children, Virginia Lee Burton,[7] introduced the unlikely combination of pastoralism and technology in her picture books through sentimentally personified machinery. Her most famous characters are emblems of industrialism: a train, a steam shovel, a snowplow. But we are made to sympathize with these machines as much as we would with the laborers they replaced. For example, in *Mike Mulligan and His Steam Shovel* (1939), Mary Anne, the obsolete steam shovel threatened with useless unemployment when gas and electric motors take over all the jobs, becomes depressed and finally breaks down crying, dramatically poised in front of a "No Steam Shovels Wanted" sign. The solution to her problem, like that of the suffocating house in *The Little House* (1942), is to move out of the big city. Surprisingly, in Popperville steam technology is not obsolete; in fact, it is so completely new to the shocked inhabitants who see Mary Anne's steam that they call the fire department: "They had seen smoke / and thought there was a fire" (28). Apparently this small town is so isolated that it has escaped modernization. Incredibly, as it unfolds, this suburban idealism simply reconciles pastoral nostalgia to industrialized modernism.

Burton created impossible rural spaces safely separate from the modernizing influence of the city. The formula worked well enough to repeat in *Katy and the Big Snow* (1943), and this time Burton sealed it with a map (figure 4). Burton's setting, Geopolis, is preserved in a detailed map that in one double-spread view shows the entire city framed by a legend-border in which close-ups of each building are numbered to correspond with flags in the larger view, affecting the simultaneous appreciation of a micro- and macro-scaled space described above.

Though based on her contemporary Gloucester, Burton selectively keyed the map to give an impression of impossible harmony. In fact, there cannot be much diversity (one church) or competition: there is one "piggery," one dairy farm, one chicken farm, one vendor for each resource and utility, and even one "factory" (we do not know what is manufactured there, but one is enough). The flags work like those of an explorer, signaling discovery and possession to the reader who can supposedly connect the numbers and learn his/her way around the city. But the map also validates a nostalgic suburban echo of the modern pastoral ideal: though no longer agrarian, this idealized rural community is satisfied and unthreatened by competition, pollution, and the "no wanted" signs of the big city. The more the world changes around Geopolis, the more we need the map to find it.

For the inventor of an imagined space, there is a constant tension between the needs for confining and authenticating it. To maintain its separateness without negating the illusion of accessibility requires careful attention to entrances and exits. Aware of the impossibility of the escape, the author must establish closure at the narrative's end to maintain the fantasy. Sarah Gilead has explored this dilemma in her "Magic Abjured: Closure in Children's Fantasy Fiction." She writes that "Writing for children [. . .] permits the adult to recuperate the familiar [. . .] and to link slippery modern culture to the lost wholeness and stability of an imagined (and largely imaginary) past. The self-doubt and anxiety behind such recuperative desire are particularly evident in the most problematic of the narrative transitions, the ending" (288).

Particularly in longer narratives, to leave a child character in a fantasy world is to sever both from the world of the reader. So the writer must negate the fantasy with the dream motif, realistically engineer a return to "reality," or leave that child and space accessible, somehow balancing an impossible illusion of entry despite its inaccessibility.

The most traditional solution to the problem is to explain away the inaccessibility of childhood and spaces invented for it by having children grow out of them.[8] In E. B. White's *Charlotte's Web* (1952), Fern Arable's involvement with the community of animals in the barnyard ends because of her entrance into the adult, sexual world. Though she was originally the one who spoke up for and saved the runt piglet Wilbur from an early death, by the time his life is in danger again, she's too busy joining a human community, indicated by her friendship with Henry Fussy, to intervene. Fern all but disappears from the narrative, as much a bystander to the intricacies of barnyard drama as the other human characters. The magical space that White created of the barnyard, with a talking, loving, totalized community of animals, is eventually nothing but a barnyard to her, associated with a childhood she is shedding: "Fern did not come regularly to the barn any more. She was growing up, and was careful to avoid childish things, like sitting on a milk stool near a pigpen" (183). Sarah Gilead points out that, rather than negating the escape, such closure can allow the fantasy that the friendly space exists to continue. The possibility of the harmonious childhood space still lingers for the reader: "if the ending abjures such childhood, relegating it to a mere stage in the progress toward adult selfhood, the ending also confesses the attraction of childhood for adults" (288). Though White effectively separates the fantastic animal world from the framing "real world" of the text, he not only leaves the reader capable of accessing the magical conversation of the animals but also makes the human world increasingly peripheral. To indulge in the fantasy world he validates the space, rationalizing its inaccessibility by withdrawing human interaction. Even traditional closure cannot always negate the fantasy.

Some authors create closure by having the child return to the "real" world, leaving the fantasy world sustained but outside of the ending narrative frame. Gilead writes, "In one sense, the return-to-reality closure asserts the conventional, ideologically mandated meanings and indeed relations between the concept pairs 'child' and 'adult,' 'fantasy' (or 'dream') and 'reality.' But to do so, it must counter a potential obscuring of such meanings and relations" (288). By displacing the fantasy world "outside" or in the subconscious, such endings can support the stark rationalist oppositions of reality vs. fantasy, adult vs. child. For example, Peter Pan is the only child in Neverland whose childhood is not threatened with growing up, and as someone free from that erasure, he might seem to obscure the distinction between fictive reality (where the Darlings live) and fantasy (the realm Peter briefly shares with them). But within the story he is set apart clearly as a "make-believe" character—ultimately his childhood must be seen as separate from the other characters': "The difference between him and the other boys [. . .] was that *they knew it was make-believe,* while to him make-believe and true were exactly the same thing. This sometimes troubled them, as when they had to make-believe that they had had their dinners" (my italics 64). And later, "Make-believe was so real to him that during a meal of it you could see him getting rounder" (71). Peter Pan is no more substantial than the air upon which he seems to feed. Neverland is clearly positioned here as unreal, in order to authenticate the fictional reality that frames it.

A contemporary example of this bifurcating process can be seen in *Jumanji,* the 1981 Chris Van Allsburg picture book turned into a film in 1996 by Joe Johnston. Though the book obscures the traditional oppositions of reality and fantasy, the film reinforces them strongly. In Van Allsburg's version, Judy and Peter find an abandoned game "for the bored and restless" and play it, briefly transforming their home into a jungle of sorts through the appearance of various wild animals. At the end of the game all disappear and the children fall asleep, but there is no indication that they have dreamed the events or simply imagined them. It is only the adults who discredit their adventure by laughing at reports of it. In Johnston's film, however, the plot and characters become far more elaborate, and the boundary between real and unreal becomes more protested. In *You're Only Young Twice,* Tim Morris points out the irony of such adaptations: "Why should the filmmakers need to add so many explanatory devices to a children's book? It makes sense that the children's story can allow rhetorical elaboration [. . .] . It makes less sense, though, to see a children's story as something needing a clearer *explanation* to an adult audience. Shouldn't a book for little kids be easy to understand?" (150).

The differences between the picture book and film reflect assumptions about intended audiences. Despite the story's origin, the film *Jumanji* was made by adults for a market controlled by adults. That it is considered acceptable family viewing is beside the point—the film is an adult fantasy about reterritorializing childhood. Screenwriters introduce two adult characters, Alan and Sarah, to play the game with child-characters Judy and Peter. The adult players, who had started playing the game twenty-six years previous to the story's primary time frame, seize their opportunity to finish it and revert to the past, becoming children again. Though the film appears to transform the home into a jungle, merging the fantasy and "real" worlds, it ends with a complete return to reality that seems to negate the events of the entire game. Alan and Sarah revert to their child-selves, and their companions, Judy and Peter, do not even exist yet. All has been erased and the notion of a validated reality prevails.

Smaller textual changes in the movie also serve adult desire. For example, the game is no longer a board game, "same as any other"—an escape from boredom—but an escape "for those who seek to find / a way to leave the world behind." Van Pelt, a character only briefly mentioned in the book, becomes the vehicle through which Alan will work through his unresolved childhood anxieties. Van Pelt is described as a "hunter from the wild / [who] makes you feel just like a child." This he does as a substitute therapist—unlike Sarah, Alan has been locked in the game and unable to seek professional help to move beyond childhood trauma (in fact, the game seems entirely there to serve his psyche). And in case the opportunity to re-enter childhood is not enough vicarious pleasure for the adult audience, Sarah and Alan have their much-anticipated kiss at the end of the game, but only once they have become children again. Sarah admits, "I'm starting to forget what it's like to be a grown-up," so she kisses him "before I start to feel too much like a kid." In service to the impossible adult dream of regained childhood, the filmmakers overlooked a bit of illogic: in creating the necessary closure with a return-to-reality negation of the game's world and events, they also close that world off from the players' memories (as the above quotations suggest, the kids are forgetting their adult experience). Yet in the film's closing scene, which jumps ahead again into the future authenticated reality, Sarah and Alan have grown (again) and married; they meet the now existing children, Judy and Peter, who they claim look "just like we remembered them." The film follows the traditional rationalist demand to seal off the fantasy but allows the adults-turned-children-grown-again-into-adulthood to have their cake and eat it too through selective memory.[9]

Many authors, however, obscure the oppositions of "adult" and "child," "reality" and "fantasy." Baum never, as MGM's *Wizard of Oz* did, negated the fantasy by turning it into a dream. Made popular by *Alice's Adventures in Wonderland*, the dream motif is actually less common in literature than Hollywood and Disney would have us believe. And when it is used, it is often done more subversively. Take, for example, the original. When Alice awakens from her first dream, in *Alice's Adventures in Wonderland* (1865), the fantasy space is negated by the reality in which she wakes, but when she awakens from her second dream, in *Through the Looking Glass* (1872), the return sparks a philosophical debate about the nature of reality itself. Earlier in the work, Carroll had toyed with the Berkleyan notion that humans cannot authenticate their own existence. Tweedledee informs Alice that she should not wake the Red King, as she is "only a sort of thing in his dream" (238). In "Which Dreamed It?" Alice can no longer dismiss her visit as a simple dream. Instead she realizes that whoever is dreaming authenticates a separate reality: "You see, Kitty, it *must* have been either me or the Red King" (344). The either/or defining of reality that sustains rationalism is threatened. Carroll leaves the reader only with the question, "Which do *you* think it was?" (344). Leaving the question unanswered suggests that it might be an impossible riddle (can't both be dreaming?), destabilizing the traditional but necessary (for rationalism[10]) divide of fantasy worlds from reality.

John Vernon describes the rationalist tendency toward either/or equations: "There is no *coincidentia oppositorum*, no unity of opposites, in classical Western thought, as there is in almost all primitive cultures. The function of static exclusivity and separation is established at the very heart of Western civilization" (4). For this reason Vernon calls the West "schizophrenic," arguing that we mentally organize our surroundings one-dimensionally, with careful attention to defining, which he spatializes with the image of the map, as opposed to the garden, which represents a comfortable embracing of opposites and contradiction.[11] When applied to fictional spaces, this "static exclusiveness" translates into what Gaston Bachelard called "the myth of outside and inside." He writes, "'This side' and 'beyond' are faint repetitions of the dialectics of inside and outside: everything takes form, even infinity. [. . .] The dialectics of here and there has been promoted to the rank of an absolutism according to which these unfortunate adverbs of place are endowed with unsupervised powers of ontological determination" (212).

Authors often use childhood spaces, as Lewis Carroll did, to thwart this absolutism—this either/or defining of "here" and "there." Even the use of fantasy maps, which seem to follow absolutes in their service to verisimilitude, can subvert their own appeal to rationalism by heightening the reader's awareness of possibilities for harmonious contradiction. Carroll satirizes rationalist dependence on continuous compossibility (Deleuze's more precise term for rationalism's "noncontradiction") with the Captain's map in "The Hunting of the Snark," which is "A perfect and absolute blank" (223). By endowing an emblem of human dependence upon abstract signification with blankness, suggesting the impossibility of static meaning, Carroll annihilates singular reading and encourages acceptance of indecipherability. Deleuze explains, "Signification does not establish the truth without also establishing the possibility of error. For this reason, the condition of truth is not opposed to the false, but to the absurd: that which is without signification or that which may be *neither true nor false*" (*Logic,* my italics, 14–15). Alternate fictive realities can be used to resist the closure of single signification and replace it with an acceptance of compossible contradiction.

Not all "returns" need negate the escape, as Gilead points out: "The return may be viewed as resolving a narrative rivalry between realism and fantasy and thus as analogous to a self that has worked out internal conflicts [as with the dream motif]. But what if the return instigates this rivalry even as it appears to offer resolution?" (278). One answer is that the subversive ending can draw attention to the impossibilities of realism and representation itself, leaving the reader carefully balancing a belief in realities otherwise defined as contradictory.

L. Frank Baum drew attention to and subverted the either/or tendency of rationalism by telling readers that Dorothy remained in Oz and could report (with difficulty) to him. Oz cannot be placed in the past or the unconscious: it simply concurrently exists exclusive from the reader's reality. At one point Baum even highlights the subjectivity of "reality," as Carroll did, by suggesting that space is constructed in the mind. In *The Patchwork Girl of Oz,* the journeying characters come up against a wall and locked gate that bars them from their path. The Shaggy Man assures them that "looks are deceiving" (160). By closing their eyes and moving forward they easily pass through what is described as "an optical illusion. It is quite real while you have your eyes open, but if you are not looking at it the barrier doesn't exist at all. It's the same way with many other evils in life; they seem to exist, and yet it's all seeming and not true" (162). Thus, even though Oz is inaccessible, Baum suggests that barriers can be mental. As we create and adhere to absolutes like "here" and "there" to define the world around us, Baum suggests that boundaries, like childhood itself, are not so easy to define. This admitted, it becomes easier to sustain an illusion of accessibility despite the rational/realist borders that surround childhood. One simply suspends defining.

Maurice Sendak achieves this balance of verisimilitude and subverted "reality" in *Where the Wild Things Are* (1963). On one hand, Max's journey is clearly indicated as a dream by visual cues. Early on we see a drawing, by Max, of a monster who will be among the wild things, suggesting that they, like the one in the drawing, are products of his imagination. Max and the monsters re-enact Max's misbehavior with his mother, including the threat "I'll eat you up!" and its punishment, no dinner. Sendak replays the dream motif, letting Max work through the conflict subconsciously, but rather than enclosing the journey by showing him asleep or awakening, he links Max's dream with his home life, keeping them on the same diegetic level by having Max smell his supper "all around from far away across the world" before he returns to find it in his room. In the written text, he goes even further in validating the fantasy by never mentioning sleep and literally counting the passage of time: "He sailed off through night and day / and in and out of weeks / and almost over a year." The illustrations also support this straightforward depiction of a real journey, showing the different phases of the moon throughout his stay with the wild things. The book allows the reader to accept both possibilities by not forcing a single definition of reality based on static exclusivity. Certainly Max's experience with the wild things occurs in a different space "across the world," yet his own room retransforms itself based on the fantasy (becoming a jungle and then a bedroom again), suggesting a single setting. Yet Sendak links the fantasy world so closely to the framing one that the reader need not question the authenticity of either.

One advantage Sendak has in deconstructing absolutist oppositions is his pictorial medium. In *Words About Pictures*, Perry Nodelman writes, "Stories occupy time, pictures space" (198). Time and narrative are linear, less capable of instantaneous contradiction, but when illustrations contradict print, we deepen our view and are encouraged to accept two contradictory realities at once. John Burningham capitalized on this opportunity in his *Come Away from the Water, Shirley* (1977), in which he distinctly isolates a child's fantasy experience by limiting it to illustration. On the left-hand pages we see Shirley's parents and read their dialogue, but on the right we see her inhabiting a far larger and more colorful space, full of open sea and sky, pirates, an island with buried treasure, and a greater passage of time in which to find it. Meanwhile, Burningham subtly links Shirley's experiences to the words of her inattentive parents by multiplying and

Figure 5. (From *MY FATHER'S DRAGON* by Ruth Stiles Gannett, copyright 1948 by Random House, Inc. Used by permission of Random House Children's Books, a division of Random House, Inc.)

overlapping possible meanings. At one point he achieves this in an auditory overlap. Shirley's parents tell her, "Careful where you're throwing those stones. You might hit someone." Opposite is a picture of Shirley and a dog diving from the pirate ship with a treasure map. One need only imagine the sound of stones hitting the water to validate the illusion of her diving in. Illustrations free the reader from the need to determine causality, sequence, or static setting. More importantly, they preemptively discourage imposing the exclusive absolutes of Western rationalism, either "reality" or "fantasy."

In novels for which illustrations seem supplemental to the narrative (unlike the inseparable effect they have in picture books or, for example, through composite stylings like that of Roald Dahl and Quentin Blake), mapping offers a similar opportunity for validating fantasy worlds. This outlet appeals to writers because it frees them from rationalist and linguistic restraints while enabling freer acceptance of relative ontologies and subjectivities. Phillip and Juliana Muehrcke write that "Writers may be especially attracted to maps because they are so well acquainted with the limitations of written communication in dealing with forms, processes, and relationships in the space-time continuum. Written language is linear [. . .] . The subject of discourse is rarely as ordered; rather, it is characterized by the simultaneous interaction of many factors" (318).

The use of an annotated map in the endpapers of *My Father's Dragon* (1948) by Ruth Stiles Gannett (figure 5) illustrates the degree to which mapping initiates a break from the necessary linearity of written text. The eye surveys the mapped territory with its own pace and pattern, while at the same time a journey is delineated with descriptions of what was done where: "my father slept under this tangerine tree," "my father doesn't know what's on this side of the island," and even "my father got here late in the afternoon and waited for dark." Though suggesting temporal events, each descriptive marker can be read anytime completely out of chronological order or entirely skipped. There is clearly a chronology, but that only becomes clear from reading the book. And when going back to the book one need not remember it—the pleasure is in the possibilities rendered, not the pace.

The picture book format enables even more "simultaneous interaction" of words, images, and the "realities" they convey, which is a possibility that contemporary writers and artists seem to be increasingly exploiting. The current popularity of composite texts, or those in which text and image are entirely interdependent for narrative and plot, and wordless storytelling, which favors image to the extent of eliminating as much written text as possible, is demonstrated by their increasing frequency in Caldecott Award winners such as *Black and White* (Macaulay 1990), *Tuesday* (Wiesner 1991), *Officer Buckle and Gloria* (Rathmann 1995), *The Three Pigs* (Wiesner 2001), and *My Friend Rabbit* (Rohmann 2002), as well as honor books like *Olivia* (Falconer 2000) and her sequels. Each of these texts plays with moments of compositeness in which image subverts or takes over the narrative function—some include many spreads without words at all. Illustrators seem to be prizing and prized for surpassing dependence upon on the written word, exploring the possibilities outside of verbal expression.

Composite and relatively wordless texts provide an outlet and medium that novels could not fully utilize even if illustrated. They disrupt literate linearity while circumventing language barriers. Their use in children's works presents more compelling evidence for the Western tendency to construct childhood outside of language, that is, if one takes the implied subject or audience of picture books to be children. Rather than insisting that truth exists only in consistent noncontradiction, such texts successfully block rationalist adult patterns of hyperliterate linearity and construct a pleasured reader (dual audience included). Roland Barthes's description of such an idealized position is apt:

> Imagine someone who abolishes within himself all barriers, all classes, all exclusions [. . .] by simple discard of that old specter: logical contradiction; who mixes every language, even those said to be incompatible; who silently accepts every charge of illogicality, of incongruity. [. . .] Such a man would be the mockery of our society: court, school, asylum, polite conversation would cast him out: who endures contradiction without shame? Now this anti-hero exists: he is the reader of the text at the moment he takes his pleasure. (3)

"Such a man" might be a mockery, but "such a child" is the anti-rationalist ideal. The kind of pleasure Barthes describes is the freedom *to not* reason singly, to think relativistically, communicate flexibly, and be happily unburdened by a need to systematize one's understanding into noncontradiction. No picture book better demonstrates this pleasure than David Macaulay's *Black and White* (1990). In it, the reader is encouraged to "endure contradiction" with pleasure.

Macaulay not only resists having a single focalization for this text, he provides four different stories, each with a separate narrative technique in a separate quarter of each spread. "Seeing Things," the story of a boy's "first trip alone" on the train, is focalized through him and told in third person;

"Problem Parents," about a brother and sister witnessing their parents in an unusually silly mood, is narrated in first person by the sister; "A Waiting Game" and "Udder Chaos" are externally focalized and almost entirely wordless, telling two stories in pictures: first, of a long wait for a train in which commuters (the choir from "Udder Chaos"?) get punchy and make paper hats out of their newspapers, singing "She'll Be Coming 'Round the Mountain" (evidenced in crossover reference in "Problem Parents"), and second, of an escaped convict (first seen on the train opposite the boy in "Seeing Things") who camouflages himself in a herd of loose Holstein cows that has delayed the train that the boy from "Seeing Things" is in and the "Problem Parents" are waiting for. Each story has its own illustrative style as well, yet they overlap in subtle ways (as my need for parenthetical explanations above contests).

No two critics seem to agree on a single holistic reading of one totalizing fictive reality or chronology (see Trites, Collins, and Kaplan), but each offers an interpretation that can be supported by the text depending upon how the reader reconciles the stories, because the text supports multiple approaches and encourages an acceptance of simultaneous contradiction. On the final endpaper, a hand and dog's nose, clearly from "Problem Parents," intrude on the scene for "A Waiting Game," echoing Alice's question, "which dreamed it?" Was the train station in one story just part of the kid's train set in another? Yes, but that does not mean they are incompossible as fictive realities.

Macaulay destabilizes our attempts to totalize a singular fictive reality, forcing us to accept its indeterminacy. Deborah Kaplan argues that Macaulay's "disruption of [literacy] codes" in *Black and White* maintains the plausibility of multiple stories, and multiple simultaneous—though possibly contradictory—truths" (38). Roberta Seelinger Trites argues that Macaulay's disruption of hyperliterate technique enables reading resistance of ideological manipulation: "Traditional linear narratives immerse the subject in the narrative's ideology. [. . .] But nonlinear or fractured texts invert that process" (100). By resisting linearity the text disables the linear and false-totalizing logic of persistent noncontradiction, encouraging multitudinous disruption.

Structurally, these narratives confront the same relativity of perspective that automatically confronts anyone writing to or of a child subject-position. Childhood is a culturally constructed and relatively defined concept. Awareness of its constructedness demands self-conscious methods for representing and addressing those being defined as children. In fiction, attempts at circumventing the inaccessibility of child-minds have resulted in modeling alternatives such as externalized focalization and spatialization. As the vehicle of socialization, language becomes seen as a defining barrier between literary children and adults, foregrounded in indirect discourse, narrative opacity, and dramatic irony, but seemingly circumvented through mapping and illustration. Resisting language (as a barrier to childhood), some fictions spatialize childhood and definitively render boundaries to child spaces in an attempt to reterritorialize them while acknowledging their inaccessibility. These methods acknowledge the culturally relative constructedness of childhood and attempt to represent the inaccessible subject position from a respectful distance. They also demonstrate how childhood can come to make us see inadequacies in realism and representation itself.

Frederic Jameson has written that Henry James, among other modern writers, foreshadowed the breakdown of structuralism and the totalized subject in a relativized view of inter-subjectivity: "Each consciousness is a closed world, so that a representation of social totality now must take the (impossible) form of a coexistence of those sealed subjective worlds and their peculiar interaction" (350). If so, this "impossible coexistence" and "peculiar interaction" is fully expressed in *Black and White* and hinted at throughout literature that attempts to represent and reterritorialize childhood with techniques that eschew the trappings of essentialism and circumvent the limitations of language. All of the above examples indicate the fragile conceptual barriers that exist and are necessary to recognize if we are to respect the inaccessible mindscapes of those we call children. Indulging in the escapist pleasure of constructing nostalgic worlds for fictional children and readers, adults are careful to bind childhood to explain its inaccessibility, yet grasp it. That childhood represents a "sealed subjective world" barred from adult experience only makes it all the more appealing, and the above constructions demonstrate attempts at envisioning an impossible coexistence with it. Anti-rationalist constructions of childhood recognize the impossibility of reterritorializing it but protest that we can at least break down the barriers that have been built through education in our own minds.

chapter 4

REVERSING
DEVELOPMENT

*W*hereas the elusiveness of childhood enables unchecked nostalgia and an imagined reterritorialization of childhood, some skeptics have found validation in seemingly more empirical approaches; however, they still find childhood out of reach. Scientific theorizing about childhood has led to its own subversions. Developmental sciences, which tend to presuppose universal and chronologically fixed stages through which children must pass toward the ideal of adulthood, have met an ongoing counter-argument in literature, the romantic "development as fall" narrative, in which growth and maturation are seen as processes of decline. According to the former view, childhood is irrational, in the worst cases primitive, and in need of taming; to the latter, it is intuitive, natural, and untainted by socialization. These contrary responses to the immeasurability of childhood have continued alongside and often in dialogue with each other. Their diluted themes are easily recognizable in popular-cultural productions. For example, Disney's version of Rudyard Kipling's Mowgli in *The Jungle Book* is a mesh of both views—he is a primitive, animalistic child who needs to be civilized, but he is also Rousseau's wise child of nature, cleaned up a little and eager to please Disney audiences. We rarely pause at the implicit incompatibilities of such constructions. We may do as Disney allows and simply think that they are cute. But developmentalist approaches and their romantic reversals have more sinister roots and ramifications than we recognize—both take a simplistic linear model that posits inexplicable childhood as a bad example or ideal, and in doing so they excuse imprecision, render any consideration of individuality unnecessary, and enable increased generalizing upon already misleading generalizations.

Ignoring the inaccuracy of these influences reduces the rhetoric of childhood discourse to a contradictory but rigid frame in which we can only speak of children in terms of rationalist absolutes.

In this chapter I will uncover some often overlooked tropes of developmentalism that pervade discourses on childhood and then consider romantic subversions in light of scientific standards. The romantic reversal of development attempts to free childhood of scientific efforts to fix it, but both views rely on similar presumptions—that development is a linear process, whether an ascension to knowledge or a descent from intuitive wisdom; that childhood as a subjective position is best understood through simple absolutes; that through studying those whom we deem children we can know them and even learn about our adult selves. These common premises reinforce each discourse's credibility and obscure their contradictions, justifying simplistic adult projections, stereotypes, and control over children's access to knowledge and power. These constructions do less to illuminate the social position we call childhood than they do to expose adult hopes and fears, suggesting the damage we might do in indulging them.

The average reader and theatergoer will recognize widespread beliefs about childhood that we have inherited from developmental psychology and the pedagogical ideologies we transmit through education. We are less likely, however, to recognize the roots of their biases in early evolutionary theories. In *The Biologising of Childhood*, John Morss points out that "the nature of Darwin's influence has not been as straightforwardly benevolent as some histories of developmental psychology would imply" (1). In fact, developmental psychology (with most of us in tow) has unquestioningly absorbed tropes from earlier "misguided biologies" and applied them in attempts to understand the maturation of social subjects. Rex and Wendy Stainton Rogers have explained the resulting bias: "Developmentalism's view of childhood as a period of primarily *biological* maturation is hardly surprising, given that many of developmentalism's best known theorists began their careers as biologists" (179). Developmental psychology, under the early influence of natural sciences, essentialized the highly variable social phenomenon of maturation to "scientifically" translate children into primitive animals who need to develop through chronologically fixed, universal stages to reach civilized adulthood. Such a generalizing approach was flexible enough to be selectively supported and applied to individuals when useful.[1] With the modern interest in individual development (expressed in literature through the popularity of *Bildungsromane*), nature and nurture conveniently conflated. Rising literacy rates and the growth of organized education in the nineteenth century provided further measures to enable seeing individual development as a linear, measurable progression from irrationality to rationality, concrete to abstract thought, uncontrolled impulses to civility, all in service to a rationalist ideal of adulthood.

Popular discourse on childhood has passively absorbed two dissonant trains of thought: that children develop in the same predictable, measured stages according to an innately fixed process, yet socialization/education is somehow necessary for ensuring the success of that process. To contemporary thinkers who have been influenced by sociology and post-structuralism, these ideas will probably seem at odds—our study of identity tends to focus less on nature/biology than nurture/socialization. But at large these ideas co-exist comfortably. Rather than calling for a nuanced analysis of childhood development, these conflicting constructions are superficially reconciled to justify a double-dealing attitude toward children that James Kincaid, Mike Males, Judith Levine, and even Michael Moore's *Bowling for Columbine* have investigated closely from various perspectives—a fearful desire to contain yet reshape the young. We desire that children be so good that they can only seem bad in comparison. We also wish for them to be bad (like Peter Pan and Huck Finn) in service of our own vicarious revisitations of youth but must chastise such behavior lest real children get the wrong idea and challenge adult authority. Though paradoxical, the call for simultaneous explanations of behavior according to nature- and nurture-narratives justifies adult control—development might be a biologically determined process, but that only proves that children are essentially inferior and in need of social reconstruction. Nature must be guided by rigorous "nurture."

Disney's cutefication of children (often done indirectly through infantilizing personifications of animals) provides an example of the condescension that results from this paradoxical justification. Characters like Snow White and Bambi are charming because they are helpless. Dopey and Dumbo are even named to emphasize their adorable stupidity. Daniel Harris, in his explication of the cute aesthetic, equates the cuteness of an object with the pity it arouses in its viewer: "Something becomes cute not necessarily because of a quality it has but because of a quality it lacks, a certain neediness and inability to stand alone. [. . .] Cuteness, in short, is not something we find in our children but something we *do* to them" (4–5). The popularity of anthropomorphism in entertainment for kids, he argues, attests to our desire to animalize them to maintain the illusion of adult superiority and power. Perhaps this is why adults often act as if threatened by precocity and independence in children. John Holt has argued that

"Children acting really competently and intelligently do not usually strike us as cute. They are likely to puzzle and threaten us. We don't like to see a child acting in a way that makes it impossible for us to look down on him or to suppose that he depends on our help" (85). By selectively falling back on essentialist explanations (nature) when children misbehave ("boys will be boys," "but her heart is in the right place") and conveniently recognizing the power of socialization (nurture) when it is useful in controlling children ("little pitchers have big ears," "what if the kids hear us?"), adults impose child ignorance as it best serves their cognitive comfort. It seems we have cast childhood as essentially undeveloped in order to justify intense control over socialization.

Two works that force an awareness of the paradoxical influence of developmentalism in our constructions of childhood are William Golding's *Lord of the Flies* (1954) and Richard Hughes's *A High Wind in Jamaica* (1929).[2] Both cast child characters in natural and remote spaces—much like their precedents, R. M. Ballantyne's *The Coral Island* (1857) and James Barrie's *Peter Pan* (1911)—but Golding and Hughes invert earlier, innocent constructions of children and childhood spaces to epitomize our unfavorable essentialization of the young in theories of human development. Their child figures are far from cute—they are uncontrolled and capable of deliberate malice.

The irreconcilable critical responses these novels receive suggest that adult desire, fear, and denial are strong when directly confronted with complex, nonconforming constructions of children. Though Golding's novel was originally written for an adult audience, *Lord of the Flies* has come to be considered a juvenile text and is frequently taught in secondary schools, probably with the belief that young readers will relate to its young characters while being exposed to "mature" themes. However, critics past and present persistently ignore it as a statement on childhood and adolescence. In their rejection of a more literal reading, many have insisted that *Lord of the Flies* is strictly to be read allegorically (as if allegory itself is meaningless at its literal level),[3] because if they recognized Golding's characters as children, they would have to acknowledge Golding's frightening construction of childhood, which, ironically, is simply an exaggeration of many prejudices we already accept. Critics and readers have responded with denial in the form of absolutes: Jack Merridew is a monster; he cannot be a kid.

In a contemporary review of *Lord of the Flies* entitled "Small Savages," Louis J. Halle described Golding's characters as "savage-civilized children (who are simply grown-ups more plainly written)," which denies the more obvious fact that what is "plainly written" involves children exclusively, not adults (qtd. in Nelson 5). If Golding is exclusively concerned with "grown-ups," why do they appear in only two of the novel's two hundred pages? This question has been relatively suppressed or simply dismissed as pedestrian. E. L. Epstein avoids the issue by immediately vaulting over it: "The implications of the story go far beyond the degeneration of a few children" (205). Even Reinhard Kuhn, whose book is on *child* characterization, limits Golding's characters to representing adults, stressing the commentary that Golding might be making about adult culture with the final rescue scene. He writes that the novel has a "radical pessimism concerning the durability of the childhood world" (159), and in doing so he sentimentally reduces the concept of childhood to fixed ignorance and nothing more. Because Golding's representation of children's violent potential violates his own definitions, Kuhn redefines the child-characters as nonchildren. *Lord of the Flies,* populated with emotionally complex and menacing children, challenges the security of adults who insist on oversimplified constructions of child innocence.

This threat to idealism clearly disturbed Halle, who objected to the manner in which it was achieved. Recognizing evolutionary overtones in the text, he seems particularly shocked that scientific discourse might infect a literary work:

> The novelist's vision conflicts with that of the textbook anthropologist [. . .] [He] sees good opposed to evil; he recognizes the existence and the utility of heroes. But the social scientist deals only with amoral phenomena. In his termite society heroes are social misfits who must come to a bad end, one suspects, to confirm the tacit assumption that maladjustment is undesirable. The intimidated novelist, thus opposed by the misplaced authority of science, dares hardly suggest even that his heroes save the honor of mankind. (qtd. in Nelson 6)

A force conspicuously surfaces—the lure of scientific authority—which challenges nostalgia for defining children as innocent. There is no room for sentimental nicety—survival of the fittest is the order of the island. Despite Piggy's and Ralph's attempts to establish and enforce rules, Jack convinces the "littluns" that might makes right. To Halle, a novel must provide a moral antidote for human barbarity, but this primal hierarchy indicates that Golding's goal was to investigate that barbarity further, and he (significantly) traces it back to childhood.

Golding reported that his novel was "an attempt to trace the defects of society back to the defects of human nature" (Epstein 204). He chose to do so by first pinning the degenerative process on children, and in the process he is perpetuating a mythology that he knew, if not as a science student, then surely through teaching children at a time when pedagogic discourse was already dominated by the outlook of biologically based developmental sciences. That critics consistently overlook Golding's potential statement on childhood reflects our culture's denial of the implications that logically follow from scientific constructions we have passively inherited from recapitulation theory.

Introduced in the 1860s and 1870s with Ernst Haeckel's "biogenetic law," recapitulation theory popularized the belief that "the development from fetus to adulthood (ontogeny) provides a brief recapitulation of the entire history of the race (phylogeny)" (Sulloway 259). Recapitulation theory was used to scientifically position children, along with women and nonwhites, as undeveloped, primitive beings. Haeckel studied the embryos of varied species, discovering a supposed common stage among them. It was assumed that if "lower animals" develop similarly as embryos, might not children replicate their development entirely? Charles Darwin seems to have also assumed this connection to some degree. His 1877 article "A Biographical Sketch of an Infant" includes observations of his newborn son, whom he consistently compares to "lower animals" in order to predict and understand the development of children in general. A disciple of Darwin, George Romanes, further investigated the human lifespan by finding similarities between human children and adults of other species.[4] In his *Mental Evolution in Man* (1888), Romanes wrote, "the emotional life of animals is so strikingly similar to the emotional life of man—and especially of young children—that I think the similarity ought fairly to be taken as direct evidence of a genetic continuity between them" (7). Romanes sparked the imagination of many scientists and psychologists (Freud, Jung, Skinner) and helped to spread the ageist tropes of recapitulation.[5]

We have inherited a scientific obsession with mapping a chronological standard of development based on the assumption that children are closer to other species than they are to the "perfected" adults of their own. This primitivizing view of children imposes a deterministic linearity to modern pedagogy and developmentalism, the relativism of which we often overlook. John R. Morss explains this as a teleological misunderstanding of evolution: "The assumption of direction and design in evolutionary change [. . .] gave rise to a linear picture of development: A single track of developmental progress, up which all organisms and civilisations have to climb" (*The Biologising of Childhood* 16). Jean Piaget mapped out universal stages of maturation in a process he called "genetic epistemology," favoring the ultimate goal of literate, rational, abstract thought: "the child must be brought through progressively higher stages of civilisation through appropriately chosen materials" (qtd. in *The Biologising of Childhood* 63). Even Freud relied to some extent on the linear and rationalist bias of developmentalism, as Peter Gay points out in *Reading Freud*. Gay compares Freud's concept of childhood to indentured slavery—a period through which the subject must develop toward the ideal of adulthood:

> [Freud's] scheme of maturation [. . .] visualiz[es] mental and emotional growth as a laborious, often disrupted, and never wholly completed attempt to escape from bondage [. . .] glorious scenarios of omnipotence that a small child enacts in fantasies [. . .] attest vividly to its impotence [. . .] Each stage of physical and mental development has its appropriate experience of servitude and its appropriate experiments in overcoming that servitude. (92)

This oppressively adult-centered vision of childhood and development still limits popular views. Tim Morris playfully points out that "even finding one's inner child, in popular psychology, is done in the service of growing up more completely" (5). Growing up "more completely," in Western modernity, means controlling emotions and developing one's ability to reason abstractly, sequentially, and systematically. In her deconstruction of developmentalism, Erica Burman blames this tendency on a gender bias: "The child study movement of the late nineteenth century prefigured the terms of developmental enquiry [. . .] . It institutionalised the ancient split between emotion and rationality, played out in the gendered practice of scientific research" (12). In favor of preserving a concept of adulthood that is rational, our constructions of childhood dismiss intuition and fall back on divisive and dehumanizing assumptions that we would otherwise find preposterous.

Lord of the Flies transmits mythologies that had been circulating for almost a century. In *Constructing and Reconstructing Childhood*, Allison James and Alan Prout write: "The scientific construction of the 'irrationality,' 'naturalness' and 'universality' of childhood through psychological discourses was translated directly into sociological accounts of childhood in the form of theories of socialization during the 1950s" (12). On some level, all Western adults are influenced by these discourses, regardless of how passively or unintentionally we transmit them. James and Prout explain the possibility of such an oversight as it concerns the construction of childhood:

86

"As heirs to a western intellectual tradition centered on scientific rationality, 'the child' represented a laboratory specimen for the study of primitive forms of cognition and, indeed, children were brought into the laboratory to be studied [...] . So much is this perspective incorporated into the everyday understanding of children [...] that it is difficult to think outside it" (12).

Golding investigates the animality of humans by populating the book with child characters—we cannot overlook the significance of this choice. He strips children of the sentimental literary construction of "innocence" and draws them as innate (ignoble) savages. Jack, for example, is constantly described in animal terms suggestive of his primitivism: "Power lay in the brown swell of his forearms: authority sat on his shoulder and chattered in his ear like an ape" (150). Why the attention to his forearms—are they longer? Without the benevolent influence of adult society, he becomes apelike. Golding falls back on these familiar tropes to underscore Jack's aggressive behavior as primitive and somehow contagious. Piggy warns, "we'll soon be animals anyway," signaling their natural retrogression (92). Jack's group, known only as the "savages," joins him in increasingly sadistic and destructive rituals. Soon they inflict these rituals on Simon, whom they not only mistake for a "beast" but circle and kill as one (153).

The only characters who recognize the boys' degeneracy are Simon and Piggy, who are, as a result, estranged and killed. Ironically, they are the only two characters described like adults. While most of the boys tan, growing wild and vibrant, Simon's "half-shut eyes were dim with the infinite cynicism of adult life" (137). Coming down the mountain, before he is brutally attacked by the others, "The usual brightness was gone from his eyes and he walked with a sort of glum determination like an old man" (146). Even though Simon is the novel's shining hope for a hero, he is unhealthy and somewhat unsympathetically sketched. As Halle has bemoaned, Golding will not give heroism a chance, and this decision indicates lack of faith in the ability of children to establish social order, do good works, and recognize what is right (for example, the wisdom of Simon) without parental guidance.

The new island order follows the circular logic of recapitulation: if children are like primitive adults, then "primitive" adults are degenerates. As Stephen Jay Gould explains in *The Mismeasure of Man*, "Recapitulation provided an irresistible criterion for any scientist who wanted to rank human groups as higher or lower. The *adults* of *inferior* groups must be like *children* of *superior* groups, for the child represents a primitive adult ancestor" (115). According to the children's hierarchy in *Lord of the Flies*, the atavistic "adult" child is inferior to the natural "savage" child. Simon must be brought under the power of savage children in order to establish and preserve their hierarchy.

Piggy is likewise cast as an adultlike outsider. He scorns the childishness of the others, taking a grown-up role. Scolding them, he yells: "Like kids! Acting like a crowd of kids!" (38). Piggy's unnatural maturity is manifested morphologically as well—he looks like a bespectacled old man. While the others grow untamable locks, "He was the only boy on the island whose hair never seemed to grow. Piggy's hair still lay in wisps over his head as though baldness were his natural state and this imperfect covering would soon go" (64). Like Simon, Piggy is one of the few characters to evoke sympathy, especially after his murder, yet he is also unnaturally aged—he does not belong, nor can he adapt, on the island. This is likely what Halle was reacting to in his assessment that "maladjustment," even when resisting corruption, "is undesirable" on the island. Piggy and Simon are the voices of reason, but they are also maladapted to this new and wild environment. However, this ambiguity makes it impossible to read as Halle wishes to, finding good and evil clearly marked and justly rewarded or punished. Instead, our frame of reference is Golding's representation of a child-powered space—the island—Neverland gone wrong.

Because Simon and Piggy appear more as primitive adults than savage children, they are considered degenerate among degenerates. Traditionally, literary children's unnatural aging has been explained as a result of the "sins" of their parents. The atavism of Simon and Piggy resembles that of Little Father Time in *Jude the Obscure* or Dickens's *Little Dorrit*. But there are no parents to blame here. Golding has inverted the adult order and replaced it with a hierarchy of savage children that silences voices of reason.

Golding sculpts children who easily slip into ritualistic roles that seem a prewritten part of their degenerate unconscious. Conscience fails to prevent violence. Jack hides behind the mask of his paint: "He began to dance and his laughter became a bloodthirsty snarling. [. . .] [T]he mask was a thing on its own, behind which Jack hid, liberated from shame and self-consciousness" (64). Even in the 1990 film version of *Lord of the Flies*, a similar recapitulationist trope is introduced when Jack stabs a simple image into a rock, resembling the artwork of early humans. This echoes E. D. Cope's argument that because children's art resembles cave paintings, children *are* savages (Gould 117).

The rituals of hunting, face painting, and rock carving connect Jack with early evolutionary ancestors in the natural world. A contemporary of G. Stanley Hall's, M. A. Starr, thought such experiences are key to child development, and he encouraged parents to support activities such as hunting and fishing (in boys, at least): "The boy in the woods building his fire [. . .] is living over again the wild outdoor savage life of his ancestors" (qtd. in *The Biologising of Children* 35).[6] This sentiment is also expressed in *Peter Pan* and *Coral Island*. But the mythology on which it is based is a "science" of *a priori* reasoning and inductive conclusions.[7] Starr's conclusion simply repeats his premise: a child relives the primitive experiences of his ancestors because he can be interpreted as acting primitively—he is a savage himself.

There is a more practical explanation for Jack's barbarity, which also explains the contagion of his rituals: fear. In an early conversation with Ralph, Jack reveals that his "savagery" is in part inspired by fear: "'If you're hunting sometimes you catch yourself feeling . . . as if you're not hunting, but—being hunted, as if something's behind you all the time in the jungle'" (53). He is becoming a part of the cannibalistic environment in which he must learn to exist. Though his methods are often cruel, Jack offers a valid alternative to remaining in fear of imaginary "Beasties" and boogiemen. To him the frightened "littluns" are "'a lot of cry-babies and sissies,'" and he advises them to be brave: "'as for the fear—you'll have to put up with that like the rest of us'" (82). Despite his toughness, Jack admits to his own fear as he desperately tries to conquer it.

But even this pragmatic interpretation of potential childhood "savagery" (children are only human, after all) was once dismissed by early theories. In Darwin's "Biographical Sketch of an Infant," fear itself became a primitive trait: "May we not suspect that the vague but very real fears of children, which are quite *independent of experience,* are the inherited effects of *real* dangers and abject superstitions during ancient savage times?" (italics added, 288). He assumes, then, that modern children have inherited instinctive but artificial fears to prepare them for the dangers of the natural world, but only "ancient savages" were in any real danger proportionate to such emotions. Given what we now know of the exploitation of children in factories and the abuse of children on the streets, in schools, and even at home, this assumption seems ill focused. Surely there is plenty for children to fear that is *dependent upon experience,* not simply residual goblins of primitive links.[8] Not to mention that fear is an understandable emotion to have when one, like many defined as children, *lacks experience* in his/her relatively new surroundings. More so, the children on the island have irrefutable reasons to be scared—their plane has crashed during a wartime evacuation. Who knows who will find them—the enemy? Even so, Golding depicts their fears as over-imaginative and superstitious—in short, as primitive. They fear the elements, as the chapter headings reveal: "Beast from Water" and "Beast from Air."

It seems that the discourses we have created concerning children force us into imposing impossible extremes: either we imagine friendly spaces for them (as discussed in the last chapter), or we throw them out of dream-like safety and call them primitive for being afraid. Perhaps the deeper fear lurks in adult egos threatened by the secret suspicion that Jack is no monster but an animal, a human animal, in fact, like all of us. Peter Hollindale notes that some adults remain shocked and discomfited by *Lord of the Flies* almost half a century after its publication. Describing a 1995 Royal Shakespeare Company stage production of Nigel Williams's adaptation of the novel, he recounts, "the man sitting next to me hid his head in his hands while Jack was daubing the other boys' faces with blood, and elsewhere in the small auditorium there was some defensive adult tittering. (The few children present appeared to be spellbound.)" (4). Critics continue, as he says, to "distort the book as a version of art because [they] cannot bear it as a version of life" (4). Whether child-characters are cute or barbarous, critics insist on seeing them as inferior to adults and thus, if not controllable, at least dismissible.

Likewise, Reinhard Kuhn points out, Richard Hughes's *A High Wind in Jamaica* (1929) presents a "rigorous demolition of the Rousseauistic vision of children as noble savages, incorruptible within a state of nature" (156). These novels reject the stifling ideal of innocent childhood by drawing on scientific tropes that allow them to construct children as inscrutable, animalistic brutes who act indifferently to the moral codes of adult society. In this sense they dignify children more than any Disney production could ever do, by allowing children to represent the complexities of human nature.

In *A High Wind in Jamaica*, Hughes exaggerates recapitulatory images to satirize the irreconcilability of science to sentiment, describing one girl as follows:

> To take a metaphor from tadpoles, though legs were growing her gills had not yet dropped off. Being nearly four years old she was certainly a child: and children are human (if one allows the term "human" a wide sense): but she had not altogether ceased to be a baby: and babies of course are not human—they are animals, and have a very ancient and ramified culture, as cats have, and fishes, and even snakes: the same in kind as these, but much more complicated and vivid, since babies are, after all, one of the most developed species of the lower vertebrates. (134)

Despite the confident classification here, the narrator injects his own awareness of children's elusiveness. In doing so he plays with the construction of a child as animalistic, but also as a human engaged in the slow process of becoming a knowable social subject. He exaggerates scientific presumptions to expose the absurdity of reliance upon measuring and categorizing:

> Possibly a case might be made out that children are not human either: but I should not accept it. Agreed that their minds are not just more ignorant and stupider than ours, but differ in kind of thinking (are *mad,* in fact): but one can, by an effort of will and imagination, think like a child at least in a partial degree—and even if one's success is infinitesimal it invalidates the case: while one can no more think like a baby, in the smallest respect, than one can think like a bee. (135)

According to this paradigm, a baby is a non-human and a child is human but mad. The narrator does not clarify when babies become children, unless it is by demonstrating a convincing resemblance to adult behavior: "Subconsciously, too, everyone recognizes they are animals—why else do people always laugh when a baby does some action resembling the human, as they would at a Praying Mantis? If the baby was only a less-developed man, there would be nothing funny in it, surely" (135). The standard of adult development discriminates the young by degrees of recognizable rationality. Though closer than babies, by definition, in their progression from animalism to maturity within the hierarchy, children are compared to lower life forms as much as babies when measured against the rational, adult ideal.

The above distinction of baby from "less-developed man" hinges on recognizing only normative behavior and exaggerates the rationalist bias in favor of interpreting play solely as a function for learning adult codes of behavior (rather than as testing, resisting, or breaking rules to create new ones)—if the baby clearly imitates adults (conforms), it is engaged in rational play; if not, it is incomprehensibly inhuman. This bias is still reflected in developmental sciences, as James and Prout indicate: "Rationality is the universal mark of adulthood with childhood representing the period of apprenticeship for its development. [. . .] The decreasing 'irrationality' of children's play as they mature is taken as a measure of an evolving 'rationality' of thought" (10–11). Of course, one could just as easily interpret more "rational" play as evidence of rule conformity learned from hard-pressed socialization rather than any essential change from within, but in order to seal our prejudice in favor of adult-defined norms, developmental sciences essentialize the difference by insisting that rationality is innately programmed. When the foregone conclusion is that adult behavior is rational, any deviance is automatically considered irrational and thus impossible to reason with or validate.

As in *Lord of the Flies,* Hughes's child-characters' fears are invalidated and pre-deemed irrational through vilification. The children are to be feared instead of pitied, especially after the novel's central character, Emily, murders a man helplessly bound under her guard in Jonsen's cabin. The pirates who are stuck on the ship with the children develop a xenophobic reaction to their inscrutability (once they realize "innocence" does not quite fit): "All tenderness towards the children vanished. Even José ceased playing with them. They were treated with a detached severity not wholly divorced from fear—as if these unfortunate men at last realised what diabolic yeast had been introduced into their lump" (155). Without the guidance of educators and parents, the children regress into a state of primitive behavior (after all, yeast is not a very advanced organism) that shocks even the pirates, who, the narrator gets the reader to overlook, might have raped Margaret and Emily.[9]

The adults in *A High Wind from Jamaica* read the children with the same absolutism that we saw in the governess's construction of Miles and Flora and in Ida's construction of Maisie. James Kincaid explains, "Idealized angels are made possible by matching devils"—in service to our schizophrenic idealism about childhood, we cannot see them as simultaneously flawed and gifted humans (*Erotic Innocence* 140). Even when the children are victims themselves, once they have victimized the adults, they are to be feared, as Emily's father realizes when reunited with her: "he realised, with a sudden painful shock, that he was afraid of her! [. . .] But surely it was some trick of the candlelight, or of her indisposition, that gave her face momentarily that inhuman, stony, basilisk look?" (233). His unforgiving reconstruction of Emily reflects an inability to categorize her as anything more complex than "good" or "bad," "human" or "inhuman," because she is a child.

Critics' responses to Hughes's depiction of childhood primitivism resemble those of critics to Golding's. Just as child-murderers are often redefined by social sentiment as adults and tried as adults in court, Emily no longer fits a construction of childhood that is sentimentally palatable to critics. When Emily accuses her former hero Jonsen and his companions of the murder she committed, Reinhard Kuhn asks, "Is she an overwrought child who does not know what she is doing and who gives way under the pressures of interrogation, or is she a calculating adult, desperately defending herself and knowingly sending others to the gallows for the crime she has committed?" (155). Once again we have a mystifying case of either/or. Kuhn presupposes that she cannot be both "calculating" *and* a child. He omits the possibility that a child can knowingly react dishonestly in fear (or malice) to protect herself from a murderer's sentence, and his redefinition betrays his denial. Constructing children as completely innocent forces us into the hypocrisy of denying the childhood we have adamantly circumscribed when confronted with exceptions to its adult-serving boundaries. This denial also rests on unstated assumptions: not only is the true child ignorant of evil, he/she is essentially honest.

Hughes's breakdown of the romantic construction has already anticipated and refuted this bias: "A child can hide the most appalling secret without the least effort. [. . .] Parents, finding that they see through their child in so many places the child does not know of, seldom realize that, if there is some point the child really gives his mind to hiding, their chances are nil" (119). Hughes, like Golding, has exaggerated the claims of biological determinism to better expose the hypocrisy of adults imposing an absolutist construction of childhood innocence. Rejecting the uncompromising binaries of developmentalism and romanticism, he opts for a construction of children as ultimately inscrutable.

American literary childhoods are even more at odds with the childhoods of our scientific (and legal) discourse. On the one hand there is the romantic tradition Leslie Fiedler described in "Come Back to the Raft Ag'in, Huck Honey!": American literature is uniquely "regressive," with an "implacable nostalgia for the infantile" (40). Yet scientific approaches to childhood in this country maintain a rigidly adult-bound, rationalist bias. Developmentalism, behaviorism, and positivism still limit the social sciences rigidly in the United States—the work of Russian psychologist Lev Vygotsky, who challenged the exclusivity of rationalist sciences, was not even translated into English until the 1970s, and psychoanalytic and phenomenological influences are not legitimated here in professional research and practice as they are in Europe.[10]

The selective but exclusionary coexistence of such seemingly contradictory extremes as scientific developmentalism and literary romanticism makes for some impossible reconciliations (especially, as we will see later, in science fiction). Neil Postman has dubbed this dichotomy of approaches Protestant and Romantic. The former allies itself with a rationalist take on development, as I have described it:

In the Protestant view the child is an unformed person who through literacy, education, reason, self-control, and shame may be made into a civilized adult. In the Romantic view it is not the unformed child but the deformed adult who is the problem. The child possesses as his or her birthright capacities for candor, understanding, curiosity, and spontaneity that are deadened by literacy, education, reason, self-control, and shame. (59)

American fiction abounds with romanticized children who through unsocialized wisdom are able to reflect maturation as a fall. Perhaps the most famous example is Huck Finn, who serves as a foil to "deformed" adults whose perceptions are limited by prejudice. Mark Twain uses his child-character to reflect social evils and force recognition of the dangers of socialization itself. Rather than needing to be formed as an adult through education, Huck tries to resist the "conscience" of his elders to do the right thing. Postman writes, "Certainly Twain attacked the presumption that children are, in any but the most superficial sense, unformed. And he mocked the claim that their character may be vastly improved by society's values" (60).

The adult values that Huck is exposed to and negotiates in his own decision-making are constantly shifting and usually hypocritical. The Widow Douglas wants to "sivilize" Huck through religion and book learning, but he sees her as having a double standard and doubts her ability to choose what is right for him. When she tells him not to smoke, Huck reports this as an example of the subjectively selective values of adults: "They get down on a thing when they don't know nothing about it. [. . .] And she took snuff too; of course that was all right, because she done it herself" (2). On the opposite end of the nurture scale is Pap, who cares little about preserving childhood innocence or nurturing Huck's education. When he discovers that Huck is learning to read, he responds, "I ain't the man to stand for it—you hear?" (15). His motives are clear—he does not want his son to surpass his own inadequate schooling.

Twain keeps the spotlight on the adult desires and socializing forces surrounding Huck at all times, even when he has gone "back to nature" by fleeing with Jim on the Mississippi. Huck's ethical reasoning always reflects an awareness of the social views he is expected to adopt. In deciding to help Jim he realizes that "people would call me a low down Abolitionist and despise me for keeping mum—but that don't make no difference" (32). Though the voice of society, or "conscience," as Huck calls it, keeps creeping into his mind, Huck tries to drown out that noise in favor of his independent conclusions. He is able to see that social mores and personal ethics can differ greatly, as he reasons, "S'pose you'd done a right and give Jim up; would you felt better than what you do now? No, says I, I'd feel bad—I'd feel just the same way I do now. Well, then, says I, what's the use you learning to do right, when it's troublesome to do right and ain't no trouble to do wrong, and the wages is just the same?" (69). He is able to see that the morality he has been taught is a socially constructed system dependent upon subjective interpretation: "It don't make no difference whether you do right or wrong, a person's conscience ain't got no sense, and just goes for him *anyway*" (175).

Through experience and observation, not what others tell him, Huck perceives that social difference is constructed much in the same way. Huck is an empiricist, not a rationalist; he constantly measures the ideologies presented to him against the world as he experiences it. Early on in their journey Huck feels a pang of conscience when Jim plans to go back for his children: "Here was this nigger which I had as good as helped to run away, coming right out flat-footed and saying he would steal his children—children that belonged to a man I didn't even know; a man that hadn't ever done me no harm" (67). But gradually he begins to understand that Jim is not property but a caring father: "he was sitting there with his head down betwixt his knees, moaning and mourning to himself [. . .] . I knowed what it was about. He was thinking about his wife and children, away up yonder, and he was low and homesick. [. . .] I do believe he cared just as much for his people as white folks do for their'n" (117). The presumption of Jim's being different (lacking human feeling) simply because of his skin color and enslavement finally gives way to Huck's realizing the constructedness of that difference. Huck's education is the Rousseauistic ideal—he escapes the trappings of "nurture" to find his own understanding at his own pace. He learns condition by condition based on observation, not a pre-reasoned belief system.

When Huck lies to protect Jim from being discovered, Twain subverts developmentalist essentializing through dramatic irony: "I knowed very well I had done wrong, and I see it warn't no use for me to try to learn to do a right; a body that don't get *started* right when he's little, ain't got no show—when the pinch comes there ain't nothing to back him up" (69). Though he plays with the developmental notion that nurture must start early to combat an uncivilized nature, the reader knows that it is because Huck was "brung up wicked" (160) or without rigorous and constant supervision that he has been spared the mentally narrowing effects of hegemonic socialization. The romantic child often becomes cast as a rev-olutionary because of his/her potential for civil disobedience. At the end of Huck's narrative, we are left with his plan to remain in a state of nature: "I got to light out for the Territory ahead of the rest, because Aunt Sally she's going to adopt me and sivilize me and I can't stand it. I been there before" (220). However, socialization *is* inevitable for most, and Twain highlights its dangers in his depiction of other child-characters (like Buck) who foil Huck's romantic isolation.

This contrast seems the most significant function of Tom Sawyer, whose immersion in society is more complete, which is especially evident in the power he wields because of his exaggerated bookishness (once again we see literacy as a measure of rationalist development). Tom uses his knowledge of adventure stories to bully others into mimicking their plots. Always the pragmatist, Huck questions Tom's elaborate schemes, but within the hierarchy of children in this text, Tom has more power because of his institutional learning. Louise K. Barnett writes, "Adults invariably place Huck in a subordinate position while peers like Tom and Buck exert leadership on the basis of their greater knowledge—knowledge which they have acquired through an acculturation process that Huck has not had" (222). But Twain inverted the developmental hierarchy through satire, portraying an unstudied intuition as most sagacious. When Ben Rogers refuses to "ransom" the "gang's" prisoners because none of them understand what the word means, Tom chastises him: "Don't I tell you it's in the books? Do you want to go to doing different from what's in the books, and get things all muddled up?" (7). Yet it is going by the books that not only makes things too complicated but also winds up enabling the cruel treat-ment of Jim in the controversial final episode at Aunt Sally's.

When the cruelty and danger of Tom's plot to imprison Jim and plan a slow escape becomes intolerable, Huck finds his practical alternatives dashed by Tom's conventional confidence: "'Well, if that ain't just like you, Huck Finn. You *can* get up the infant-schooliest ways of going at a thing. Why, hain't you ever read any books at all?'" (180). Regardless of the absur-dity of Tom's ideas, he remains an authority for Huck, who is less schooled and thus, it is assumed, less intelligent and mature.[11] This legitimating of literate nonsense over spoken wisdom reflects the sometimes skewed hier-archy of developmentalism, which can be traced back to Locke, whose metaphor of child as *tabula rasa* evolved in nineteenth-century American pedagogy into the contrasting ideal of adulthood as well written and well read. Postman contrasts the Lockean (rationalist) view, instrumental in pedagogy, to the romantic view, expressed more often in literature: "Locke wanted education to result in a rich, varied, and copious book; Rousseau wanted education to result in a healthy flower" (60). Clearly Tom is becoming a "copious" but confused book, and Twain favors the natural wisdom that is budding in Huck.

Steven Mailloux, writing about the last half of the nineteenth century, states that public discourse about literacy "assume[d] a close cultural connection among moral order, mental development, and bodily exercise" (136). One need only think of the importance of reading to moral development in *Little Women* (1868) to get an idea of American pedagogy at the time. Jo's gothic reading is considered dangerously imaginative, but Marmee starts the girls safely on *Pilgrim's Progress* (1678), and not only does Alcott's narrative follow that text—chapter headings come from Christian's journeys—but the girls also model their development on the suggested path of Bunyan's book: "reading *as* self-reform takes place while the daughters read *about* self-reform. Consuming books like *Pilgrim's Progress* helps the girls re-figure the disorderly process of growing up as an orderly progression of moral development" (Mailloux 144). Mailloux calls this process "rhetorical self-fashioning," which is precisely what Tom Sawyer does with adventure novels, interpreting them as direct models for behavior and repeating plots as if by rote. Twain's rejection of self-fashioning is more than a case of romantic anti-intellectualism—his satire suggests that reading in itself (regardless of "quality") cannot provide models for maturation, that is, if we want to encourage young readers to think for themselves and regard reading as a critical, not simply passive didactic activity.

Through Tom's reading, Twain may have also snubbed the quality of "boys' books" available in his time, many of which were under reconsideration through pedagogical reforms.[12] Along with the mania for children's reading existed a concern about what kinds of books were "molding" children, as can be seen in Marmee's selectivity above. For some time this care applied primarily to reading for girls. However, Thomas Bailey Aldrich's *The Story of a Bad Boy* (1870) and George W. Peck's *Peck's Bad Boy* (1883) popularized the figure of the boy rebel, and "many adults were convinced that real bad boys were made out of juveniles subjected to bad fiction" (Mailloux 148).

For the most part, however, Twain seems to mock this fear with his threat that "persons attempting to find a moral [. . .] will be banished" ("Notice" iv). And his inversion of developmentalism is complete—the fact that his two wisest characters, his heroic civil-disobedients Huck and Jim, are also the least educated speaks for itself. But this inversion might not have spoken to his censors, who likely underestimated the book's critique of the limiting process of socialization and its dangerous by-products—superstition, hypocrisy, racism, and cruelty. According to Mailloux, "the cultural conversation of the mid-1880s demonstrated less anxiety about race relations then [*sic*] it did about juvenile delinquency [. . .] [C]ensors reviewing *Huckleberry Finn* were preoccupied less with racist segregation practices than with the 'Bad-Boy Boom' and the negative effects of reading fiction" (135). This prioritizing would suggest that Twain's contemporaries felt more threatened by Huck's example than Tom's, focusing on his "bad boy" truancy, smoking, and "uncivilized" manners rather than his "good boy" behavior in helping out his enslaved friend. Parents may have feared the influence of Huck's behavior on their own potential "bad boys." Yet Huck is the quintessential romantic child in America, as Fiedler has indicated: "The Good Bad Boy is, of course, America's vision of itself [. . .] crude and unruly in his beginnings but endowed by his creator with an instinctive sense of what is right; sexually as pure as any milky maiden, he is a rough neck all the same, at once potent and submissive" ("Eye of Innocence" 483).

That Twain's censors concentrated on Huck's minor transgressions and overlooked Tom's cruelty to Jim indicates more than how silenced racial fairness was at the time; it also reveals a common hypocrisy in our tradition of constructing childhood. To parents worried about imitations in their own children, Huck was not a suitable model because "Huck is closer to Jim than to Tom—that is, closer to what the white world of gentility fears and excludes than to what it condescendingly indulges in the child" (Fiedler, "Eye of Innocence" 484). Tom represents the child we can control—a model for our own children—but Huck has the childhood adults want to reinhabit themselves. Perhaps this double standard explains the close coexistence of such opposing extremes as developmentalism and romanticism: developmentalists promise to mold children into perfectly socialized adults, while romantics (to spin a quip of Alison Lurie's) want to *be* children.

Both literary critics and developmentalists have recognized their own projection onto and possessiveness toward childhood. Fiedler reminds us that "the child remains still, what he has been since the beginnings of Romanticism, a surrogate for our unconscious, impulsive lives" ("Eye of Innocence" 511). Just as a child can be imaginatively linked with a nostalgic past, he/she is also cast as a primitive link to pre-social human experience, representative of an essential or "inner" self. In fact, to many humanists the concepts of childhood and individual selfhood originated and evolved together. Carolyn Steedman makes this a founding premise of *Strange Dislocations:* "The interiorised self, understood to be a product of a personal history, was most clearly expressed in the idea of 'childhood,' and the idea of 'the child'" (5). Scientifically, children constructed in discourse have served in an indirect investigation of our adult selves. Erica Burman writes, "The study of infants in the mid-nineteenth century, along with that of 'primitives' and of natural history, was motivated by the quest to discover the origins and specificities of mind, that is, the human adult mind" (10).

That such investigations have hinged on assessing children's cognition reflects the rationalist equation of knowledge with power. Attempts to control or empower children depend upon definitions of knowledge and belief in a child's potential for comprehension. Tapping that potential became an interest of modernists, as Fiona Björling points out:

> The modernist artist [. . .] attempts to channel despair into creation and turns the child into primitive man as a source of inspiration. The creativity of the child consists in the fact that he passes from a state of complete ignorance at birth to a state of knowledge. It is the actual moment of transition from ignorance which bears witness to creativity; knowledge once obtained becomes automatic and loses value. The process and not the object of seeing and knowing for the first time is of value. (5)

Many modern writers eulogize the pre-social, supposedly integrated self by concentrating on such a process or transition. The fall of development backlights most of James Baldwin's fiction—especially in characterization. In his tale of two brothers' coming of age, "Sonny's Blues" (1965), practically every page contains a reference to childhood. Characters' faces are described in terms of perceived age: when light or smiling, their faces are childlike; when sad and fallen they are old. Michael Clark has said, "The implicit assumption here is that childhood is a holistic state, whereas the process of growing older maims the individual. Indeed, there is frequent evidence throughout the story that Baldwin sees childhood as a touchstone by which to judge the shortcomings of adulthood" (198). Metaphorically speaking, Clark has characterized adulthood as fragmented (as I did in my discussion of *White Mule*); thus, again, we see the fall as one in which experience brings loss of totalization and wholeness.[13] Baldwin depicts a child as being aware of an inevitable loss increasing with experience, as in the scene in which Sonny's brother (the narrator) remembers being a child in a room full of adults and knowing that the security of childhood was waning with every nightfall:

The silence, the darkness coming, and the darkness in the faces frightens the child obscurely. [...] Something deep and watchful in the child knows that this is bound to end, is already ending. In a moment someone will get up and turn on the light. Then the old folks will remember the children and they won't talk any more that day. And when light fills the room, the child is filled with darkness. He knows that every time this happens he's moved just a little closer to that darkness outside. The darkness outside is what the old folks have been talking about. [...] The child knows that they won't talk any more because if he knows too much about what's happened to *them*, he'll know too much too soon, about what's going to happen to *him*." (115)

Baldwin idealizes childhood as a state of grace (Sonny's niece, significantly named Gracie, dies young, thus avoiding the fall). The transition from innocence to knowledge reveals also that childhood is isolated discursively (in order to postpone it, the parents stop talking when they remember his presence, yet he wants them to talk about their experience). The modern romantic figuration of childhood is prelapsarian but not entirely unknowing—at once celebrated for innocence and curiosity. A seeming paradox emerges: children are seen as unencumbered with knowledge and thus have more open potential for wisdom.

Developmentalists are not completely free of this paradoxical romanticism. Erica Burman indicates that both approaches hold the idealized child up as a key to wisdom that is inaccessible to adults:

> By virtue of being very young, and having had less opportunity to learn, the infant is seen as close to nature, devoid of the trappings of adult training and (Western) "civilisation." In contradictory ways, romantic and scientific models combine to locate within the child both *more* knowledge ("the child is father to the man") and (by virtue of the child's lesser and different understanding) the *route* to knowledge. In this, developmental psychology naturalises the romantic fiction of children as innocent bearers of wisdom by producing them as objects and subjects of study. (10)

Developmentalism might allow for seeing children at least as trainable rather than "too young to understand," but it still situates their experience as distinctively different—a tantalizing otherness and curious object for analysis. Burman's comparison is important in understanding a romantic trend in science fiction, of constructing children as aliens or new subspecies—sometimes menacing, at other times innocent—always somehow intellectual/evolutionary superiors to their parents and elders.

This theme was a favorite of Henry Kuttner, who often wrote with his wife, C. L. Moore, under the pseudonym Lewis Padgett. In their Carroll-inspired "Mimsy Were the Borogoves" (1943), Kuttner fully developed his pet theories about children. One of the child-characters, Scott Paradine, finds a box of interactive, educational toys that have time-traveled through another dimension to 1942 from millions of years in the future. As Scott and his infant sister, Emma, play with the toys, they become conditioned to think in terms of an advanced logic that their parents cannot understand. Before the Paradines realize what is happening, Scott and Emma have successfully decoded the formula for returning to the future in another dimension and disappear (amusingly, the key is in the poem, "Jabberwocky," which the story implies was taught to Lewis Carroll by Alice Liddell after she found a similar box of toys).[14]

According to James Gunn, "a favorite Kuttner character [is the] reasonable, rational, university professor," and such a character is the perfect contrast to his child-characters, whose lack of rational rigidity is their strength (200). In "Mimsy Were the Borogoves" the professor is a child psychologist, Rex Holloway, who explains the Paradine children's odd behavior to their parents. He starts by quoting none other than Hughes's *A High Wind in Jamaica:* "'Babies have minds which work in terms and categories of their own which cannot be translated into the terms and categories of the human mind'" (79). But unlike Hughes, whose narrator comically interpreted this difference along recapitulatory, developmentalist lines as a sign of primitivism, Kuttner neo-romantically twists the difference into a sign of great future potential. Holloway explains the process by which development, ironically, limits the human brain: "The brain's a colloid [. . .]. We don't even know how much it can grasp. But it is known that the mind becomes conditioned as the human animal matures. It follows certain familiar theorems, and all thought thereafter is pretty well based on patterns taken for granted" (79).[15] As Björling stated above, "knowledge once obtained becomes automatic"; thus we are limited by our lack of inquiry and loss of opportunities for (re)discovery.

The comfort of knowing keeps adults from seeking alternatives, even if they are better ones. Holloway seems to envy the Paradine children as he describes one of their toys: "Our minds, conditioned to Euclid, can see nothing in this but an illogical tangle of wires. But a child—especially a baby—might see more. [. . .] Only a child wouldn't be handicapped by too many preconceived ideas" (80). With less to unlearn, the baby, Emma, becomes their mental leader, and Scott verifies all of his plans through her.

The hierarchy of age and power is inverted so that now the least educated member of the Paradine family has the greatest mental potential and thus holds the power. With her instruction, she and Scott transport themselves to another dimension.

According to a surprisingly frequent motif in science fiction, babies do not resemble primitive ancestors; they represent something (human? alien?) more evolved. According to Gary Westfahl,

> Writers informed by modern science may celebrate children on alternative grounds. Biological evolution often progresses by means of neoteny, the retention of juvenile features in adulthood. Since *Homo sapiens* resemble baby apes in their hairlessness, large heads, and restless curiosity, it is logical to assume that the advanced human beings of the future—*Homo superior*—will emerge from and closely resemble the baby humans of today. In science fiction, then, children may represent not a link to a blissful past, but the vanguard of a strange and unknown future. (x–xi)

Both developmental and romantic notions of childhood hinge on development perceived as a process moving in a linear, temporal pattern (either child as link to past, or child as link to future). Science fiction, as might be expected, tends to biologize childhood through developmentalist themes. But science fiction also tends to be unexpectedly unscientific, revising developmentalist themes with sincere romanticism by replacing the associations of recapitulation (by which children represent our evolutionary past) with neoteny (by which children represent our evolutionary future), thus shifting from projecting a rigid determinism to speculating in awe.

Neoteny justifies an empowering view of the young and the roles they might ideally play in their larger environment. Stephen Jay Gould explains the child-centered shift: "Under recapitulation, adults of inferior races are like children of superior races. But neoteny reverses the argument. In the context of neoteny, it is 'good'—that is, advanced or superior—to retain the traits of childhood, to develop more slowly. Thus, superior groups retain their childlike characters as adults" (120). In a neotenous interpretation of human evolution, children become vehicles for the improvement of the species—emblems of what we are striving, whether consciously or not, to become.

In "Mimsy" one of the children's toys is an anatomical doll that, being from the future, represents a more evolved human form. The parents see it as imperfect: "'The digestive tract's too short. No large intestine. No appendix, either'" (73). But as the story progresses, it is clear that the doll belongs to a future phase in human evolution that will include Scott and Emma. Scott's questions about the life cycle of salmon reveal his awareness of belonging to a vaster world: "'They're born in the river, and when they learn how to swim, they go down to the sea. And they come back to lay their eggs, huh?'" (88). The pattern is also a metaphor for the superchild's development. There is a sinister hint of Scott's dwarfing super-status in his description of home (earth?): "'This is only—part—of the big place. It's like the river where the salmon go. Why don't people go on down to the ocean when they grow up?'" (89). Kuttner's point is that we cannot. But the superchild can. Scott and his little sister possess capabilities that adults have lost the ability to comprehend. Through them, Kuttner fantasizes an alternative to the limitations of individual human intelligence.

One could argue that the authors discussed here construct childhood in order to soothe metaphysical anxieties—where do I come from? (Apes.) What comes next? (Superchildren.) Howard Hendrix offers this as his explanation for the popularity of childhood themes in science fiction in his essay "Baby's Next Step: *Überkinder* and the Burden of the Future." He writes that "the way these Otherly offspring are made part of the human universe, how they are integrated into the macroself of human history and human cultural tradition, is a metaphor for how the future itself is to be humanized" (107). Here we see a reversal of the process we saw in William Carlos Williams's *White Mule*, where Gurlie projected her nostalgia for "the old world" and a simpler, agrarian past onto her child, Flossie.

In science fiction this projection speculatively peers into the future. Many authors have created plots surrounding the development of *Überkinder*, superchildren who represent a next step in evolution, "each characterized not only by his superiority but also by his essential unique-ness, aloneness, beyondness, and Otherness" (Hendrix 106). Through them, authors and readers can project themselves into the future while soothing anxieties about the unknown. Hendrix explains, "Education is how we use the past to shape the future, how we use the known to shape the unknown [. . .] . And just as the future is other than what we are yet still informed by what we are, the same is true of the *Überkinder* of science fiction or even the ordinary children of consensus reality" (106). But unlike "ordinary children," the *Überkinder* are constructed as powerful usurpers (intellectually, technologically) rather than passive inheritors of adult cul-ture. Through them, adults can bemoan the decreased potential for dis-covery and mental inflexibility of adulthood.

In his "Infant Joys: The Pleasures of Disempowerment in Fantasy and Science Fiction," Eric Rabkin suggests that such projections express that the power and knowledge of adulthood are often perceived as too burden-some and thus require an outlet. The myth of development as a fall, then, could be seen as a fantasy of disempowerment: "Regression may be a balm for the disappointed" (11). On a more personal and perhaps narcissistic level, the *Überkinder* function as superpowered wish fulfillments—through them we imagine escaping mortality and time.

Arthur C. Clarke's child-characters become vessels of collective memory as well as fears for the future. Take, for example, his *Childhood's End* (1953), in which children are transformed into an emotionally and intellectually unrecognizable next evolutionary generation—mutants, aliens, of sorts—who will replace the last, dying generation of *Homo sapiens*. This novel enacts a fantasy of disempowerment for the readers—adult civilization on earth becomes dependent on the protection and administration of Overlords from outer space. They become, as the character George Greggson surmises, "like children amusing themselves on some secluded playground, protected from the fierce realities of the outer world" (150). But playtime cannot last. In fact, the adults are being protected from the realization that their civilization has come to its end.

Children in the story mentally mutate into a telepathic network that will eventually inhabit and change the earth entirely. The transition is an explicit reversal of developmentalism through neotenous mutation. As in "Mimsy," only the young can evolve. An Overlord explains, "All we have discovered is that it starts with a single individual—always a child—and then spreads explosively [. . .] . Adults will not be affected, for their minds are already set in an unalterable mould" (184). Jeff is the "single individual" who carries the "telepathic cancer": "into his mind was flooding knowledge—from somewhere or somewhen—which would soon overwhelm and destroy the half-formed creature who had been Jeffrey Angus Greggson" (179). However, like Scott Paradine in "Mimsy," Jeff is too old to learn as swiftly as his little sister: "To all outward appearances, [Jenny] was still a baby, but round her now was a sense of latent power so terrifying that [her mother] Jean could no longer bear to enter the nursery" (178).

This construction indicates, again, our need to know and control childhood. Clarke, like most of the writers I have discussed, targets a language and logic barrier as the first source of estrangement. The Overlord's description to parents of the next generation highlights their difference to the extreme: "You have given birth to your successors, and it is your tragedy that you will never understand them—will never even be able to communicate with their minds. Indeed, they will not possess single minds as you know them. They will be a single entity, as you yourselves are the sums of your myriad cells. You will not think them human, and you will be right" (184). This description dramatizes extreme inaccessibility, introducing another unique motif (and solution) in science fiction—specifically, *Überkinder* as a "gestalt consciousness." This theme has been intricately developed by Theodore Sturgeon in *More Than Human* (1953). In part 2, "Baby Is Three," the main character, Gerry, discovers his own gestalt nature, as he describes to a psychologist: "I'm the central ganglion of a complex organism which is composed of Baby, a computer; Bonnie and Betty, teleports; Janie, telekineticist; and myself, telepath and central control" (115).[16] Then he realizes that the five children who comprise his self lose their holistic identity if separated: "Oh, the parts would live on: two little colored girls with a speech impediment, one introspective girl with an artistic bent, one mongoloid idiot, and me—ninety per cent short-circuited potentials and ten per cent juvenile delinquent" (115). Together the children have powers (supernormal powers) that complement each other's handicaps, so that they complete each other, but apart they would lose the identity they have developed as a whole. They would also lose their sense of a shared reality that comes from having their subjective worlds merged, or "bleshed," as Gerry calls it. Sturgeon is totalizing a future child by piecing together an otherwise fragmented "self." The gestalt ideal of an inter-subjective unit posits the impossible merging of what would otherwise be, in Jameson's terms, "sealed subjectivities."

To sustain the illusion of totalization, Sturgeon temporally limits childhood potential. With age, education, and socialization, one loses the ability to "blesh." Gerry tells the therapist that individual physical growth has threatened his organism's communications, so the baby (being youngest, of course, the boss and brain of the unit) compensates through body language:

> Janie [. . .] said she used to be able to hear the twins thinking [. . .] and they could hear Baby. So she would ask the twins whatever she wanted to know, and they'd ask Baby, and then tell her what he said. But then as they grew up they began to lose the knack of it. Every young kid does. So Baby learned to understand when someone talked, and he'd answer with this semaphore stuff. (76)

Once again, the inaccessibility of childhood is explained by the myth of development as a fall. But the disappointment of inaccessibility is answered with the promise of neotenous evolution. The gestalt consciousness of which Gerry is a part will be the first of a more powerful and flexible race.

Notice, again, that the vehicle of corruption is language, and the unit's resolution is to communicate without spoken or written forms (to be discussed in more detail in chapter 5).

Virginia Hamilton creates a more optimistic model in her sci-fi trilogy, the Justice cycle. *Justice and Her Brothers* (1978), *Dustland* (1980), and *The Gathering* (1981) follow the formula of neotenous/gestalt evolution—featuring a telepathic unit of kids, of which the youngest is the leader. The unit, like Sturgeon's, includes twins, brothers Levi and Thomas, who are thirteen; their eleven-year-old sister and leader, Justice; and their twelve-year-old neighbor Dorian. As in the above stories, the mutating team is estranged from (and even feared by) their elders, as revealed in these words of "comfort" from their father to their mother: "It's better you consider them forever strangers. [. . .] Our kids, our own flesh and blood, are the race to come" (*Dustland* 210). These superkids escape the influence of and surpass their elders seemingly without effort: "Their alteration must have been an accident. The difference in one chromosome was enough to alter a few inherited characteristics. Into existence could come sensory and physical changes, the release of genetic information far beyond the ordinary" (*Justice* 210).

One might wonder, considering their extraordinary powers, why these superkids depend entirely upon each other and upon unit formation in order to effect change—why the gestalt form is necessary. One answer can be found in further theorizing on human neoteny. Anthropologist Weston La Barre reasons that human evolution is neotenous because bipedality and use of tools freed human hands and gradually increased brain size, at the same time increasing dependence upon knowledge for safety and survival. Dependence upon knowledge increases time needed for development in order to learn necessary life skills and amass understanding—neoteny slows down the process of maturation to enable education. La Barre calls this process "alloplastic or 'other-substance' evolution" (12). According to neotenous interpretations of human evolution, as upright tool-users we retain juvenility longer out of dependence on tools and the training required to use them. We also form families to support prolonged dependence. This dependence might explain the pervasiveness of teaming in neotenous science fiction. The mutants are constructed to represent another step in the evolution of human brainpower, but they are still interdependent upon each other's special skills to free themselves in order to fully develop their own. They also create their own families, breaking biological kinship and replacing it with a kinship of inter-dependence based on specialized powers and shared knowledge.

The Celester (a cyborg who reports his past to the unit in their future) tells Justice and her brothers, "Information constantly increases. [. . .] We do not have time for ordinary evolution" (*Gathering* 79). The alloplastic nature of human evolution seems exaggerated in neotenous science fiction in order to accelerate and dramatize the mutants' superpowered progress. Hamilton is also essentializing the process by having Justice reflect changes physically. This seems a logical consequence of merging romantic and developmentalist narratives. Evolution rests on knowledge, but only the young can amass the most recent knowledge without having to unlearn first. And, as they, in that youthful state, represent our future, it logically follows that the future must look more juvenile. In fact, Justice noticeably "evolves" in her own lifetime when she returns from the unit's second journey to Dustland; her neck has lengthened and her head and eyes are larger, suggesting, at least in the latter features, an exaggeration of juvenile proportions (*Dustland* 190–93).

It is not the aim of this chapter to suggest that developmentalism is always at odds with romantic constructions of children. In fact, I would argue (and the underlying momentum of this book attests to this fact) that romanticism is implicit in the notion of childhood itself. Though often opposing in their applications, both approaches to the human subject place hope in youth—either as an ideal representation of the past or as an indication of the future's potential. One work that negotiates this commonality closely is *2001: A Space Odyssey*. The novel, written by Arthur Clarke in 1968, repeats and refines some of his themes from *Childhood's End*. He projects into the past as well as the future, combining developmental recapitulation and romantic neoteny. This is not an easy task: the implications of the former are that children are primitive, of the latter, that they are more advanced. So Clarke manages a synthesis in his narrative by modeling evolution as cyclical rather than linear. Howard Hendrix describes how the astronaut Bowman journeys into both his biological past and future: "In the film, Stanley Kubrick further complicates this sequence of deaths and rebirths by having Bowman both retrogress back to childhood and infancy, and also move forward into his geriatric future. But both film and novel end with infancy as the next step in human evolution" (103). Kubrick's interpretation is certainly in keeping with Clarke's chapter, "Recapitulation," which indulges in the paradoxical fantasy of linking both past and future in a progression of development. In it, Bowman "was retrogressing down the corridors of time, being drained of knowledge and experience as he swept back toward his childhood. But nothing was being lost; all that he had ever been, at every moment of his life was being transferred to safer keeping" (*2001* 230). Held in an alloplastic liminal space, Bowman is retrogressing but retaining knowledge.

One way of making this paradox seem reasonable is to speed up evolution into a one-generational, single-specimen, and socially controllable phenomenon. To this end, Clarke resurrects antiquated misapplications of evolutionary theory. Echoing the century-outdated Lamarckian premise that learned traits are inheritable, Clarke makes knowledge the key to evolutionary change, possible in a single generation. In the beginning of his novel, the famous monolith, TMA-1, instructs primitive humans in the use of tools, implying that each individual's genes change with learning: "the very atoms of his simple brain were being twisted into new patterns.[17] If he survived, those patterns would become eternal, for his genes would pass them on to future generations" (17). Likewise, the adult hero and superchild-to-be, Bowman, acquires knowledge for the next step in evolution (as if it is transmittable):

> With eyes that already held more than human intentness, the baby stared into the depths of the crystal monolith, seeing—but not yet understanding—the mysteries that lay beyond. [. . .] Beyond this moment lay another birth, stranger than any in the past. [. . .] With the instincts of three million years, he now perceived that there were more ways than one behind the back of space. (233)

Knowledge is "instinctive" here, but more strangely, it is amassed and passed on genetically over "three million years." This (science) fictional formula provides a teleological balance to the romantic view of loss in learning, reconciling it with the implicit developmentalist belief in human perfectibility. Howard Hendrix writes that such a relapse toward Lamarckism is already implicit in developmentalist theory because it "tends to conflate or collapse the distinction between evolution and education. This is perfectly understandable, given that the educational enterprise, at least since the advent of humanism, has also been informed by an ideology of human improvement and perfectibility" (102). Beyond the comfort of such a hopeful position lies the opportunity to protect against the unknown. Essentializing knowledge as inheritable circumvents the slow necessity of alloplastic evolution, reducing the process to our cells not effort. If children are supposed to progress, they will as intellectually programmed. Such a construction eliminates adult accountability just as reversals of the fall narrative free us of the possibility of understanding.

Superchildren allow us to bemoan our present mental limitations, project our unrealistic hopes onto children, and find comfort in the sense that there is some kind of divine plan/desired end. Such a response can be expected, as the cult of childhood began with the rise of secularism and science—yet another result of a cultural crisis of faith. In this light, it is no surprise that Hamilton's young leader Justice is first mistaken for a god when her unit visits the future (*Dustland* 42).

Consider the example of educator Maria Montessori. She was a disciple of the developmental sciences, a recapitulationist in her own right (she tried measuring skulls and forearms to categorize children's intellectual potential), and a keen observer with an empiricist bent. But she was equally romantic about a child's potential, constructing him/her as a revolutionary: "We must have faith in the child as a messiah, as a savior capable of regenerating the human race and society. We must master ourselves and humble ourselves in order to be able to accept this notion" (14). In combining the vocabularies of science and religion, her words reflect something behind all of the above constructions: more than simply a hope for better futures through children, a need for unburdening ourselves through (blind) faith in their wiser and eventually more promising power.

Donna Haraway writes, "Every story that begins with original innocence and privileges the return to wholeness imagines the drama of life to be individuation, separation, the birth of the self, the tragedy of autonomy, the fall into writing [literacy], alienation; i.e. war, tempered by imaginary respite in the bosom of the Other" (2295). Certainly our constructions of childhood attempt, impossibly, to make up for the perceived losses that Haraway lists. She provides an emancipatory model of subjectivity (cyborgian) and agency (writing) as an alternative narrative: "Cyborg writing must not be about the Fall, the imagination of a once-upon-a-time wholeness before language, before writing, before Man. Cyborg writing is about the power to survive, not on the basis of original innocence, but on the basis of seizing the tools to mark the world that marked them as other" (2293). Whereas romantic constructions of childhood mourn a supposed loss of innocence, the implication of Haraway's argument for young people is that the inevitable, infinitely deferred hope of regaining the imagined wholeness of youth dooms adults to incurable dissatisfaction, and the young they envy and/or try to control (even out of love) can only resist by subverting the definitions that adults impose upon them.

Perhaps the best example of Haraway's emancipatory project can be seen in comic book superheroes, who often gain their superpowers literally by using the tools of their oppressors to empower themselves (Hulk, Cloak and Dagger, Wolverine). More pertinent here, however, are those to be found in the *New Mutants* (1983–91) and *Power Pack* (1984–91), both of which play on the theme of neoteny, endowing children and adolescents with superpowers. As in "Mimsy Were the Borogoves," Simonson and Brigman, the creators of the *Power Pack,* pay homage to Lewis Carroll, naming the enemy aliens "Snarks" (who even look snakish and have shark-ish fins, as the portmanteau term might suggest) and explaining why the "snark-fighters" intervene on behalf of human safety: "We cannot allow those who gave us *Alice in Wonderland* to be destroyed" ("Power Play" 4). The kids are given superpowers by another alien, Whitey, reminiscent of the Carroll-figure chess-piece, or White Knight, in *Through the Looking-Glass.* Like the children in "Mimsy," "Baby Is Three," *Childhood's End,* and the Justice cycle, the youngest (Katie) advances most quickly, realizing her power briefly before the others, and, at least to my mind, she, too, is endowed with the most potentially destructive/defensive power. The oth-ers have powers that in combination can transport the four siblings and/or disguise them, but Katie, or the energizer, alone has the ability to throw futuristic equivalents of godlike lightning bolts.

New Mutants, a spin-off of the *X-Men* series, concentrates on the next generation of young superpowered mutants who go to Xavier's Academy for Gifted Youngsters to learn how to control their powers usefully and carefully. The film, *X-2* (2003), reduces the age of many original X-Men and likewise focuses on their school years, opening with the theme that they represent a future evolutionary stage of humans, *Homo superior,* when Charles Xavier (Patrick Stewart) asks in the introductory voiceover, "are mutants the next link in the evolutionary chain?" Certainly in the ideal-ization of youth power these figures "seize the tools" of their own othering and represent a break from fall narratives, but our empowering construc-tions of youth still provide "imaginary respite in the bosom of the Other."

The X-Men, like Justice and other neotenous figures, grow into their powers (usually in adolescence) and have to come to terms with unex-pected physical and paranormal changes. Often their powers, or "gifts," are for the benefit of the larger group (peers, parents, society), particularly in the case of empathic healers like Dorian in the Justice cycle and the Scab (from the graphic novel *X-Men: Children of the Atom*[18]). Similarly, the con-cluding installment of Lois Lowry's trilogy of utopia/dystopia novels, *Messenger* (2004), makes the role of the "gifted" young protagonists of the preceding novels clearer—each serves his/her community with a gift that will help lift them out of oppression. In *The Giver* (1993) Jonas risks his life to revive the emotional and cultural life of the community he lives in (but must leave). In *Gathering Blue* (2000) Kira decides to stay and help those in her hamlet when she comes to understand the ways in which they have all been deceived and dominated. In *Messenger* Matty heals the ailing forest and his community poisoned by it. Jonas, now the leader in Matty's community, tells him that his gift should not be wasted but saved for those who need it: "If it comes without your summoning it, it is because of need. Because someone needs your gift" (92). Lowry's protagonists are redemptive "mutants"—embodiments of their culture's needs. Their power is not their own.

We do not stop at burdening youth with our hopes for something better; however, we simultaneously expect their submission to what we think is best. Even romantic, empowering constructions of childhood, like those resulting from a neotenous interpretation of evolution, wind up justifying adult control through prolonged necessity of interdependence and education. A belief in perfectibility can be used, as it has in imperialist ideology, as justification for taking absolute control in the name of "improving" others. Ironically, this has, in turn, looped back to justify the more dominant construction of children as primitive.

Many scholars argue that the protective patronization of children that emerged from Enlightenment and romantic ideals provided a model of power for imperial domination. Claudia Castañeda puts this view clearly in the perspective of recapitulatory practices: "Not only has the child-as-primitive represented both the individual and racial past to the West [. . .] but the unequal child-parent relation in Western society has also provided a foundation for the colonial/imperialist order" (14). Essentializing childhood as underdeveloped (or advanced but in need of harnessing) allows us to justify institutionally enforcing "improvement."

Post-colonial materialist Ariel Dorfman illustrates how conflating child (individual) development with historical (national) imperatives reinforces domination in two ways:

> This confusion of individual psychological life with national historical life enhances the dominating dimensions of both. You get treated like a child for your own good, and that's how the indigenous and backward must be treated too. [. . .] [A]nd all those little people need is education and technology in order to gain access to the Western, Christian, adult world. By biologizing social stages and socializing bodily growth, the familial system (and colonial and neocolonial systems, too) creates a certainty that, as far

as peoples-who-are-the-same-as-children are concerned, there is only one river flowing to success: namely, established values. (45)

Childhood, here, is the measure of powerlessness. And just as colonial subjects are coerced by the standards of another culture, children are "molded," "brought up," "disciplined," and "guided" to accepting the values established by adults. Even our language reflects that education is not the same as learning but rather institutional socialization. Dorfman's comparison of colonial and childhood discourses highlights the American penchant for compartmentalizing the marginalized, as "biologizing social stages" is one of the most consistent absolutist symptoms of American discourses on childhood.[19]

We still regulate development by equating calendar ages with levels of maturity, labeling "age-appropriate" audiences, debating age of consent/age of majority, and defining grade levels. Lois Lowry investigates this extreme tendency toward essentializing development on a micro-scale in *The Giver* and *Gathering Blue*. The latter posits an oral-based culture in which the status of individuals is measured by physical signs of biological maturation—secondary sex traits in puberty, full body strength in adulthood, gray hair in middle age, physical decline in old age—each stage recognized by adding a syllable to a person's name. In this setting, as in Ariès's and Postman's hypotheses on less technologically, medically developed oral cultures, children do not get special protection. But in the futuristic setting of *The Giver*, maturing is measured more closely, and childhood is valued as a necessary, special, but inferior phase preceding adulthood. As in U.S. developmental and pedagogical discourse, child identity is carefully defined according to chronological (consistent, culturally defined, measurable), not biological (unpredictable, physical, individual), time.[20] Here the roles defined by age are more limiting—each year is strictly signaled by particular dress, activities, and possessions. Young people are identified almost entirely by their chronological age; their roles are defined by the number of their years. The main character Jonas's little sister is "only a Seven," but "very soon [Jonas] would not be an Eleven but a Twelve, and age would no longer matter. He would be an adult, like his parents, though a new one and untrained still" (5, 51). As each Twelve gets his/her career assignment, the Chief Elder says, "thank you for your childhood," as if it has been a source of entertainment and interest but now must be left behind (56). In this culture, childhood is comfortably controlled by rigid expectations defined in a carefully enforced pace of development[21]—set by an abstract system (time) that is orderly but empirically invalid.

The more abstract we make the concept of maturation, the more corruptible it becomes—*and* the easier to fit on unwitting (and ill-fitting) subjects. The highly variable biological transition of puberty, or "stirrings," is completely omitted through medication in Jonas's community, so that their definition of childhood is unthreatened by the unclear boundaries of natural diversity. And though each child's course of development seems, by the discourse of their culture, pre-determined and easily marked, the clear division of child and adult experience justifies extreme control and demands extensive adult-focused training. In both texts Lowry indicates that essentializing identity by age reduces the young to prescribed roles and robs them of their right to define themselves.

In *The Commodification of Childhood,* Daniel Thomas Cook links the twentieth-century penchant for ageist categorizing in the United States to its consumer economy: "especially with the extension of capitalist modes of production, clock time as well as the timing of the life course takes on finely graded forms" (98). He traces the shift toward essentializing development by age rather than task to compulsory education and increased literacy:

> By the 1870s, age-graded schooling was standard, though by no means universal, in the United States. Its structure initially reinforced the old categorizations offered by textbooks, used for at least a century prior, which were loosely graded according to the relationship between age and reading ability. This curriculum allowed students to move on to another level or reader once he (or, increasingly, she) mastered the previous level. Eventually, in the 1880s, textbooks began to be produced specifically for the graded system, helping to fix chronological age closely with school grade. Once established, an assumed or proposed trajectory of development can function as an argument in favor of its own transcendent reality. For instance, one effect of the emergent age-based systematization of knowledge and ability was to make intellectual precocity suspect, thereby placing, through institutional means, limits on how much children could achieve "beyond" their years. (99)

From Cook's description of this shift, Lowry's settings could be seen as highlighting the contrast before (in *Gathering Blue*) and after (in *The Giver*) the absolute internalization of an age-based "trajectory of development" in U.S. institutions and popular discourse. In this light one can see Jonas's community as an exaggeration of our own. And it would follow, then, that Kira's community, which seems at first a dystopia unsafe for children, from the viewpoint of child rights, might not be as bad as Jonas's. At least it seems a meritocracy rather than sheer technocracy.

It is no surprise that the more literate of these two fictive cultures violates child liberty the most (I am assuming, by the fact that Lily already signs pledges at the age of six, that this culture has high regard for the written word—despite the limit on books—at least as a means of control, as can be seen with the stringent demand for precise diction). Neil Postman credits, as I would blame, literacy for adult control, providing a genealogy of epistemological change caused by the emergence of literacy as a standard: "the underlying structural change—was that through print and its handmaiden, the school, adults found themselves with unprecedented control over the symbolic environment of the young" (45). Two measured but malleable concepts, chronological age and literacy, have functioned as a rationalist gauge and developmentalist justification for coercive institutionalization of the young. A hidden consequence, John R. Morss explains, is that "these regulatory processes are concealed, and the talk about 'natural' development is part of that suppression" (*Growing Critical* 134). When we rationalize development as biologically determined, we deny cultural responsibility while justifying adult/institutional intervention at the same time.

By conflating nurture and nature narratives we are far from naturalizing childhood; we are "scientifically" constructing it with impossible boundaries and denying our complicity. Developmental constructions of childhood satisfy our desire for control and soothe our fears, all the while enabling what Gayatri Spivak has called a "collective ideological refusal" to perceive the rights of those we marginalize (286). One might ask, "can a child speak?" But it might not be worth asking unless adults can hear a child answer. Romantic reversals, at the very least, indicate the extent to which developmentalism, like its ideological spin-off, imperialism, must constantly be deconstructed in order to liberate the subjects of its discourse.

chapter 5

DISRUPTING DISCOURSE

$\mathcal{G}$illes Deleuze asks, in *The Logic of Sense,* "how much must one pay in order to be able to speak?" (236). This question resonates with the primary issues of the preceding chapters: we are linguistically isolated until we pay the price of conforming to standards of development, which continue to cost us, as in order to gain a voice in one context we commit ourselves to the prelimited range of ideologies expressible in that context (embedded and transmitted through language) at the expense of others. When we gain a voice we silence others. There is no truly egalitarian dialogue where linguistic power is enacted, only the ideal of more enlightened listening.

Deconstructing misleading dichotomies of Western childhood discourses is only a beginning; the field of childhood studies needs to make a constant effort to decenter the unearned authority of adulthood itself. The spaces silenced in the process of legitimating discourse enclose potential for resistance and disrupting from within that goes unsuspected because of our own exclusionary biases. If in vigilantly deconstructing our age-biased discourse about children we can only reconstruct them, at least we should do so with respect for the potential resistances built into that discourse for those excluded from it.

P. L. Travers's *Mary Poppins* (1934) indulges in such an empowering reconstruction (and indulges us in the fantasy of a dialogue with it) when we eavesdrop on the "conversation" of two infants, a bird, the sunshine, and Mary Poppins. Barbara is confused by the way adults speak around her, and John explains, "It's only the idiotic way they have of talking.[. . .] I don't believe I'll ever understand Grown-ups. They all seem so stupid" (138). They deride their older brother and sister, Michael and Jane Banks, for not understanding their own communication, or that of the starling and the wind. But Mary Poppins shocks them with the news that Michael and Jane once understood as well as the infants do now. The starling expounds: "You'll forget [too] because you just can't help it. There never was a human being that remembered after the age of one—at the very latest—except, of course, Her" (140). Mary Poppins is the adult version of Peter Pan—a gatekeeper to a magic space inaccessible to other adults. She is, as the starling explains, "the Great Exception," the embodied dream of adult anti-rationalist nostalgia. She is also the exception who reaffirms the rule that language creates a gradually receding barrier that surrounds and defines childhood. This receding linguistic barrier is perhaps the most commonly embedded distinction in definitions of "childhood"—any dictionary will remind you that "infant" comes from the Latin and French for "not yet speaking."

In this chapter I will look back on many of the texts already discussed in earlier chapters, along with some fresh examples, to consider more closely children's discursive agency in them. Though disallowed engagement by lack of necessary language skills or willing (able?) adult listeners, literary children are frequently idealized as sites of resistance to the inflexible, systematizing logic of adult discourse. Anti-rationalist nostalgia casts child-figures as excluded from adult discourse but advantaged by their outside position. Such figures illustrate possibilities for passive resistance in disrupting rather than engaging adults on the level of their own discursive trappings.

All of the techniques we have seen for isolating and imagining access to those we call children pivot around a perceived language barrier. Mary Galbraith has described this problem in terms of experience: "Experience may be always already saturated with language, but language is always already saturated with experience" ("Hear My Cry" 193). In other words, linguistically indoctrinated subjects are more likely to carry the biases their language has available for making sense of their experiences, whereas less socialized subjects will be less saturated with the built-in biases of a language, necessarily depending less upon it to categorize and communicate their experience. Their lack of linguistic ability, therefore, could be seen as a cognitive (empathic) strength (inaccessible, of course, to adults). But adult discourse occludes recognition of that potential strength. Children are continually dismissed as irrational, crude, and prelogical when they have not yet mastered the means (language) to communicate any disproof of these assumptions.

The apparently insurmountable self-interest of adult discourse and power is limited to consciousness expressed in terms of rationalist logic, as Daniel Dennett has granted: "The preeminent work of consciousness is dependent on sophisticated language-using activities" (qtd. in Sheets-Johnstone 251). He, like most academics, assumes that linguistic sophistication is a necessary condition for worthy conscious thought when, in fact, it might merely be a limited means for expressing it. This oversight in the works of Piaget and other developmentalists has come to be recognized as a flaw by progressive child psychologists, yet in literary study we often bow to the logo-determinism that still pervades post-structuralist theory and discursive analyses in cultural studies. Cathy Urwin traces the linguistic isolation of children through this critical tradition:

> One of the most frequent debates focuses on the relative importance of nature versus nurture, inbuilt as opposed to environmental factors, or other versions of this familiar see-saw. Representing a particularly clear example of the individual-social dualism . . . at the core of this view of development is an implicitly or explicitly assumed unitary subject which knows and exists outside of, or prior to, its entry into the social world. This assumption is particularly evident in the study of language development, where there is a marked if not universal tendency to view language as an object outside the child. (264)

Only when children begin using language that we comprehend do we tend to acknowledge them as language users (no matter how much Roman Jakobson dignified babbling). Questions of language acquisition seem to provide the critical axis around which theory can pivot (in the case of linguistically relativistic theories like those of Kristeva and Vygotsky) or take root (as in rationalist accounts such as Piaget's and Chomsky's). But Urwin indicates a common tradition among them all—a tendency to dichotomize the self as individual or social, preverbal or speaking.

Jacques Lacan's reading of Freud's "Fort-Da" analysis spotlights this threshold: "the moment in which desire becomes human is that in which the child is born into language" (103). This manner of defining dismisses the identity of a preverbal infant almost as sharply as recapitulation dismisses its humanity. Michel Foucault's model of discursive power (in knowledge) is sometimes seen as sharing this bias because knowledge depends upon language, which confines thought. He writes, in *The Order of Things*, "The grammatical arrangements of a language are the *a priori* of what can be expressed in it. The truth of discourse is caught up in the trap of philology" (297). If we acknowledge that language is a flawed vehicle for "truth" and knowledge, we must consider the implications of this "trap" for the study of children. Rex and Wendy Stainton Rogers provide a rubric: "Applying analytics of textuality [. . .] to children/childhood is to argue that whenever we see or recognize, portray or represent a child (or children or childhood in general), we do so at one remove. Spoken or written, the child in text is a child 'in other words': a child already worked upon, a child re-presented—*a word child*" (187). All we can do in discourse is deal with word children, but that does not mean that all young subjects placed by discourse into a position of "childhood" are solely and absolutely determined by (or even accessible through) our words.

In recognizing the constructedness of identity through language, contemporary scholarship and theory respectfully keep their analytical focus at the level of language, yet for this reason theorists usually ignore the potential of asystematic verbalization and nonverbal consciousness. Lev Vygotsky wrote against this bias, as Alex Kozulin explains in his introduction to *Thought and Language:* "A child's development knows pre-intellectual speech as well as nonverbal thought" (xxxii). Certainly the trend of teaching pre-speaking babies sign language suggests that infants are linguistically capable before they have the phonetic mastery necessary for recognized speech—only the tools, not the intelligence, necessary for communication are missing.[1] Even if we tolerate a logo-determinist bias, we at least have to recognize that nonspeaking infants have communicable thought earlier than generally acknowledged, and that such a state or means to accessing that thought is highly relative and indefinable.

Presenting herself from the rhetorically rare position of being both in and "outside of language," autistic writer Temple Grandin exemplifies that thought is not limited to speech-ready language. Her experience reveals the extent to which our normative social practices neglect nonlinguistic cognition. In *Thinking in Pictures* she explains, "One of the most profound mysteries of autism has been the remarkable ability of most autistic people to excel at visual spatial skills while performing so poorly at verbal skills" (19–20). Such thinkers, like nonspeaking (or linguistically inexperienced) children, can easily be overlooked as unsophisticated. (Incidentally, Piaget, D. W. Winnicott, and Vygotsky each made comparisons of autistic thought to early developmental stages in pre-speaking children.) For nonautistics she articulates her thought processes in terms that she admits are rarely translatable:

> Autistics have problems learning things that cannot be thought about in
> pictures. The easiest words for an autistic child to learn are nouns, because

they directly relate to pictures.[2] [. . .] When I read, I translate written words into color movies or I simply store a photo of the written page to be read later. [. . .] When I am unable to convert text to pictures, it is usually because the text has no concrete meaning. [. . .] Growing up, I learned to convert abstract ideas into pictures as a way to understand them. (29–33)

Her description shows that her primary epistemological mode is visual, not verbal. And although she is forced to adapt verbally to communicate, Temple Grandin uses her advantage as a "visual thinker" to excel where "language-based thinkers" cannot.

"Visual thinkers," or any thinkers independent from verbal composition and articulation, can be seen as having an unnoticed advantage over those who depend upon normalized methods and do not recognize alternatives. Feral children have often been idealized as embodying this epistemologically independent space, which might explain the seeming correlation between cultural interest in feral children and revolution (in France, for example, there was great intellectual fervor over the "wild boy" Victor d'Aveyron in the last quarter of the eighteenth century and in Germany, over foundling Kaspar Hauser in the first quarter of the nineteenth). Feral children, representing pre-social alinguistic experience into much later ages than socialized kids, have been found throughout history (undoubtedly existing in greater numbers before they got such attention) but were not always the target of media focus and intellectual fantasizing. Research on feral children frequently crosses over with that of autism. In fact, in two of the more famous cases, those of Victor d'Aveyron and Kaspar Hauser, it is hypothesized that the boys were severely and mildly autistic, respectively—whether as a cause or effect of their abandonment is unknown. Both became the subjects of critically acclaimed films,[3] also at a time of cultural revolution, the 1970s.

Despite occasional cultural curiosity about thinking from outside of conditioned reason enabled by lack of linguistic experience, Western discourse, especially in the United States, seems steeped in disregarding possible thought outside of language. Maxine Sheets-Johnstone states directly how this bias limits our constructing of childhood: "The infant or child in our culture is typically undervalued because it does not speak; only adults speak. In turn, an infant or child does not *know;* only adults *know.* Until a child accedes to language, it has no value" (243). If we equate speaking with knowing, we risk ignoring the consciousness of young people who are yet to work or still working their way into language. Perhaps such a position cannot be voiced, but its potential (and the limited domain of adult discourse) should be recognized and respected.

The inaccessibility of the pre-articulatable mind is key to Julia Kristeva's conception of early development: "The impossibility that beset [*sic*] [. . .] an attempt at gaining access to childhood" stems from the condition that "the real stakes of a discourse on childhood within Western thought involve a confrontation between thought and what it is not, a wandering at the limits of the thinkable" (276). That which is thinkable without language is supposedly unthinkable to adults. But authors who legitimate a childhood silenced by our discourse often suggest that what is inexpressible in discourse may be thinkable to those outside of it. Toni Morrison foregrounds this challenge in *Beloved* (1987) when she asks through her title ghost-child-character: "How can I say things that are pictures?" (210). Dramatizing a mental process like that Grandin has described, Morrison preserves that which is thinkable at the borders of language and beyond with images, turning her inaccessible child-character into a visual, not verbal thinker.

Beloved, the ghost of a baby who died seventeen years prior to her reappearance, returns in the body of a young woman but is characterized as an unsocialized child who must learn not only how to talk but also walk and use a toilet. (In an interview with A. S. Byatt, Morrison refers to her as having an "eight-year-old mind.") Morrison recognizes the impossibility of speaking as a child—she even addressed this issue in the afterword to her first novel, *The Bluest Eye* (1970), in which she describes narrating as children an "attempt to shape a silence while breaking it" (216). She admits that when it came to developing a voice for her ghost-child, Beloved, she had writer's block for three to four months: "You only have those twenty-six letters in the alphabet—that's all you've got. [. . .] I couldn't get Beloved's language, which means I couldn't see the way she would see things" (interview). Eventually Morrison exploited the power of image to create a credible ghostly-childhood position: "Her voice is all image—all picture. [. . .] Everything she says is a picture, how it looked, how it was, or how it smelled. There's no sort of ramification or descriptive thought in between—no judgment" (interview). Syntax and punctuation are disrupted to break any sense of sequence. What results is not an empowered voice as legitimated discourse would recognize it, but a collage of images that might reflect the vast space Beloved represents. Beloved says (thinks), "There is no place where I stop" (210). The images that float throughout her montage are fragmented views of a slave ship, her mother, flowers, song, and disease—in short, collective memory. Like James's

Maisie, Beloved is limitless in what she can reflect. Morrison respects the impossible inaccessibility of her child character (complicated also by her deathliness), yet in her portrait she provides an original twist on traditional approaches to that inaccessibility, inviting us to imagine what one outside of discourse might see.

Morrison confronts and circumvents the imposition of representing a child linguistically through her reliance on image. She is particularly sensitive to the exclusionary and domineering effects of language use because she is already focusing on socially marginalized characters. As Lynda Koolish says, "Images are crucial in [*Beloved*] because Morrison writes of a people bereft of language" (422).[4] Morrison situates authority on the side of language and sympathizes with the other side. In her afterword to *The Bluest Eye* (1970), she writes of Pecola's voicelessness: "Since the victim does not have the vocabulary to understand the violence or its context, gullible, vulnerable girlfriends, looking back as the knowing adults they pretended to be in the beginning, would have to do that for her, and would have to fill those silences with their own reflective lives" (214). In order to avoid imposing her adult view through the impossible guise of representing Pecola's, she relies on the reconstructed childhood memories of Pecola's friends now that they have the means of expressing them, foregrounding the adult mediation of events through memory. This device of explicitly accessing one child's experience through the selective and unreliable memories of outsiders honorably recognizes the immediate inaccessibility of Pecola's traumatic childhood and respects the unmediated boundaries that result.

In *The Narrator's Voice: The Dilemma of Children's Fiction*, Barbara Wall surveys other techniques writers use to represent and address children in light of more everyday language barriers. (The challenge therein already evidenced by the infrequent use of children as self-narrators before the second half of the twentieth century—Huck Finn being the most notable exception.) In literature for children, some authors seem to have applied Henry James's method by experimenting with narrative immediacy. Wall credits Ivan Southall with modifying free indirect discourse into the present tense for children's prose: "In *Josh* (1971), for which he won the Carnegie Medal, the use of the present participle instead of a finite verb dominates the narration, and enables the writer to gain an immediacy which suggests not only that events are happening at the moment at which they are read, but also the fragmentary nature of Josh's imperfect understanding of what is going on" (250). In the adult canon, Alison Lurie's *Only Children* (1979) experiments with different levels of immediacy to a similar effect when articulating Lolly's thoughts. For example, in the pastoral passage discussed earlier, Lurie not only uses free indirect discourse,[5] she reduces verbs simply to the present participle for a greater sense of immediacy: "Virginia loving Anna's house, surrounding it holding it hugging it safe forever. Green-veined soft hands, hundreds of them" (41). Like Morrison's Beloved, Lurie's child-centers, Mary Ann and Lolly, break conventions of syntax and mechanics to desophisticate the language so that it appears less mediated.[6] Like Travers's infant Barbara, Lurie's child-centers are mystified and shut out from the secrets of adult speech. Lolly considers language dangerous: "*Panties,* that are safe named and clean and folded in the bottom drawer, suddenly falls apart: into *aunties,* a word for aunts that aren't real aunts; into *pant, ants, pants,* words that are safe by themselves, but they can come together and make you sick. [. . .] No words are safe" (151).

In empowered adult discourse, words are weapons, but they are weapons that can be turned against their users. This is demonstrated repeatedly in the silenced subversive space cut out for children in literature. One excluded from discourse can disrupt it without necessary awareness of contextual meaning, formal logic, or even grammar, as E. B. White's Charlotte illustrates by weaving words that Templeton collects from garbage labels in her web to save Wilbur's life in *Charlotte's Web* (1952).

Authors who struggle to represent children and stop short at the language barrier often deconstruct the assumptions that back adult discourse with unwarranted power in order to pinpoint its vulnerability. White does this by stripping the words, as mentioned above, of contextual meaning and clear syntactic function in the spider's web, but he also decenters the power-context in which words are used. Fern's mother visits Dr. Dorian for advice on her daughter's apparent delusion that she can understand the farmyard animals speaking. Dr. Dorian not only lays bare adult prejudice but also exposes the falsely centered power of Mrs. Arable's viewpoint: "It is quite possible that an animal has spoken civilly to me and that I didn't catch the remark because I wasn't paying attention. Children pay better attention than grownups. If Fern says that the animals in Zuckerman's barn talk, I'm quite ready to believe her. Perhaps if people talked less, animals would talk more" (110). Though he is talking about animals, he incorporates a hint about children as well—his subtext reads: perhaps if adults listened, children would have more voice. White is drawing attention to the one-sided nature of adult discourse, showing that adults disregard as unreal what they do not see or understand.

As a convention in childhood literature, talking to animals often effects this point. For example, in Frances Hodgson Burnett's *The Secret Garden* (1911), the idealized child of nature, Dickon,

> could speak robin (which is a quite distinct language not to be mistaken for any other). To speak robin to a robin is like speaking French to a Frenchman. Dickon always spoke it to the robin himself, so the queer gibberish he used when he spoke to humans did not matter in the least. The robin thought he spoke this gibberish to them because they were not intelligent enough to understand feathered speech. (274)

In "The Power of Speech: Life in the Secret Garden," Claudia Marquis claims that "Language is here the site of infantile development and the medium of recuperation. [. . .] Language is equally the locus of an ideological display of male power" (169). I see the discursive power in this novel as more aged than gendered, but Marquis has fittingly described an important theme in literature representing children. Exclusive language predicates power but also initiates the limiting mechanisms of ideology. Like the Banks infants in *Mary Poppins,* the robin is excluded from human talk and so assumes it is unintelligent and unimportant. This dismissal draws attention to the flipside fact—that adults make the same easy assumptions about children's language or lack thereof.

Even when the one we define as a child is gaining proficiency in language and attempts to engage adult discourse, the tendency in adults is to be skewed by their own constructions of the innocent, or ignorant, child rather than listening to his/her actual import. In "Is Anybody Out There Listening?" Maria Tatar argues, "Children can indeed raise their voices, but virtually no one bothers to listen" (276). We may say "that's precocious *for his age*" and laugh, or simply ask, "*where* did she get that?" without once recognizing that we have positioned things worth saying *elsewhere* through our own prejudice.

E. B. White illustrates the absurdity of our logocentrism the first time Charlotte weaves words in her web. Led by her text, not her action, the onlookers read, gasp, and repeat, "Some Pig" with unreflective awe. In a following conversation between the Zuckermans, White points to the irony of the situation. Mr. Zuckerman insists there has been a miracle, "and we have no ordinary pig." Mrs. Zuckerman replies, "It seems to me we have no ordinary *spider*" (80). This moment of insight is eclipsed, however, when for the rest of the novel she and other adults obediently repeat and accept without question Charlotte's simple web-words and never again question how they got there.

White has provided a literary enactment and mockery of the logode-terminism that has become a defining premise of post-structuralist theory: language structures thought, thus, we are able to perceive only that which our language allows us to think. It is this limiting effect in the language of presumed power that gives the discursively disempowered a vantage point. Accordingly, many authors endow their own word-children with extradis-cursive power. Again, the definitive example comes from Lewis Carroll, when Alice, defending the Cheshire cat, tells the King of Hearts, "'A cat may look at a king'" (114). The elusive cat's semi-invisibility is not unlike the cloak of invisibility provided children when overlooked. Alice's imper-atives might lack the weight of the King's orders, but at the center of power, like adults, the King is exposed to penetrating eyes. Observation is sufficient fuel for subversion. The young, inexperienced, or even semi-invisible cat-subject has the opportunity to question based on what he/she sees, unburdened by systematized thinking—that is the advantage those empowered yet limited by legitimated discourses overlook, creating a blind spot that makes us even more vulnerable to probing eyes and ears.

Childhood potential for spying is the central premise of Louise Fitzhugh's *Harriet the Spy* (1964). Harriet spies on Mrs. Plumber, a wealthy, spoiled woman on her "spy route," by hiding in the dumbwaiter in her home. Harriet writes in her journal, "RICH PEOPLE ARE BORING. [. . .] IF I HAD A DUMBWAITER I WOULD LOOK IN IT ALL THE TIME TO SEE IF ANYBODY WAS IN IT" (45). The passage humorously reminds an adult reader of how easy such spying must be for smaller per-sons, because larger people overlook the spaces they cannot occupy them-selves. It also should remind us that we are potential targets. If we refuse to acknowledge our vulnerability and falsely centered power, we might cre-ate enemies in our own camp.

The freedom of being overlooked makes child figures popular social critics (thus the success of poster children). In Ernst Bloch's vision of a Marxian utopia, childhood can harbor gentle revolution, particularly because of a child's potential for hiding, seeing unseen, and speaking from a silenced space: "Here too the fun of being invisible ourselves. We seek out a corner, it protects and conceals. . . . The hidden boy is also breaking out, in a shy way. He is searching for what is far away, even though he shuts himself in, it is just that in breaking free he has girded himself round and round with walls" (22–23).

The discursive space children occupy is bound but easily overlooked, which draws many to interpret children's literature, likewise carefully cat-egorized and kept in its place, as a subversive genre. As Tim Morris points out, "Juvenilizing children's books and genre fiction alike serves to repress concerns of great importance, relegating them to a land of children's literature where nothing is really taken seriously—and therefore where almost anything can be said, the privilege of both child and courtly fool" (6). Authors for and about children often indulge in this freedom vicariously. Unsuspected and overlooked, literary children demonstrate the ability to upset adult authority through honest observation and thinking from outside of established language and logic (or the common "sense" against which nonsense is defined). The psychologist in Henry Kuttner's "Mimsy Were the Borogoves" (1943) warns accordingly: "Children are different from the mature animal because they think in another way. We can more or less easily pierce the pretenses they set up—but they can do the same to us. Ruthlessly a child can destroy the pretenses of an adult. Iconoclasm is their prerogative" (Padgett 74).

Disruption can occur simply by a child turning the tables. Consider Fern's plea to Mr. Arable to keep Wilbur as a pet: "The pig couldn't help being born small, could it? If *I* had been very small at birth, would you have killed *me?*" (3). Or the dose of your own medicine, as in *Peter Pan* (1911), when Mr. Darling persuades his son, "Michael, when I was your age I took medicine without a murmur. I said 'Thank you, kind parents, for giving me bottles to make me well'" (16). Innocently (?), Wendy finds the bottle and gives her father some to take in order to set a cooperative example for his son. Mr. Darling complains that "it isn't fair," and Wendy reminds him, "I thought you took it quite easily, father" (17). Her comment exposes that her father's power comes not from sounder reason but from the fact that he is an adult and he "says so."

These disruptions often characterize adult thought as rusty and ideologically constraining. In Theodore Sturgeon's "Baby Is Three" (1953), for example, Gerry realizes that his gestalt self (described in chapter 4) is threatened by the imposition of Miss Kew's power as adult caretaker: "'We all woke up at the same time. We all did what somebody else wanted. We lived through a day someone else's way, thinking someone else's thoughts, saying other people's words'" (99). Again, the vehicle of her control comes down to language. And it is clear that unlike the paranormal gestalt unit formed by Gerry and the other children, Miss Kew, as a grown-up, is blinded by her own systematized thought. When a display of their paranormal powers threatens her sense of reality, she simply denies what she sees: "[The twins] could pop from one place to another right in front of Miss Kew's eyes and she wouldn't believe what she saw" (93). When they defend themselves against Miss Kew's attempts to break up the unit by sending Baby away, they communicate telepathically and fight on their own terms: "We'd tried our best to be good according to her ideas, but, by God, that time she went too far. She got the treatment from the second she slammed her door on us. She had a big china pot under her bed, and it rose up in the air and smashed through her dresser mirror. Then one of the drawers in the dresser slid open and a glove came out of it and smacked her in the face" (95). Their means of communicating their needs and intent is non-verbal, which Miss Kew can then rationalize away, explaining, "Something struck the house. An airplane. Perhaps there was an earthquake" (95). Like the Banks infants, the children who make up the gestalt self have their own means of communication but are misunderstood by those who would have power over them. When the kids tell Miss Kew that Baby is happy with them, she retorts, "As if he could talk, the poor little thing!" (94). She cannot understand their voiced needs because she accepts her own reasoning over what she observes (rationalism again). As her denial robs them of a means of engaging in a productive and fair debate with her to promote their preservation, Gerry finds no alternative but to kill her.

Rationalist discourse in particular seems to force disruption from without more than within—those who devalue reason are discredited easily as irrational, making it more difficult to legitimate a break. This is demonstrated in *The Enigma of Kaspar Hauser* (1974),[7] when a professor tests Kaspar's ability to reason by presenting him with a version of the Epimenides paradox. The professor tells Kaspar that there is a village of liars and a village of people who only tell the truth, and Kaspar must divine which of the two someone comes from: "In order to solve this problem logically, there is only one question, and only one. What is the question?" The "one question" the professor seeks from Kaspar is to ask if the person is from the village of liars, whereby through a double negative a liar will be revealed. Kaspar, however, comes up with a different question: "I should ask the man if he is a tree frog." The professor's response exposes the rigid limits of the professor's abstract system of reason: "I cannot accept that. [. . .] There's no other question by the laws of logic. [. . .] In logic we do not understand things; we reason and deduce them." Kaspar, who thinks with little training on his own to a less complexly reasoned but more practical solution, successfully debunks the professor's rationalism and mocks the blind spots in understanding caused by trusting systematized reason over intuition or simple observation. The scene also demonstrates the ways in which more experience with language and logic can tie us up with impractical particulars, losing sight of the not so easily categorized reality around us, confusing the systematization of thought and its expression with knowledge itself.

In *The Marvelous Land of Oz* (1904), a particularly apt example (pertaining to language barriers) occurs when the Scarecrow and Jack Pumpkinhead recruit a child, Jellia Jamb, to be their interpreter. Developing a theme common to Baum, on the blind adherence to ideas in light of their obvious ridiculousness, adult figures rationally follow through with faulty premises to demonstrate the foolishness of trusting reason over observation. The Scarecrow and Jack assume, because they come from different countries, that they speak different languages. This they discuss, clearly understanding one another, deciding to have Jellia interpret for them. Overlooking the obvious fact that they are communicating directly, they depend upon Jellia's account of what each is saying, but Jellia mocks them by misinterpreting their remarks to each other as insults, thrusting their folly in their faces. When Jellia finally tells them that they are speaking the same language, Jack takes the blame for assuming their difference. The Scarecrow returns, "This should be a warning to you never to think" (52). But they are "thinking" based on abstract presumptions rather than common sense. Baum demonstrates the inadequacies of rationalism in comparison to empiricism: there is danger in valuing the singular consistency of logic over the constant multiplicity of possible observations.

What Louise K. Barnett has said of Huck Finn's experience applies here: "Public language is committed to *a priori* positions which often require a falsification of experience" (221). Baum exaggerates the adult-figures' dependence upon (pre)systematized thought to indicate Jellia's fortunate isolation and freedom from it. To Baum, the cause and means of ideological deception is language, another example being in the willingness of Emerald City's inhabitants to wear green glasses. In *The Wizard of Oz* (1900) the wizard explains to Dorothy that it is all done in the service of naming: "I thought, as the country was so green and beautiful, I would call it the Emerald City, and to make the name fit better I put green spectacles on all the people, so that everything they saw was green" (161).

The wizard "makes the name fit," seeming to fit reality to his ideas, but he also uses language to disguise reality on falsely centered authority. In literature for and/or about children, adults are frequently heard using language arbitrarily to fit their interests. Lewis Carroll's Humpty Dumpty (a seeming caricature of age with his bald, round shape) tells Alice, "When *I* use a word, it means just what I choose it to mean—neither more nor less" (269). This arbitrarily applied subjective authority is not much of a stretch from that which Lolly Zimmern responds to in her elders in *Only Children*.

She ponders the unpredictability of their meaning: "Things are suddenly called a different name that makes them change invisibly and be smeared with invisible dirt. [. . .] Or other times the word holds still and the thing changes behind it and some ordinary word is wrong and awful" (149–50). Mary Ann appreciates her teacher Anna as an exception: "When you talk to Anna she looks at you instead of at things behind you like most grown-ups" (22). Both Lolly and Mary Ann are aware of the slippage in meanings "behind" words and that this slippage is contextually dependent on adult desires and perceptions.

Often child characters disrupt discourse by turning adults' presumption of power and linguistic bullying back on them. Dorothy rhetorically disrupts the Wizard's bullying, when he demands that she and her friends kill the Wicked Witch of the West in order to earn his gifts, by flinging his own words back on him: "If you, who are Great and Terrible, cannot kill her yourself, how do you expect me to do it?" (110). She exposes his hypocrisy and decenters his power by reminding him of her presumed lack of power.

This decentering of power and disruption of discourse became the trademark of Louise Fitzhugh's Harriet, who takes up the weaponry of words to cultivate her independent selfhood and to provide a ready defense. Her parents worry that she writes too much, which is not surprising considering that Harriet's use of the language constitutes a kind of passive resistance toward (or escape from) the influence of their words. Their fears resemble nineteenth-century parental concerns about corruption from books that I discussed in chapter 4. Both seem to reflect a desire to control child access to and use of literate knowledge and, thus, power. In this light, Harriet is a successful subversive, as J. D. Stahl indicates: "Louise Fitzhugh creates a child who appropriates adult forms of literacy and transforms them to suit her purposes" (120).

Her parents suspiciously eye her journal, but they fail to directly address Harriet, who writes, "WHY DON'T THEY SAY WHAT THEY MEAN?" (171). The novel follows her struggles with straightforward language against the confusing layers of meaning surrounding her. In her writing she is frank and uncensored, as Miss Golly has advised her to be. But when her classmates steal her journal and read it aloud for all her peers to hear, they are hurt and desert her. Betrayed by her own words, she turns for advice to the following lines from Golly's letter:

> Naturally those notebooks should not be read by anyone else, but if they are *then*, Harriet, you are going to have to do two things, and you don't like either of them:

1) You have to apologize.
2) You have to lie. (275)

In such examples, the power of language lies in the power to deceive. By lying Harriet will learn an important skill in negotiating her interests and better intentions more successfully. Fitzhugh arms her child-character with a growing knowledge of how to use words in her own defense.

The lying child is a literary representative of the romantic philosophy that language itself is unavoidably deceitful (or a "prison-house," to Wordsworth). The most famous example is, of course, Huck Finn. Unlike Harriet Welsch and Lolly Zimmern, who wish to decode and counter the deception "behind" adult talk, Huck's skill in lying seems possible because of his rejection of the social codes preset "behind" language itself. Louise K. Barnett describes Huck as a "linguistic outsider" for this reason: "Huck lacks the veneration of socially prescribed labels ordinarily acquired through acculturation. In society's view he is aberrant because he sees the activity without the social meaning which an official label provides" (222). According to this description, he uses words simply without attention to meanings "behind" them. His rejection of social contextualization constitutes subversive self-empowerment—for example, he disembodies the "conscience" that haunts him from its usage in a wider racist context, developing his interpretation of what "conscience" means (66). He succeeds because he thinks outside of the prescribed meanings of his own culture's language (as the definitive American romantic child, so he can enact this seemingly impossible ideal of independent interpretation).

One of the most common techniques of subversion in literature for and about children does this to an extreme. Hyperliteralism strips phrases of their contextually dependent meaning, thereby enabling a disruption of normative control over interpretation. For example, in Horatio Alger's *Ragged Dick* (1868) the title character uses figurative phrases in a literal sense to divert attention from his homelessness and fashion himself as successful. When Dick jokes with a shoeshine customer about his lodgings the man asks, "So your house is on Fifth Avenue, is it?"(5). Dick responds, "It isn't anywhere else," which, of course, is literally true but evasively denies the more common meaning of the phrase. When Mr. Whitney mentions that Dick's face is dirty, he replies, "They didn't have no wash-bowls at the hotel where I stopped. [. . .] The Box Hotel" (21). In fact, he has slept in a box, but his joke briefly, literally masks the truth. Alger seems to use this device simply for humor, or at most to indicate that Dick is self-conscious about his untidy homelessness. But more often hyperliteralisms point to a child's exclusion from language by misinterpreting phrases that, like jargon and euphemism, seem to say something different from what they mean.

Alison Lurie makes this especially clear in *Only Children*. When Bill Hubbard's job is threatened by a depressed economy, he assures his family that he won't lose his job, but "his office might get smaller" (18). His daughter, Mary Ann, sensibly asks, "How could it get smaller?" She imagines the room shrinking. In the slippage that causes such miscommunications the dependency of meaning on context is revealed. When she tries to make sense of her parents' language, she incorporates what she is learning of their contexts in the definition: "They are agnostics, which means they think God probably doesn't exist but they are too polite to say so to people who believe he does" (158).

The reader most keenly feels Mary Ann's exclusion from the language of adult business. When she overhears her father mentioning that he has been asked to sit on the school board, she "wants to ask what board, and why Anna wants Bill to sit on a board at Eastwind, [. . .] but she decides to wait till later. If she says anything now they'll remember she is there and know she is listening" (246). Lurie demonstrates the literally confusing and contextually dependent meanings likely to occur in unmastered language, as well as a child's exclusion from understanding them and resulting awareness of the silent space cut out for spying.

Edith Wharton uses the same device to show how literal misunderstandings can seem threatening to the uninitiated. In *The Children* (1928) Beechy and Bun's biological mother boasts, "When Astorre and Beatrice come to live with me the first thing I shall do is to make them both co-operate" (255). Beechy (Beatrice) embraces her brother Bun (Astorre): "'No—no, you bad wicked woman, you musn't! You shan't operate on Bun, only on me—if you *must!*'" Ironically, Beechy's misunderstanding foregrounds that their mother *is* threatening an invasion of another sort—she is eager to experiment with child-rearing strategies she has learned from (yet again) child psychology.

Some literary children resist such mental meddling and refute adult constructions. They are constructed as understanding and resenting adult constructions of themselves, showing that "age" itself is a *context* of empowered speech. Wharton's primary theme in *The Children* is the difficulty of defining children (for her, this difficulty especially relates to sexual knowledge, and her tale reads like a subtle prototype for *Lolita*). The main child figure, Judith Wheater, has an ambiguous role in society: she is prepubescent and unworldly, but she is also the chief caretaker of her many younger siblings, which forces her into difficult decision-making and responsibility. When she explains to Martin Boyne, her self-appointed guardian, that her mother is fond of her tutor, Martin is scandalized because he considers this a blunt revelation of Judith's knowledge about her mother's sexual improprieties. However, the extent of her understanding is unclear. Even so, Martin, always pressing to preserve an image of her innocence, says angrily: "'You've said something exceedingly silly. Something I should hate to hear if you were grown up. But at your age it's merely silly, and doesn't matter.'" Her response reveals her resentment of his stereotyping and disrespect for her opinion: "'My age? My age? What do you know about my age? I'm as old as your grandmother. I'm as old as the hills. I suppose you think I oughtn't say things like that about mother—but what am I to do, when they're true, and there's no one but you that I can say them to?'" (59). Though aware of her chronologically defined age, she is expressing to Martin that such measures inaccurately reflect what they aim to—they are relative at best. Like Maisie, she's learned that "age" is a culturally defined and ever-shifting concept. Judith's experience demands that she behave responsibly, "like an adult," so she perceives how socially constructed the concept of "old" can be. She also refuses to let Martin strip her words of their weight by adding a false context—her "innocence."

Jean Baudrillard idealizes the resulting potential for subversion from such an ambiguously perceived position: "The child has a *double strategy*. He has the possibility of offering himself as object, protected, recognized, destined as a child to the pedagogical function; and at the same time he is fighting on equal terms. At some level the child knows that he is not a child, but the adult does not know that. That is the secret" (*Baudrillard Live* 111). Judith knows that the identity adults impose upon her is an inadequate and simplistic representation of her true experience and responsibility. She resists Martin's presumptions (not to mention his veiled sexual advances), taking refuge in her position as a protected "object." Her question, "What am *I* to do?"—one that is repeated in many variations throughout childhood literature—reveals that she is using the only power allowed her in the given context by invoking her marginalized status. She forces him to consider the opportunity he affords her for more adult conversation but reminds him of the relative helplessness of her condition.

Others, as Baudrillard suggests, more aggressively take advantage of adult blind spots. British *Bildungsromane* set a precedent for American literary children in this category. In Charlotte Brontë's *Jane Eyre* (1847), Mr. Brocklehurst comes to interview the young Jane, who has been labeled a liar and cast off by her Aunt Reed to Brocklehurst's school, Lowood. He tells Jane that the wicked go to hell and asks, "What must you do to avoid it?" (25). Jane elusively replies, "I must keep in good health, and not die" (26). She refuses to play into his simplistic construction of the innocent child and mindlessly repeat his fed doctrine. Further pressing her reform, Brocklehurst quizzes her knowledge of the Bible. She admits a preference for "Revelations, and the Book of Daniel, and Genesis, and Samuel, and a little bit of Exodus, and some parts of Kings and Chronicles, and Job and Jonah," but her claim that "Psalms are not interesting" challenges Brocklehurst's expectations for malleable children, so he can only react in a negative and infantilizing manner: "Oh, Shocking! I have a little boy, younger than you, who knows six Psalms by heart: and when you ask him which he would rather have, a ginger-bread-nut to eat, or a verse of a Psalm to learn, he says: 'Oh! the verse of a Psalm! angels sing Psalms,' says he; 'I wish to be a little angel here below.' He then gets two nuts in recompense for this infant piety" (26). Charlotte Brontë is satirizing the use of rote learning and revealing that Brocklehurst is probably being duped by his son. It would seem logical that this "pious infant" plays the role because he knows he can get twice as many cookies that way. Why not be "a little angel" if as a "protected object" one is safer and spoiled? Imposing innocence reinforces such a masquerade.

Brontë's passage reveals three important things about relationships between adults and those constructed as children: first, that adults are naïve in imposing a state of innocence/ignorance on children, who for all they know may have something very intelligent to say or a critical insight or question to be acknowledged; second, that in imposing our own limited constructions of childhood we encourage hypocrisy in children; third, that even the "pure" child who appears to follow the rules can act subversively in his/her own interest.

Adult-child relations are complex in their constant redepictions of vulnerability and power, dependence and subversion. The child psychologist in "Mimsy Were the Borogoves" puts it this way: "Children are helplessly dependent on the caprice of those who give them birth and feed and clothe them. And tyrannize. The young animal does not resent that benevolent tyranny, for it is an essential part of nature. He is, however, an individualist, and maintains his integrity by a subtle, passive fight" (Padgett 74). Subversive literary children maintain the fight through a passive (and unknowing?) resistance enabled by overlooked loopholes in the oppressive logic of adult discourse.

Both Judith Wheater and Jane Eyre, in the examples above, seem to resent and resist the constructions that adults would pin on them. Resistant efforts are particularly strong when children must defend themselves *and* the "benevolent tyrants" who care for them. Pearl in *The Scarlet Letter* (1850) is one of the most estranged child-figures I know of in the American canon (except Pecola Breedlove in *The Bluest Eye*), and she serves as an early precursor to modern child rebels. Within the society in which she lives all are hostile and condemn her mother. As a "child of sin," she is not spared their antagonism. When the Governor threatens to take Pearl away from Hester, a local minister is called in to "examine" the love-child. He asks Pearl, "Canst thou tell me, my child, who made thee?" (134). Her reaction, like Jane's above, challenges the discourse of adults present and, incidentally, the teachings of the church:

> Now Pearl knew well enough who made her; [. . .] But that perversity, which all children have more or less of, and of which little Pearl had a tenfold portion [. . .] took possession of her, and closed her lips, or impelled her to speak words amiss. After putting her finger in her mouth, with many ungracious refusals to answer good Mr. Wilson's question, the child finally announced that she had not been made at all, but had been plucked by her mother off the bush of wild roses, that grew by the prison door. (134)

Pearl does more than simply disrupt adult order and expectations during the examination. Aside from expressing her obvious resentment toward those in power, her response, ironically, draws attention away from the contentious issue of her creation that continually punishes her mother. She not only defends her own dignity but her mother's as well. In *Uncle Tom's Cabin* (1852) Topsy evades the same issue by saying, "Never was born!" (356). Both examples echo the subversive effect of Hans's version of Hanna's creation and reinforce Freud's theory that the most universal deception children first experience and continue to resent is being lied to about their own conception with unsatisfying, evasive mythologies.

The most effective way to disrupt adult discourse and yet be sheltered by the imposed guise of innocence is in the form of a question.[8] It is an assumed natural right of children to ask questions, for questions hasten learning and can be seen (by those who need it) as respecting authority. Pearl demonstrates such subversive power through her questions that she effects change and demands justice in the events of the narrative that influence all of the main characters. It is Pearl, not her mother, who makes the greatest strides toward forcing Dimmesdale's confession and uniting her parents. When the two plan to steal away together and live as a family with Pearl, the girl asks, "Will he go back with us, hand in hand, we three together, into the town?" (228). She insists, in her own subtle ways, on vindicating her mother's honor by forcing Dimmesdale's honesty. It is not enough for him to accept her as a daughter; he must first endure what Hester has and be socially recognized as her father. She overtly refuses him any voluntary sign of affection until he climbs the scaffold in public and invites Hester and Pearl to join him (229). Dimmesdale seems to have been led by a need for Pearl's approval, and when he has confessed, he asks her, "Dear little Pearl, wilt thou kiss me now? Thou wouldst not yonder, in the forest! But now thou wilt?" (268). That she does finally kiss him at this moment confirms the rightfulness of his decision, and "a spell was broken. The great scene of grief, in which the wild infant bore a part, had developed all her sympathies [. . .]" (268).

Pearl functions in the novel much more complexly than stock redemptive child-characters, such as Eva in *Uncle Tom's Cabin*. She is often the cause of her mother's pain and aggravates her mother's effort to protect her. She is described as dangerous and otherworldly, frequently signified by her incomprehensible language. When taunted by local children she throws stones at them, making "shrill, incoherent exclamations" that seem to be "witch's anathemas in some unknown tongue" (117–18). When she is angry at Dimmesdale's failure to come forward, she tricks him into close attention as if to answer a question: "Pearl mumbled something into his ear, that sounded, indeed, like human language, but was only such gibberish as children may be heard amusing themselves with, by the hour together. [. . .] The elfish child then laughed aloud" (176). Here she disrupts his attempt to get information with elusive language, but she makes clear that he is being punished for his own lack of forthrightness: "Thou wast not bold!—Thou wast not true!" (176). Her consistent role in these scenes is critical and subversive, not simply redemptive. She is the only character in the novel with the freedom to be an individualist.

Pearl is an idealization of the subversive potential of being overlooked and silenced within legitimated discursive spaces—through her Hawthorne articulates a critique of hypocrisy and power. But the silenced subversive discursive space is truly ineffable, at least to those of us empowered by discourse. That does not change the fact that we create such an opportunity for subversion by enacting power in discourse—an unprovable reality that Lindsay Camp nonetheless demonstrates in his picture book, *Why?* (1998), illustrated by Tony Ross.

In it, Lily incessantly asks the question that she is entitled, from a position of unknowing, to ask: "Why?" Her father sometimes gets frustrated

Figure 6. (From *WHY?* by Lindsay Camp, illustrated by Tony Ross, copyright © 1998 by Lindsay Camp, text; 1998 by Tony Ross, illustrations. Used by permission of G. P. Putnam's Sons, A Division of Penguin Young Readers Group, A Member of Penguin Group (USA) Inc., 345 Hudson Street, New York, NY 10014. All rights reserved.)

realizing how infinitely deep her rounds of questioning can go—until a Thargon spaceship lands practically at their feet, and the aliens threaten to destroy the planet (figure 6). Lily asks them why:

ALIEN: WHY? Because that is our mission, of course.
LILY: Why?
ALIEN: Because destroying puny planets brings glory to the mighty Thargon Empire.

LILY: Why?

ALIEN: Because . . . well, because our Great Leader, the Imperial Tharg, says so.

LILY: Why?

ALIEN: Because . . . he just does, Small Female Earthling, he just does. *Hmmm.*

Once Lily has opened up a dialogue the Thargons look critically at their own rhetoric, deciding to leave and rethink their leader's plans: "Your questions show disrespect to our great leader. However, we realise destroying planets hasn't done us much good."

Did Lily just deconstruct Thargon imperialism in one word? Such a swift breakdown might be idealistic, but Camp's point is concrete: legitimate discourse is empowered by the silences that prevent its self-deconstruction by constant questioning. Every time we get to a point where we have to say that someone "says so," we have exposed the reliance of our truths upon subjective authority—authority whose centering of power we must question. Camp's book demonstrates the great potential of unknowing. Attempting to think from such a position (recognizing and homing in on what we do not know, asking questions, and listening more as a means of understanding) of self-aware unknowing, we might come to more fairly recognize those we silence and are silenced by.

Questioning from a position of unknowing protects the discursive child from accountability and forces empowered speakers to lay bare their own reasoning to the point of exposing the centering of that context's discursive power. It is no wonder, then, that so many authors have used child-characters to "voice" their social criticisms. Rebel child-figures are often paired with marginalized underdogs in order to help reflect their struggles for justice. In fact, children seem to be the only primary characters (usually middle- to upper-class) to befriend servants in the British tradition from *Jane Eyre* to the Harry Potter series, a tendency that is Americanized to include enslaved and exploited laborers and domestic workers in *The Adventures of Huckleberry Finn*, the *Wizard of Oz* series, *The Secret Garden*, *Pollyanna*, *To Kill a Mockingbird*, and *Harriet the Spy*.

Eleanor Porter's title character in *Pollyanna* (1913), in particular, is a vehicle for criticizing the idle rich and their methods of "charity." She innocently asks her aunt if she has ever received a barrel of donated clothes from the church and is quickly reminded by her aunt's displeasure that her aunt would have no need: "I forgot. Rich folks never have to have them. But you see sometimes I kind of forget that you *are* rich—up here in this room, you know" (46). Innocently she draws attention to the poor condition of her own attic room, but "rich" takes on an ironic meaning as well, hinting that her aunt's life is not so plentiful in activity and friends. Her comments have the effect of not only illustrating a common theme, that money alone does not bring happiness, but also, in the form of an apology, criticizing her aunt's lack of generosity.

Porter's narrator always stresses that such criticisms are unintentional on Pollyanna's part. For example, in the passage above, she was "plainly unaware that she had said anything in the least unpleasant" (46). When Pollyanna overhears the Ladies' Aid group arguing over their decreased fund for missionaries in India, Pollyanna's criticism is phrased, much as the questions above, as confusion: "It sounded almost as if they did not care at all what the money *did*, so long as the sum opposite the name of their society in a certain 'report' 'headed the list'—and of course that could not be what they meant at all!" (93). However, Pollyanna knows the consequences of the women's narrow-minded charity and public vanity. She dreads having to tell her own charity cause, the street orphan Jimmy Bean, that "they would rather send all their money to bring up the little India boys than to save out enough to bring up one little boy in their own town, for which they would not get 'a bit of credit in the report,' according to the tall lady who wore spectacles" (93). Pollyanna eventually finds a home for Jimmy Bean, and as if that is not enough, she manages to reunite her aunt with a former lover in the mix. Porter makes it clear that her motif on the necessity of "a child's presence" is more than sentimental—in the small fictive world of Pollyanna, a child can be redeemer of the rich and Robin Hood to the poor.

Like other authors discussed here, Porter reminds us that though her child character affects change, she is excluded from adult discourse and only indirectly or unknowingly doing so.[9] When she pleads Jimmy's case to Mr. Pendleton, she reveals that she has misunderstood Nancy's comment that Pendleton has "a skeleton in his closet": "Maybe you think a nice live little boy wouldn't be better than that old dead skeleton you keep somewhere. But I think it would!" (154). Without revealing his secrets or explaining Nancy's figurative meaning, Pendleton agrees to see Jimmy. At her most influential moment, Pollyanna is excluded from understanding the contextual meaning that determines her influence on Pendleton, as he admits: "I *know* that a 'nice live little boy' would be far better than—my skeleton in the closet. Only—we aren't always willing to make the exchange. We are apt to still cling to—our skeletons" (154–55). It is clear that he means more in this statement than he assumes she knows. But his realization also carries the anti-developmental sentiment that adults get rusty in their thought, along with the flipside notion that children are free thinkers, because they are excluded from adult discourse and power, outside of which they can think and act subversively.

Scout, in Harper Lee's *To Kill a Mockingbird* (1960), effects even more dramatic disruption and turn of events yet, like Pollyanna, seems free of accountability for her influence. She demonstrates the literary child's propensity to ask many questions early on. When she asks her Uncle Jack what a "whore-lady" is, he dodges her question, but her father, Atticus, warns him, "Jack! When a child asks you something, answer him, for goodness' sake. But don't make a production of it. Children are children, but they can spot an evasion quicker than adults" (87). Atticus is aware of the power in simple questions, and Scout asks plenty. The climactic scene of the novel (even more so in the film) revolves around this fact. Atticus, who is surrounded and threatened by a white mob for protecting a prisoner (Tom Robinson) they want to lynch, tells his son Jem to take Scout home. One man from the mob grabs Jem to hurry him along, and Scout defends her brother from him: "I kicked the man swiftly. Barefooted, I was surprised to see him fall back in real pain. I intended to kick his shin, but aimed too high" (152). She is ignorant of her reasons for triumphing here but triumphs all the same. More astonishing is the effect of her questions once she recognizes a familiar face among the mob: "Hey, Mr. Cunningham. How's your entailment gettin' along?" (153). A slew of her innocent questions silences the crowd: "Don't you remember me, Mr. Cunningham? [. . .] I go to school with Walter [. . .] He's your boy, ain't he? Ain't he, sir? [. . .] Tell him hey for me, won't you?" (154–55). Oblivious to the danger her father and his client are in, she acts just politely enough to shame the mob into retreating. Her presumed innocence protects her from the anger of the mob, but her questions remind them of their own culpability.

In a penetrating moment of social criticism, Scout asks Jem about racist comments she's overheard: "How can you hate Hitler so bad an' then turn around and be ugly about folks right at home—" (247). Such questions, and the indirect disruptions cited above, expose contradictions in adult discourse. What Susan Stewart has written of nonsense applies here: "When a fiction concomitantly presents two domains of reality as the set of voices in conflict with one another, irony results. In irony the text begins to demonstrate the relative nature of provinces of meaning" (20). Recognizing relative meaning destabilizes rationalism, of which a fundamental tenet is that truth is found and upheld through noncontradiction. Antirationalist constructions of childhood indulge in moments of forced contradiction in order to dismantle this absolutism. They force awareness of the relativity of meaning and systems of meaning (ideology), idealizing a childhood free of the trappings of socialized subjectivity.

This and preceding chapters have demonstrated various uses of hyper-literalism, dramatic irony, "innocent" questions, and paradox to indicate word-children's estrangement from, misunderstanding of, and potential to disrupt adult discourse. When we recognize adult power we must also recognize the power to resist it. As Foucault suggests in "The Subject of Power," this resistance might be purely intellectual or even unintentional: "The relationship between power and freedom's refusal to submit cannot [. . .] be separated. The crucial problem of power is not that of voluntary servitude (how could we seek to be slaves?)" (790). Empowered discourse imposes and enforces varied constructions upon children—but that does not mean that subjects are powerless to reject, subvert, or even ignore the constructing.

Mikhail Bakhtin has written that "every act of world history was accompanied by a laughing chorus" (474). Writers for and about children have turned to their subject often as part of that laughing chorus, critiquing and healing more legitimated, "serious" forms of discourse associated with the adult world of consequential action. Creating a space in which to laugh at ourselves as hyper-rational adults or to fancy ourselves children, we reveal more about our language, anxiety, and desire than we do about the youth they target. That attempts at portraying childhood tend toward anti-rationalism is not surprising when thrown in the light of Western history. Kristeva writes, in *Desire in Language*, "Western reason perceived that its role of being servant to meaning was imprisoning. Wishing to escape, it turned toward and became haunted by childhood. [. . .] [A]nalytic discourse was given a privileged foil, a nexus of life and language (of species and society)—the child" (271). Adulthood, born of the age of reason, its ensuing literacy and empowerment of knowledge, is accompanied in response by the concept of childhood as unreasoning, speechless, and disempowered; but in the latter position we imagine a freedom from what Foucault might call the danger of abstraction. In *Madness and Civilization* he explains the connection between childhood and madness (both developed as negative contrasts in the Age of Reason), and he argues that insisting upon noncontradiction can become obsessive and isolating:

> If the progress of knowledge dissipates error, it also has the effect of propagating a taste and even a mania for study; the life of the library, abstract speculations, the perpetual agitation of the mind without the exercise of

the body, can have the most disastrous effects. [. . .] Knowledge thus forms around feeling a milieu of abstract relationships where man risks losing the physical happiness in which his relation to the world is usually established. (217–18)

This unhappiness is demonstrated in chapter 3 by characters like Colin from *The Secret Garden* and Gurlie in *White Mule*. It is also the unhappiness that Boo Radley avoids in *To Kill a Mockingbird*. Like other holy simpletons (Isaac Bashevis Singer's "Gimpel the Fool," Jerzy Kosinski's Chance[10] in *Being There*, and Forrest Gump) he resembles a child-figure. Excluded from the adult social reality of Maycomb, his medium is silence and irony. Jem, who is older than Scout and more jaded by the trial, wrongful conviction, and murder of Tom Robinson, reveals this when, at one point, he contradicts Scout's optimism about equality: "If there's just one kind of folks, why can't they all get along with each other? [. . .] I think I'm beginning to understand why Boo Radley's stayed shut up in the house all this time . . . it's because he *wants* to stay inside" (227). By rejecting education and society, Boo Radley is trying to escape adulthood, much as authors and their readers may desire when idealizing childhood, escaping frustrations through nostalgic indulgence.

I quoted Eric S. Rabkin earlier as saying that "regression may be a balm for the disappointed," relating such nostalgia to the burdens of language and abstract thought (11). If we believe, as Western rationalism teaches, that the highest truth is only knowable through reason, then the burden of knowledge is entirely upon us as individuals seeking answers in our minds with limited reference to empirical proofs. The burden of rationalism is therefore great, and through nostalgic constructions of childhood it is vicariously lightened. In fictional realms where children initiate change and force recognition of relativity, we can believe, briefly, in an unthinkingly totalized "ever after." But we must check ourselves from taking advantage of the inaccessibility of childhood by imposing an impossible notion of innocence to nostalgically soothe away the very complex responsibilities we in turn deflect onto children without giving them credit to control or room to differ.

Developmentalism laid the paradigmatic groundwork for a family épistémè in which adult power over children is ideologically inherent, locking in a paradoxical disclaimer against any dissention or radical questioning from within (and thus, by ideological means). Those of us falsely empowered (adults) within this épistémè are the very subjects who must alter our thought. If we could only accept the impossibility of reterritorializing childhood, molding children, and appropriating child culture, then we might stop expecting our constructions of childhood to materialize and start learning from the ideals we are projecting through them instead. By following the example of our own anti-rationalist idealizations of childhood as an intuitively primed position of unknowing receptivity, we might be more primed, ourselves, for self-criticism and engaging in more self-conscious, self-revising discourse.

Claudia Castañeda points out that what is required of us is to rethink not only children but also the actual *ways we define the knowledge* we use to center power and delegate authority:

> The newborn's existence cannot be known fully by adults because that existence is the effect of an agency that is excessive to adult knowledge (though perhaps not to our experience). [...] To re-theorize the subject in terms that do not make use of the child as the adult's presubjective other means establishing an un-knowing—the impossibility of total knowledge and of a total claim on the real—that is the condition of knowledge itself. (168)

If we embrace our inability to know childhood, and even empirically accept limitations to our understanding posed by a dependence upon language, we might find a different kind of empowerment in a position of unknowing and, likewise, encourage those less socialized and linguistically limited than ourselves (whom some will call children) to open questioning and ongoing discovery.

THE POSSIBILITIES OF UNKNOWING

*I*n the preceding chapters I hope to have demonstrated that children in literary discourse are generally constructed as linguistically, and thus narratively, isolated—more desirable because of their remote unknowability, enviable for their lack of schooling in a culture dominated by hyperliterate rationalist adults, and in turn idealized as flexible sites of possible resistance to rationalism (dependence upon systematized thought) and ideology (thought-systems themselves). Pressing for this idealized position, we imagine liberating childhood spaces for "children" while at the same time maintaining limits by controlling approaches to the institutionalized process that defines children, development. Seemingly freeing children to nurture their own development, we can vicariously indulge our own desires for freedom while saddling the young with our own standards.

As writers, readers, and consumers, we must be ever vigilant in promoting rhetoric that seems to empower and recognize multiplicity in those it situates (if necessary) as children, reducing the adult-serving biases we are able to detect. The closest example literary scholars have of a method for avoiding biased adult mediation is probably in the work of Peter and Iona Opie, nonacademics who entered schoolyards like an anthropological field, recording rhymes volunteered by young students. Of course, their completed manuscripts came from entirely outside of the schoolyard context, but the Opies set an example of the direction the most committed students of child culture might take if trying to circumvent barriers between themselves and the culture of those they call children. Another area of production that seems less exclusively mediated and one-sided than the literary canon is the comic book genre.[1]

Comics create an illusion of immediacy with young readers, uniting with them against the adult-world order. Alex Scobie explains that "as a medium the comic book strives more than any other printed literature to create the intimate rapport between producer and reader which is aimed at by oral storyteller and his listener-participants" (73). Perhaps for this reason such popular publications, including some interactive sites on the Internet today, can give us a better idea of what works with young readers and why. Comic books represent a more interactive genre "in the same way as an oral storyteller shapes his oral narrative in response to his listeners' favourable or unfavourable reactions to his on-going performance," by "inviting readers to write to the story editor [. . .] and express their views on any aspect of the comic from one issue to another. One page in every issue prints a selection of readers' letters accompanied by editorial response" (79). Many challenge readers to find narrative inconsistencies or suggest future plotlines by writing in, giving a forum to their readers' voices. This democratic reciprocity is achieved by "simulating oralcy," which means, in the context of my analysis, rejecting more literate codes of narration.

In *Power Pack* (introduced in chapter 4) correspondence with the audience is published on the last page in a section called "The Pick of the Pack." Significantly, readers have provided specific advice there concerning the linguistic representation of children, as in the following samples:

Dear Louise, June and Bob,

I bought POWER PACK #1 and I'm glad I did because it's the best thing to come from Marvel since the return of X-Men.

But I have one complaint—Katie's way of talking! For a girl who looks five, she has a heck of a good vocabulary! I figure she should speak the way most other kids her age speak. For instance, she should say something like, "I shine bright. Me shoot stars at bad snakes!" Something to that effect!

—Joseph E. Perez ("Secrets")

And

Dear People that Pack Powers,

I love POWER PACK! I'm 12 and I think POWER PACK is totally awesome! And I think you guys are narly and thanks a lot for making this comic book! It's the best thing since electricity. I got all my friends to collect it [. . .]

But could you ask Alex something—why does he always say "Gee" instead of "Wow" or "Narly" because "Gee" is old!

Thank you,
Jeff Butler ("The Kid Who Fell to Earth")

One must wonder what Henry James would have done with such criticisms of his own work.

The difference this immediate rapport makes is clear in the graphic novel *Shelter from the Storm* (1989), which joins the Power Pack with Cloak and Dagger to help two young runaways. Its opening scenes introduce the main characters, Marjorie and Juan, by stressing the potential tyranny of adults. Juan is introduced in an archetypal struggle between abusive father and growing boy—he strikes his father to protect his mother and for the first time overpowers him. Meanwhile, Marjorie discovers that her parents have hidden her acceptance letters from Yale, Princeton, and Columbia to keep her close to them. She packs to run away, sobbing: "Their love is just a prison!" (5). Both teens flee their homes and meet at the bus station, where their adventure begins. Even the Power Pack children, who have a nurturing relationship with their parents (whom they "protect" from knowing of their superpowers), are introduced commenting on the frightening reality that parents can and do abandon children, suggested by a bedtime reading of "Hansel and Gretel" (10). The graphic novel so earnestly takes up the plight of the young that it even includes an ad for runaway safe-houses in the endpapers.

Creators of comics often assume that their audience needs to be listened to. They take on stock psychological themes as a form of group (reading) therapy. For example, in another scene Marjorie is actually imprisoned by a superpowered villain, and she reconsiders her decision to run away in a new light: wasn't being imprisoned by love better than real walls? Her burst of emotion reveals the duplicity of adult power when it is one-sided—she imagines her parents calling her a "parasite" if she were to return, even though the lifestyle they tried to force on her was hyper-dependent, parasitic. From this point of view, a parent's "love" is shown as being at odds with emancipation. The incongruity of developmentalism here is implicitly deconstructed: if we too simplistically equate guidance with maturity, we confuse love with control.

These examples point to a dangerous aspect of our nostalgia, not just in that we impose it, but that it also carries the threat of our envy—we indulge in it as our own escape but impose it to prevent the escape of others. In our efforts to nurture and protect children, we enable full-scale solipsization of youth. Compulsory education also standardizes performance, to the point of stigmatizing those who "develop" slowly, and holds others back, as Daniel Cook has pointed out: "one effect of the emergent age-based systematization of knowledge and ability was to make intellectual precocity suspect, thereby placing, through institutional means, limits on how much children could achieve" (99). Protecting them from a right to work when they want to might also prolong idleness and postpone engagement with the community. What Viviana Zelizer has revealed about the flipside of child labor reform applies here on many levels: "For reformers, true parental love could only exist if the child was defined exclusively as an object of sentiment and not as an agent of production" (72). Denying any young person access to certain types of knowledge, or the right to choose a vocation at any age (rather than helping him/her to unionize or fight exploitation), is an infringement, not protection—it is robbing another person of their rightful *agency*—but we have morally twisted the imperative of protecting the innocence of childhood to the point that we usually fail to see it clearly, and even more rarely do we feel comfortable questioning it, lest we be accused of harshness toward those we should protect.

Rebekka Habermas dates this paradoxical paradigm from a shift in the nineteenth century, from necessary full-family involvement in labor to the ideal of disinterested or "selfless parenting," which grew with the middle class as a result of its new affluence. Her analysis of German culture also applies to American experiences (and many have pointed out that in rural areas reciprocal family work existed as a norm longer). Although earlier families maintained more equity and balance out of interdependence, parental affluence changed that. Habermas compares two generations of a family exemplifying such a shift:

> The Roths' grandparents still believed themselves to be linked to their children by a relationship based on reciprocity, in which children contributed not only to the material and social but also to the emotional capital of their parents (and vice-versa), and also openly discussed these links as a form of mutual dependence. The Roths by contrast saw themselves as parents who were all-powerful, completely devoid of any needs on their side, and unselfishly loving, thereby reducing their children to the status of passive, willing, objects of this love. (46)

The latter remains a current (and problematic) paradigm of parenting, as seen in Robert Munsch's *Love You Forever* (1986), which protests this "selfless parenting" so much that it reeks of a caging possessiveness that makes love seem like a compulsive desire to stalk children and render them unconscious. A mother sings to her son (but only "if he was really asleep," we are told repeatedly), "I'll love you forever / [...] As long as I'm living / my baby you'll be." The direct message of the book, "I won't stop loving you," becomes an indirect threat as the child grows to be a man (after all, as long as she is living, he is supposed to be a baby), followed by "But sometimes on dark nights / the mother got into her car and drove / across town" (with a ladder on her car to gain access to her son's [still] single bed upstairs). Despite this disturbing display of possessive and *selfish* parenting, the book has, according to the press release on amazon.com, "sold more than 15 million copies in paperback and the regular hardcover edition (as well as hundreds of thousands of copies in Spanish and French)." It has also been featured on an episode of *Friends*. Why? Because it flatters parents' sentiments, not their children's.[2] Once children become, as Zelizer is quoted above as saying, "objects of sentiment" rather than agents of their own choosing, there seems no end to the projections and impositions that can be made in the name of nurturance.

These include robbing children of the agency to gain knowledge and freedom on their own terms. Ideal parental love, in its sentimental literary expressions, is far from disinterested—*Love You Forever* demonstrates the extent to which we ask child readers to take everything uncomfortable on faith to make ourselves comfortable. It is so focused on congratulating the mother for her tolerant and unending love that it elides the very fear most parents think they buy the book to address: fear of losing a parent. "As long as I'm living" might seem an admission that love has some conditions, like mortality, but the entire book testifies that Mother is not going anywhere—and neither is her son; she'll always find him. The book even avoids the usual conflicts of "family romance" and the challenges of gender-identification by showing only mother and son, and then, his daughter (who comes as a surprise, as he seems to have no partner and the birth of the baby is not explained). We expect child readers to accept this unrealistic, uncomplicated, and over-secure image of the world they live in to make ourselves more comfortable with the lack of it.

Perhaps the acute awareness of this lack explains why we push for unquestioning belief in magic so much in texts where we indulge it. Take, as an example, Chris Van Allsburg's *The Polar Express* (1985), in which a child journeys to the North Pole, meets Santa, and gets a bell from his sleigh as a gift.³ On Christmas morning the boy discovers that his parents cannot hear the bell, which is consistent with the romantic construction of development as a fall. In the end, the boy, now an adult and our narrator, tells us that "At one time most of my friends could hear the bell, but as years passed, it fell silent for all of them. [. . .] Though I've grown old, the bell still rings for me as it does for all who truly believe." Once again adult nostalgia cuts out an adult figure who is the exception to the rule; he does not fall from belief when growing up. But there is a double subtext here for the target audience. The boy still hears the bell because he *knows* it is magic—he went to the North Pole, saw the bell on Santa's sleigh, and by still hearing it can remember the midnight magic journey that, in turn, is reified by the bell. However, what he suggests for his readers is necessarily different from knowing; it is to take his story on faith. Encouraging belief over validation is the same as pressing for acceptance rather than questioning—it is yet another infantilizing extension of romantic innocence/ignorance. After all, what is belief but an acceptance of not knowing in order to reduce a seemingly impossible desire to know?

Just like Marjorie's parents' imprisoning love, the sharp edge of our nostalgia often works against the freedoms of those we call children while the saccharine side hides our complicity, even from ourselves. We encourage the acceptance of a wish for something to be real over the reality itself. This agenda is often more pronounced in Disney and American film productions than the texts that inspire them—as in film adaptations of *Peter Pan* (not to mention, for those of us who remember, the peanut butter commercial), which dramatically expand the theme that wishing alone suffices, found in Tinkerbell's near-death scene where "she could get well again if children believed in fairies" (125). In the most recent film adaptation, *Peter Pan* (2003), we no longer clap our hands but endlessly repeat a mantra (isn't that useful in brainwashing?). Repeat after me: "I *do* believe in fairies." Repeat. Again.

Perhaps the assumption is that belief is less dangerous than questioning. Questioning can lead to both knowledge and skepticism, neither of which has been encouraged in those we wish to keep "innocent." Asking children to believe in magic postpones their need to question. Anthropologist Galina Lindquist equates magic with nostalgia (expressed as kitsch, in her study) because it "presents more than represents, evoking simple, but recognizable and widely shared, emotional states and experiential moods, feelings that are strong, basic and unreflected—this is what sentimentality is all about" (340). According to Weston La Barre, insisting on belief in magic, like superstition and religion, is a "group defense mechanism," like any "beliefs we still hold onto willy-nilly, regardless of common sense and experience, because they comfort us psychologically, or hide some unpleasant fact" (45). In fact, he interprets this stubbornness as a sign of human neoteny, retaining juvenile features in adulthood (although he could also be stereotyping juveniles as superstitious where convenient rather than pointing to a potential mental continuity between youth and age). If we accept the common tendency among all ages to "hold onto beliefs willy-nilly," then we have to ask why magic is relegated to children's books and religion is legitimated in more public contexts. What bias explains the dividing line? Adult choice.

Consider the following contrast. Edward Eager's *Half Magic* (1954), the book that inspired the characterization of the Power children in the *Power Pack* series, indulges in the development-as-fall sentiment in its closure of the fantasy by eroding belief. The children can use a magic token because they are young enough to believe and understand, but they know that "no grown up ever will credit any story that has magic in it" (127). Yet an adult character *does* emerge as the exception to the rule. Mr. Smith is "sensible about magic, not like most grown ups at all," and so, Jane, Mark, Katherine, and Martha trust him with using the magic token, too (147). Adult indulgence or mere coincidence? The book shows belief as something relative, eroding with age, but still (impossibly) within reach of adult choice.

In *Power Pack,* however, there are no adults who function as mediators or exceptions to the rule, no adults who can choose to be included in their heroics or even understand them. The kids are alone, without an adult mediator in their midst.[4] In fact, reader Chris Saunders wrote in with the following suggestion: "I think that the Power Pack need *some* adult to guide them through the rough spots because they almost blew up their basement in #7!" ("Sea Hunt"). But their freedom is one of the greatest strengths of the series, as another reader, Robbie Thurman, gratefully puts it: "To the pack behind the Pack, Thank you for making the Power Pack kids not adults" ("Man and Dragon Man").

The Power kids, like their literary predecessors, protect their parents from exposure to what they might not understand, in this case, their superalien powers, endowed by Whitey (a Kymellian snark fighter) before he died. Whether to take things on faith becomes an explicit matter of choice *for the children,* who can question amongst themselves and debate freely. In an issue entitled "Rescue," Jack tells Katie that "only stupid babies believe in the tooth fairy!" After giving her tooth as a gift to Whitey's father, she finds a Kymellian coin under her pillow, clearly the workings of her now

Figure 7. (POWER PACK: TM & © 2005 Marvel Characters, Inc. Used with permission. Art originally published in 1988 POWER PACK series.)

adopted "grandfather." Yet they still refer to the giver as "she," even though Katie points out that Jack has never even believed in a tooth fairy. The episode ends with the point that both children have the freedom to disagree and choose to believe what they want individually.

In a market and genre dominated by adults, it is impossible to eliminate our presence, but we can mediate less and withdraw adult-serving nostalgia and sentiment where we recognize it. Characterization in the *Power Pack* series is an example of what might result. Alex, the Mass Master, consistently says hurtful, stubborn, and nasty things. Katie throws seemingly sourceless tantrums, which is considerably dangerous in the beginning because she has not learned to control her lightning bolts (figure 7). She burns Alex's hand when he tries to stop her fall, almost burns their spaceship, Friday, and burns her own way through a floor out of fear, and early in her development of her superpowers, when her powers save the moment, it is as much due to accident as experimentation. But, because she and the others are free to interpret and learn from their mistakes, they seem invigorating—each is a believable adventure, a new challenge to overcome.

As cultural critics and readers, few of us are directly engaged in producing texts with "children" or collecting "authentic" child-lore. We may not enter the schoolyard, or publish kids online, or write comics with their input. We can, however, in contrast, see how far we have to go to avoid imposing our own standards while we read. And we can encourage this awareness in educators and parents who insist on reading texts for "children" with an impossibly conflicting set of adult-serving standards. Even in the context of my children's literature classes, where I emphasize the dangers of generalizing about those we inconsistently define as children and the political suspiciousness of prescribing readings, I still have students mid-semester asking questions about such classics as *The Emerald City of Oz,* like, "can children understand this?" and objecting to *Pinocchio* on the grounds that "we're supposed to entertain children, not scare them." Our complete lack of objectivity becomes perfectly clear when we catch such detractors admitting to having loved the same books when they were young.

Joseph Zornado explains this contradiction and critical challenge as it plays out in his classrooms:

> Claiming that children do not pick up on everything around them masks adult resistance to their own history as children. My students resist the idea that children pick up on everything, and no one resists this idea more than those who work with or parent small children. We get defensive because we love our children and are invested in seeing ourselves as efficient and effective rulers of our petty kingdoms. To give up on this fiction means that I have to give up [. . .] my culturally bound, ego-driven claims to power over them [children], and moreover, that I must give up my ideological belief that [. . .] I own my children. (195)

We seem to cringe at our hypocrisies and unfairness as adults when we see it in print, and we have trouble accepting that just because we love certain individual children, that does not mean that we can absolutely know what is best for them and children in general, so we disregard popularity with current young readers as an indicator of literary success and worth. But, as

Gerard Jones suggests in *Killing Monsters: Why Children Need Fantasy, Super Heroes and Make-Believe Violence* (2002), we need to give up our attempts at predicting what young readers will like and why, instead giving them the chance to use texts as suits them best.

Cynicism and constructivist agendas aside, one cannot help but reconstruct childhood in deconstructing it, if only between the lines. If we romantically reverse developmental definitions of childhood so that it becomes an unavoidably eroding social space of pre-verbal and pre-ideological possibility, unknowable from an adult position and accepted as unknown, we cannot help but see in it unlimited subversive possibilities. Not simply subjects, objects, or outsiders but intermittently occupying each position, children could be defined as those who are "becoming."

The most common distinguishing factor in Western definitions of children is level of language use. From the perspective of Gilles Deleuze, "becoming is itself coextensive with language" but "becoming unlimited" is an ideal directed by always recognizing the slippage and difference born with each utterance (8–9). In order to foster humans "becoming" on their own terms, negotiating their best interests in the world in which they will have to live, we have to learn to look at ourselves and re-evaluate our rhetoric for a keener detection of the arbitrary limitations we impose.

notes

Notes to Introduction

1. As a point in case, Roberta Seelinger Trites describes this bias in *Disturbing the Universe:* "adults are responsible for protecting children. The assertion is one I believe in so firmly that it feels to me like Truth rather than ideology. Nevertheless, it is a sentiment that I recognize as one that directs power away from adolescents and toward adults" (80).

2. One might consider the telling irony that adults often think nostalgically of their own experiences when they were considered children, but no one confuses being "treated like a child" with anything desirable.

Notes to Chapter 1

1. Beverly Lyon Clark gives comprehensive commentary on this phenomenon in "Kiddie Lit in Academe."

2. An excellent source on this issue is Victor Watson's "By Children, About Children, For Children."

3. Karen Coats describes the book as "an example of Childhood Studies gone wrong" ("Venting the Child" 206).

4. Although the term "child studies" was suggested by works such as Carolyn Steedman's *Strange Dislocations,* the alternate "childhood studies" better reflects the field's attempt to avoid essentializing the concept of "the child" by focusing on the position or concept of childhood.

5. Of these rubrics, that of rationality will be most relevant to my study, as the nostalgia of frustrated intellects tends to cast childhood in an anti-rationalist light.

6. The shift in childcare attitudes that might explain this difference is the focus of "Parent-Child Relationships in the Nineteenth Century" by Rebekka Habermas. In this article she describes the emerging bourgeois sentiment of "disinterested parenting" by which parents could see themselves as loving children selflessly because any need for "mutual dependence" or "reciprocity" (money, labor) in their relations with children was eliminated by their rising affluence (46).

7. In "Structure, Sign, and Play," Jacques Derrida explains that play is "permitted by the lack or absence of a center [. . .]. The movement of signification adds something,

which results in the fact that there is always more, but this addition is a floating one because it comes to perform a vicarious function, to supplement a lack on the part of the signified" (*Writing and Difference* 289). In this sense childhood studies is self-conscious play—a floating discourse of further supplementation to the absence of a verifiable "child."

8. Recognition of the literariness of Freud's case studies is considered "commonplace" by Peter L. Rudnytsky, who describes the Hans case as a "multilayered text, much like a work of modernist fiction" (39).

9. Consider the contrast evidenced in "real" children observed by Kenneth Wexler et al.: "two thirds of utterances made by mothers to their infants are either imperatives or questions, and only one third are statements, yet the utterances of children are overwhelmingly statements" (paraphrased by Bryson, 27). It would seem our literary children are idealized with more subversive interrogative power than their real-world counterparts.

Notes to Chapter 2

1. Historian David I. Macleod reports that "If we define adults as all people age 20 and older and the young as those 19 and younger, there were 128 white young people for every 100 white adults in 1830. But there were only 79 white young people for every 100 white adults by 1890 and just 66 in 1920. The proportion of young people among African Americans was considerably higher but declined sharply, from approximately 117 for every 100 adults in 1890 to 86 by 1920" (3). By the twentieth century, children were outnumbered.

2. In a letter to Mrs. Humphry Ward, dated July 26, 1899, James expounds on his views against "going behind" the character. To do so convincingly, he argues, would require "extreme and calculated selection, or singleness" in order to avoid the appearance of careless speculation (*Letters* 324). More importantly, he reveals his resulting preference for dramatic representation in narrative.

3. Likewise, she will later tell Mrs. Grose that when Flora goes on an outing, supposedly to visit the ghost of Miss Jessel, "at such times she's not a child" (68).

Notes to Chapter 3

1. According to Virginia Wolf, Laura Ingalls Wilder creates, in her retelling of her childhood, an ever-shifting, enclosed but "felicitous space" ("Magic Circle" 169).

2. The *locus amoenus* is linked with nostalgia from its inception in Western worldviews—for example, the edenic-garden representation of innocence and the golden age of ancient Greece.

3. For a parallel example see chapter 13, in which Des Esseintes has no appetite but sees a boy in a garden enjoying a simple sandwich and instantly orders the same as comfort food (156).

4. John Fiske describes the quest for novelty as a natural extension of rationalist humanism: "the origins of the desire for the new can be traced back to the ideology of progress that has pervaded the economic, political, and moral domains of post-Renaissance Christian capitalist democracies" (377).

5. For a detailed reading of Baum's color-coded territories, see Gretchen Ritter's "Silver Slippers and a Golden Cap," in the *Journal of American Studies* 31:2 (1997):

171–202. Ritter posits that the coloring reflects the racialist and sectionalist discourses of Baum's time.

6. Stuart Culver (1988) applies this term from Adorno and Horkheimer to Baum's Oz, particularly in the inhabitants' knowing agreement to wear green glasses.

7. Denis Wood considers Burton an important examplar in the spatial-visual socialization of children through picture books, particularly as it relates to symbolizing hill structures (167–70).

8. In the definitive exception to the rule of impossible returns, J. M. Barrie allows his Peter Pan to dodge the inevitable growth that comes with experience by having him "always forget" (88). In this way Peter Pan remains free to return to Neverland.

9. Richard Burt brings up a parallel example of adult appropriation of childhood: "The end of childhood is marked in movie-making . . . by the way that even the few G and PG movies that do get made seem geared to adult fantasies about their own childhoods, as in the case of Steven Spielberg's Peter Pan spin-off, *Hook* (1993). In Spielberg's retelling, Peter is a grown-up, Yuppie neglectful father who redeems himself (and saves his kidnapped kids) by becoming Peter Pan once again" (236). Is it a coincidence that Robin Williams plays *Jumanji's* Alan, Peter Pan, and a literal child in an adult's body in *Jack?*

10. The fundamental tenet explaining rationalist dependence upon reason as the means to truth is Aristotle's principle of non-contradiction: "It is impossible for the same thing at the same time to belong and not belong to the same thing at the same time and in the same respect." Contradictions are seen as proof of incompossibility.

11. As in Baudrillard's *Simulations,* the map stands here for simulacra to emphasize its constructed (manmade) knowability in contrast to the complex unknowability of nature.

Notes to Chapter 4

1. Unchecked generalizing is a consistent problem with childhood discourse on every level. Even today, the most politically correct parents have no qualms stereotyping children as a group when they bring up examples from their own children's behavior to empirically answer questions about *all* children.

2. I begin here with British examples because there are none so clear in American literature. U.S. culture is more deeply committed (without much awareness of genealogies) to rationalist developmental thought and as a result is unlikely to examine it so explicitly and brutally. I think these texts set up a fine contrast.

3. For a sample of such criticism, see S. J. Boyd, E. L. Epstein, and Bernard S. Oldsey and Stanley Weintraub.

4. Note the adult-centered method of inquiry. There is no consideration of comparing adult humans with animals of any kind. Perhaps animalizing children was part of a selective defense against accepting our own animal natures in adulthood.

5. For more on this progression of influence, see John Morss, Frank Sulloway, and Peter Gay.

6. Hall notes that "predatory organizations culminate from eleven to fifteen, and are chiefly among boys" (351). Likewise, the mythology that surrounds "primitive" children and recapitulation revolves more around "frogs and snails" than "sugar and spice." Could *Lord of the Flies* harbor a feminist critique of masculine socialization? More

research needs to address the gendering of recapitulation and adventure-story constructions of children. As such, *A High Wind in Jamaica* would provide a feminizing counterpoint to *Lord of the Flies*.

7. For example, in Darwin's "Sketch" he concludes, after studying only his two sons' and one daughter's frequency of throwing, that "a tendency to throw objects is inherited in boys" (288).

8. Consider a relevant insight of Marcia Jacobson's in *Being a Boy Again* concerning the recapitulatory trope in capitalist American culture: "In so neatly compartmentalizing boyhood, the recapitulation theory also comfortably obscured the central fact of everyday adult male life in the period: that it was ferociously competitive" (15).

9. Emily may have escaped Jonsen's drunken advances (pp. 120–23), but Margaret does not. At best she willingly takes up with the sailors, is deflowered, and in the final scene is pregnant (p. 226).

10. For a contrast, see the work of the British scholars of anti-developmentalist psychology Erica Burman and John Morss.

11. Even Tom's choice of words in expressing his condescension reveals a typical developmental essentialism—equating grade level with maturity and wisdom, as if mental development is a universal and chronologically measurable phenomenon.

12. Golding likewise creates an implicit critique of Twain's contemporary, Ballantyne, for lack of realism in *Coral Island*. *Lord of the Flies* is, in many senses, a dark parody of the earlier work.

13. One could argue that post-structuralist theories of identity merely retranslate the romantic narrative of development as a fall—socialization is seen as a process that leads to fragmentation. If Jameson serves as an applicable model, post-modernist theory seems a continuation on the same theme (see references to Jameson in chapters 2 and 3).

14. A similar use of Carroll's nonsense as sci-fi secret-coding occurs in "Chaos Coordinated" by John MacDougall (pseudonym for Robert Lowndes and James Blish).

15. Holloway's (Kuttner's) concept of conditioning resembles Althusser's *méconnaisance* and Jameson's "sealed subjectivity."

16. I must comment on the surprising frequency of psychologists in fiction concerning children. It seems that the authors are ensuring the presence of an "objective" interpreter while continuing in the adult tradition of imposing constructions through mediation.

17. Once again, only the young "evolve": "This was a younger, more adaptable specimen; it succeeded where the older one had failed" (13).

18. This graphic novel pays homage to *Childhood's End*, among other sci-fi empowerments of youth, by titling chapters in allusion to them.

19. If one considers the language of the No Child Left Behind Act and the Bush administration's crusade for higher standards, it is uncannily similar.

20. The fact that I feel I have to clarify the difference here is proof of how deeply we conflate nature and nurture: what we usually call "biological age" is, in fact, far more abstract and culturally constructed—we develop biologically at varied paces—but it is often confused with our *chronological* age, the convenient absolute by which we are most often defined.

21. Those who develop too slowly are euthanized.

Notes to Chaper 5

1. For more on this trend, see the bibliography for titles by Linda Acredolo and Susan Goodwyn as well as earlier work edited by Margaret Bullowa.

2. This explanation sheds more light on the speech patterns of Lurie's Lolly and Morrison's Beloved.

3. François Truffaut directed and even acted the part of Dr. Itard in *L'Enfant sauvage* (1970). Werner Herzog cast an autistic actor, Bruno S., to play Kaspar Hauser in his film, *The Enigma of Kaspar Hauser* (1974), with striking impact.

4. *Beloved*'s entire community sees Beloved as "a rememory," reflecting the past experience of a macroself—Morrison herself reports that she constructed her so to articulate and soothe the pains of history—an interesting inversion of the futuristic functioning of superchildren seen in chapter 4.

5. One might point out that this reads even more specifically like a narrated monologue, or psycho-narration, but in keeping with my earlier reading of Henry James, I am trying to maintain a particular awareness of the fact that Lurie avoids the explicit intrusion of representing her thoughts, of course, all the while speculating and implying what they might be.

6. Mark Twain's choice to represent Huck Finn through slang and dialect shows an early example of this strategy. The difference is that Lurie's writing is not dialect but a pictorial style more akin to the favoring of concrete words like nouns, as Grandin describes.

7. Kaspar Hauser, though seventeen when found wandering in 1828, had been confined for at least twelve years and had learned very little language. In Herzog Wernor's film he exemplifies the subversive potential of escaping socialization.

8. Harry Potter's Muggle relatives must realize this, as their policy for him is "Don't ask questions" (*Sorcerer's Stone* 20).

9. Jerry Griswold aptly applies Ihab Hassan's term "radical innocence" to describe this process, using Pollyanna as his exemplar.

10. Kosinsky actually uses his innocent fool character as a satiric device much like Maisie, a blank slate whom all the other characters construct as they wish.

Notes to Chapter 6

1. Much earlier instances of youth self-representation are the subject of Paula Petrik's "The Youngest Fourth Estate: The Novelty Toy Printing Press and Adolescence, 1870–1886."

2. For evidence in support of this claim, see the reviewers' responses to the text on amazon.com. The reviews read like a rhetorical profile of "selfless" parenting (in which adult indulgence in and projection of sentimentality become quite clear).

3. For an interesting source on the role that commercialized Christmas has played in Western (particularly German) child-rearing, see Hamlin's "The Structures of Toy Consumption," in which he points out that "Toys were [. . .] the beneficiaries of the ambivalences of what Gunilla-Frederike Budde terms the 'pedagogic double ideal' of bourgeois life: children were allowed to be children but simultaneously they were to be educated to be good middle-class citizens" (859). And, "The ties of obligation and

affection which flowed from and were represented by gifts reflected the interiorization of the bourgeois family" (862).

4. Harry Potter noticeably often avoids the aid of accessible adult figures during conflict, despite sometimes benefiting from it without asking, which might speak to the popularity of the series. Consider the contrast in recent films similar to Power Pack, where instead the parents both know of and take part in the kids' superheroic activities to some degree: *Spy Kids* (2001, 2002), *The Incredibles* (2004).

⚜ bibliography ⚜

Acredolo, Linda, and Susan Goodwyn. *Baby Signs: How to Talk with Your Baby Before Your Baby Can Talk.* Chicago: Contemporary Books, 1996.

Adams, Gillian. "Medieval Children's Literature: Its Possibility and Actuality." *Children's Literature* 26 (1998): 1–24.

Alcott, Louisa May. *Little Women.* 1868. New York: Signet Classics, 2004.

Aldrich, Thomas Bailey. *The Story of a Bad Boy.* 1870. Hanover, N.H.: University Press of New England, 1996.

Alger, Horatio. *Ragged Dick, or Street Life in New York with the Boot-blacks.* 1868. New York: Signet, 1990.

Althusser, Louis. "Ideology and Ideological State Apparatuses." In *Lenin and Philosophy.* Trans. Ben Brewster. London: New Left Books, 1971.

American Beauty. Dir. Sam Mendes. DreamWorks SKG, 1999.

Anno, Mitsumasa. *Anno's Alphabet: An Adventure in Imagination.* 1974. New York: Thomas Y. Crowell, 1975.

Ariès, Philippe. *Centuries of Childhood: A Social History of Family Life.* Trans. Robert Baldick. New York: Vintage Books, 1962.

Avi. *Poppy: A Tale from Dimwood Forest.* Illus. Brian Floca. New York: Avon, 1995.

———. *Ragweed.* Illus. Brian Floca. New York: HarperCollins, 1999.

Bachelard, Gaston. *The Poetics of Space.* 1958. Trans. Maria Jolas. Boston: Beacon Press, 1994.

Bakhtin, Mikhail. *Rabelais and His World.* 1965. Trans. Helene Iswolsky. Bloomington: Indiana University Press, 1984.

Baldwin, James. "Sonny's Blues." In *Going to Meet the Man.* New York: Dial Press, 1965.

Ballantyne, R. M. *The Coral Island.* 1857. New York: Puffin Books, 1995.

Barnett, Louise K. "Huck Finn: Picaro as Linguistic Outsider." *College Literature* 6 (1979): 221–31.

Barrie, James. *Peter Pan.* 1911. New York: Bantam, 1985.

Barthes, Roland. *The Pleasure of the Text.* 1973. Trans. Richard Miller. New York: Hill and Wang, 1975.

Bâsíc, Sonja. "From James's Figures to Genette's Figures: Point of View and Narratology." *Revue française d'études americaines* 8:17 (1983): 201–15.

Baudrillard, Jean. *Baudrillard Live: Selected Interviews.* Ed. Mike Gane. New York: Routledge, 1993.

———. *Simulations.* 1975. Trans. Paul Foss, Paul Patton, and Philip Beitchman. New York: Semiotext(e), 1983.

Baum, L. Frank. *The Emerald City of Oz.* 1910. New York: Ballantine, 1979.

———. *The Marvelous Land of Oz.* 1904. New York: Scholastic, 1970.

———. *The Patchwork Girl of Oz.* 1913. New York: Dover, 1990.

———. *The Wizard of Oz.* 1900. New York: Ballantine, 1992.

Bell, Millicent. *Meaning in Henry James.* Cambridge, Mass.: Harvard University Press, 1991.

Bender, John. *Imagining the Penitentiary: Fiction and the Architecture of Mind in Eighteenth-Century England.* Chicago: University of Chicago Press, 1987.

Biles, Jack I. *Talk: Conversations with William Golding.* New York: Harcourt Brace, 1970.

Björling, Fiona. "Child Narrator and Adult Author: The Narrative Dichotomy in Karel Polácek's *Bylo nás pêt.*" *Scando-Slavica* 29 (1983): 5–19.

Bloch, Ernst. *The Principle of Hope.* 1959. Trans. Neville Plaice, Stephen Paice, and Paul Knight. Vol. I. Cambridge, Mass.: MIT Press, 1986.

Boyd, S. J. *The Novels of William Golding.* New York: St. Martin's, 1988.

Bradley, Ben S. *Visions of Infancy: A Critical Introduction to Child Psychology.* Polity Press, 1989.

Broderick, Dorothy. *Images of the Black in Children's Fiction.* New York: R. R. Bowker, 1973.

Brontë, Charlotte. *Jane Eyre.* 1847. New York: Bantam, 1981.

Bryson, Bill. *Mother Tongue: English and How It Got That Way.* New York: Avon, 1990.

Bullowa, Margaret, ed. *Before Speech: The Beginning of Interpersonal Communication.* 1979. Cambridge: Cambridge University Press, 1980.

Burman, Erica. *Deconstructing Developmental Psychology.* New York: Routledge, 1994.

Burnett, Frances Hodgson. *The Secret Garden.* 1911. New York: HarperCollins, 1990.

Burningham, John. *Come Away from the Water, Shirley.* New York: HarperCollins, 1977.

Burt, Richard. *Unspeakable Shaxxxpeares: Queer Theory and American Kiddie Culture.* New York: St. Martin's Press, 1998.

Burton, Virginia Lee. *Katy and the Big Snow.* Boston: Houghton Mifflin, 1943.

———. *The Little House.* 1942. New York: Scholastic, 1988.

———. *Mike Mulligan and His Steam Shovel.* 1939. Boston: Houghton Mifflin, 1967.

Camp, Lindsay. *Why?* Illus. Tony Ross. New York: G. P. Putnam's Sons, 1998.

Carroll, Lewis. *The Annotated Alice: Alice's Adventures in Wonderland and Through the Looking Glass.* 1865, 1872. Ed. Martin Gardner. New York: Meridian, 1960.

———. "The Hunting of the Snark." In *Alice in Wonderland* (2nd Norton Critical Ed.). New York: W. W. Norton, 1992. 217–34.

Casey, Joe. *X-Men: Children of the Atom.* New York: Marvel Comics, 2001.

Castañeda, Claudia. *Figurations: Child, Bodies, Worlds.* Durham, N.C.: Duke University Press, 2002.

Chatman, Seymour. "Characters and Narrators: Filter, Center, Slant, and Interest-Focus." *Poetics Today* 7 (1986): 189–204.

———. *Story and Discourse: Narrative Structure in Fiction and Film.* Ithaca, N.Y.: Cornell University Press, 1978.

Childress, Alice. *A Hero Ain't Nothin' but a Sandwich.* New York: Penguin, 1973.

Clark, Beverly Lyon. "Kiddie Lit in Academe." *Profession* (1996): 149–56.

———. *Kiddie Lit: The Cultural Construction of Children's Literature in America.* Baltimore, Md.: Johns Hopkins University Press, 2003.

Clark, Michael. "James Baldwin's 'Sonny's Blues': Childhood, Light and Art." *College Language Association Journal* 29:2 (1995): 197–205.

Clarke, Arthur C. *Childhood's End.* 1953. New York: Del Rey, 1990.

———. *2001: A Space Odyssey.* 1968. New York: Penguin, 1993.

Claremont, Chris. *New Mutants.* New York: Marvel Comics, 1983–1991.

Coats, Karen S. "Keepin' It Plural: Children's Studies in the Academy." *Children's Literature Association Quarterly* 26:3 (2001): 140–50.

———. "Venting the Child: The Limits of a Polemic." *Children's Literature: Annual of the MLA Division on Children's Literature and The Children's Literature Association* 31 (2003): 206–14.

Cohn, Dorrit. *The Distinction of Fiction.* Baltimore, Md.: Johns Hopkins University Press, 1999.

———. *Transparent Minds: Narrative Modes for Presenting Consciousness in Fiction.* Princeton, N.J.: Princeton University Press, 1978.

Collins, Louise. "The Virtue of 'Stubborn Curiosity': Moral Literacy in *Black and White.*" *The Lion and the Unicorn* 26 (2002): 31–49.

Conrad, Joseph. *Heart of Darkness.* 1902. New York: Dover, 1990.

Cook, Daniel Thomas. *The Commodification of Childhood: The Children's Clothing Industry.* Durham, N.C.: Duke University Press, 2004.

Coveney, Peter. *Poor Monkey: The Child in Literature.* London: Richard Clay, 1957.

Culver, Stuart. "What Manikins Want: *The Wonderful Wizard of Oz* and *The Art of Decorating Dry Goods Windows.*" *Representations* 21 (1988): 97–116.

Darwin, Charles. "A Biographical Sketch of an Infant." *Mind* 2:7 (July 1877): 285–94.

Deleuze, Gilles. *The Logic of Sense.* 1969. Trans. Mark Lester. New York: Columbia University Press, 1990.

Deleuze, Gilles, and Félix Guattari. *Kafka: Toward a Minor Literature.* 1975. Trans. Dana Polan. Minneapolis: University of Minnesota Press, 1986.

de Man, Paul. *Blindness and Insight: Essays in the Rhetoric of Contemporary Criticism.* New York: Oxford University Press, 1971.

———. *The Resistance to Theory.* Theory and History of Literature, Vol. 33. Minneapolis: University of Minnesota Press, 1986.

Derrida, Jacques. *Writing and Difference.* Trans. Alan Bass. Chicago: University of Chicago Press, 1978.

Dorfman, Ariel. *The Empire's Old Clothes: What the Lone Ranger, Babar, and Other Innocent Heroes Do to Our Minds.* New York: Penguin, 1983.

Eager, Edward. *Half Magic.* New York: Harcourt, Brace and World, 1954.

Eisenstein, Elizabeth L. *The Printing Press as an Agent of Change: Communications and Cultural Transformations in Early-Modern Europe.* Vol. 1. London: Cambridge University Press, 1979.

The Enigma of Kaspar Hauser. Dir. Werner Herzog. 1974. Anchor Bay Entertainment, 2001.

Epstein, E. L. "Notes on *Lord of the Flies.*" In *Lord of the Flies.* New York: Perigee, 1954.

Falconer, Ian. *Olivia.* New York: Atheneum, 2000.

Fass, Paula S., and Mary Ann Mason. *Childhood in America.* New York: New York University Press, 2000.

Fiedler, Leslie. "Come Back to the Raft Ag'in, Huck Honey!" In *The Critical Response to Mark Twain's Huckleberry Finn.* Ed. Laurie Champion. New York: Greenwood, 1991.

———. "The Eye of Innocence." In *The Collected Essays of Leslie Fiedler.* New York: Stein and Day, 1971. 471–511.

Fiske, John. "Shopping for Pleasure: Malls, Power, and Resistance." *The Consumer Society Reader.* Ed. Juliet B. Schor and Douglas B. Holt. New York: New Press, 2000. 306–28.

Fitzhugh, Louise. *Harriet the Spy.* 1964. New York: HarperCollins, 1992.

Flynn, Richard. "The Intersection of Children's Literature and Childhood Studies." *Children's Literature Association Quarterly* 22:3 (1997): 143–45.

Foucault, Michel. *Madness and Civilization.* 1961. Trans. Richard Howard. New York: Random House, 1965.

———. *The Order of Things.* 1966. New York: Random House, 1970.

———. "The Subject of Power." *Critical Inquiry* 8 (1982): 777–95.

Freud, Sigmund. "Analysis of a Phobia in a Five-Year-Old Boy." 1909. *Standard Edition of the Complete Works of Sigmund Freud,* Vol. 10. London: Hogarth Press, 1955.

Galbraith, Mary. "Hear My Cry: A Manifesto for an Emancipatory Childhood Studies Approach to Children's Literature." *The Lion and the Unicorn* 25 (2001): 187–205.

———. "What Everybody Knew Versus What Maisie Knew: The Change in Epistemological Perspective from the Prologue to the Opening of Chapter 1 in *What Maisie Knew.*" *Style* 23:2 (1989): 197–212.

Gannett, Ruth Stiles. *My Father's Dragon.* Illus. Ruth Chrisman Gannett. New York: Random House, 1948.

Gay, Peter. *Reading Freud: Explorations and Entertainments.* New Haven, Conn.: Yale University Press, 1990.

Genette, Gérard. *Fiction and Diction.* Trans. Catherine Porter. Ithaca, N.Y.: Cornell University Press, 1993.

———. *Narrative Discourse: An Essay in Method.* 1972. Trans. Jane E. Lewin. Ithaca, N.Y.: Cornell University Press, 1980.

———. *Narrative Discourse Revisited.* Trans. Jane E. Lewin. Ithaca, N.Y.: Cornell University Press, 1988.

Gilead, Sarah. "Magic Abjured: Closure in Children's Fantasy Fiction." *PMLA* 106:2 (1991): 277–93.

Golding, William. *Lord of the Flies.* New York: Perigee, 1954.

Goodenough, Elizabeth, Mark A. Heberle, and Naomi Sokoloff, eds. *Infant Tongues: The Voice of the Child in Literature.* Detroit, Mich.: Wayne State University Press, 1994.

Gould, Stephen Jay. *The Mismeasure of Man.* New York: W. W. Norton, 1981.

Grandin, Temple. *Thinking in Pictures: and Other Reports from My Life with Autism.* New York: Doubleday, 1995.

Griswold, Jerry. *Audacious Kids: Coming of Age in America's Classic Children's Books.* New York: Oxford University Press, 1992.

Grunes, Dennis. "The Demonic Child in *The Turn of the Screw.*" *Psychocultural Review: Interpretations of Psychology of Art, Literature, and Society* 2 (1978): 221–39.

Gunn, James. "Henry Kuttner, C. L. Moore, Lewis Padgett et al." In *Voices for the Future.* Ed. Thomas D. Clareson. Bowling Green, Ohio: Bowling Green University Press, 1976. 185–215.

Habermas, Rebekka. "Parent-Child Relationships in the Nineteenth Century." *German History* 16:1 (1998): 43–55.

Hall, G. Stanley. *Adolescence: Its Psychology and Its Relations to Physiology, Anthropology, Sociology, Sex, Crime, Religion, and Education.* Vol. 1. New York: Appleton, 1904.

Hamilton, Virginia. *Dustland.* New York: Harcourt Brace Jovanovich, 1980.

———. *The Gathering.* New York: Greenwillow Books, 1981.

———. *Justice and Her Brothers.* New York: Greenwillow Books, 1978.

Hamlin, David. "The Structures of Toy Consumption: Bourgeois Domesticity and Demand for Toys in Nineteenth-Century Germany." *Journal of Social History* 36:4 (2003): 857–69.

Hanson, Ellis. "Screwing with Children in Henry James." *GLQ* 9:3 (2003): 367–91.

Haraway, Donna. "A Manifesto for Cyborgs: Science, Technology, and Socialist Feminism in the 1980s." *The Norton Anthology of Theory and Criticism.* New York: W. W. Norton, 2001. 2269–99.

Hardy, Thomas. *Jude the Obscure.* New York: Penguin Books, 1998.

Harris, Daniel. *Cute, Quaint, Hungry, and Romantic: The Aesthetics of Consumerism.* New York: Da Capo Press, 2000.

Hart, Roger. *Children's Experience of Place.* New York: Irvington, 1979.

Haviland, Virginia. *Children and Literature: Views and Reviews.* Dallas, Tex.: Scott, Foresman and Co., 1973.

Hawthorne, Nathaniel. *The Scarlet Letter.* 1850. New York: Penguin, 1986.

Hendrix, Howard. "Baby's Next Step: *Überkinder* and the Burden of the Future." *Nursery Realms: Children in the Worlds of Science Fiction, Fantasy, and Horror.* Ed. Gary Westfahl and George Slusser. Athens: University of Georgia Press, 1999. 100–110.

Hollindale, Peter. "Lord of the Flies in the Twenty-First Century." *The Use of English* 53:1 (2001): 1–12.

Holt, John. *Escape from Childhood: The Needs and Rights of Children.* Cambridge, Mass.: Holt Associates, 1995.

Hoople, Robin P. *Distinguished Discord: Discontinuity and Pattern in the Critical Tradition of* The Turn of the Screw. London: Associated University Press, 1997.

Hughes, Richard. *A High Wind in Jamaica,* or *An Innocent Voyage.* 1929. New York: Time Inc., 1963.

Hunt, Peter. "Landscapes and Journeys, Metaphors and Maps: The Distinctive Feature of English Fantasy." *Children's Literature Association Quarterly* 12:1 (1987): 11–14.

Hurst, Mary Jane. *The Voice of the Child in American Literature.* Lexington: University Press of Kentucky, 1990.

Huysmans, J. K. *Against the Grain,* or *Au Rebours.* 1884. New York: Dover, 1969.

The Innocents. Dir. Jack Clayton. 20th Century Fox, 1961.

Iskander, Sylvia Patterson. "Lost in Space: The Child in the American Landscape." *The Image of the Child: Proceedings of the Eighteenth Annual Conference of the Children's Literature Association.* Battle Creek, Mich. (1991). 257–62.

Jacobson, Marcia. *Being a Boy Again: Autobiography and the American Boy Book.* Tuscaloosa: University of Alabama Press, 1994.

————. *Henry James and the Mass Market.* Tuscaloosa: University of Alabama Press, 1983.

James, Allison, and Alan Prout, eds. *Constructing and Reconstructing Childhood: Contemporary Issues in the Sociological Study of Childhood.* New York: Falmer Press, 1990.

James, Henry. "The Art of Fiction." In *The Art of Criticism: Henry James on the Theory and the Practice of Fiction.* Ed. William Veeder and Susan M. Griffin. Chicago: University of Chicago Press, 1986. 165–96.

————. *The Complete Notebooks of Henry James.* Ed. Leon Edel and Lyall H. Powers. New York: Oxford University Press, 1987.

————. *The Letters of Henry James.* Ed. Percy Lubbock. Vol. 1. New York: Scribner, 1920.

————. "Preface to *The Ambassadors.*" In *The Art of Criticism: Henry James on the Theory and the Practice of Fiction.* Ed. William Veeder and Susan M. Griffin. Chicago: University of Chicago Press, 1986. 361–75.

————. "Preface to *The Aspern Papers.*" In *A Casebook on Henry James's* The Turn of the Screw. Ed. Gerard Willen. New York: Thomas Y. Crowell, 1960. 95–101.

————. "Preface to *The Awkward Age.*" In *The Art of Criticism: Henry James on the Theory and the Practice of Fiction.* Ed. William Veeder and Susan M. Griffin. Chicago: University of Chicago Press, 1986. 300–315.

————. *The Turn of the Screw.* 1898. New York: Dover, 1991.

————. *What Maisie Knew.* 1897. Introduction by Paul Theroux. New York: Penguin, 1985.

Jameson, Frederic. "Cognitive Mapping." In *Marxism and the Interpretation of Culture.* Urbana: University of Illinois Press, 1988. 347–57.

Jenkins, Henry, ed. *The Children's Culture Reader.* New York: New York University Press, 1998.

Jones, Gerard. *Killing Monsters: Why Children Need Fantasy, Super Heroes and Make-Believe Violence.* New York: Basic Books (Perseus), 2002.

Jumanji. Dir. Joe Johnston. Columbia TriStar Home Video, 1996.

Kaplan, Deborah. "Read All Over: Postmodern Resolution in Macaulay's *Black and White.*" *Children's Literature Association Quarterly* 28:1 (2003): 37–41.

Kazin, Alfred. "A Procession of Children." *American Scholar* 33 (1964): 171–83.

Kincaid, James R. *Child-Loving: The Erotic Child and Victorian Culture.* New York: Routledge, 1992.

————. *Erotic Innocence: The Culture of Child Molesting.* Durham, N.C.: Duke University Press, 1998.

Koolish, Lynda. "Fictive Strategies and Cinematic Representations in Toni Morrison's *Beloved:* Postcolonial Theory/Postcolonial Text." *African American Review* 29:3 (1995): 421–38.

Krips, Valerie. "Imaginary Childhoods: Memory and Children's Literature." *The Critical Quarterly* 39:3 (1997): 42–50.

Kristeva, Julia. *Desire in Language: A Semiotic Approach to Literature and Art.* 1977. Trans. Thomas Gora, Alice Jardine, and Leon S. Roudiez. New York: Columbia University Press, 1980.

Kuhn, Reinhard. *Corruption in Paradise: The Child in Western Literature.* Hanover,

N.H.: Brown University Press, 1982.

Kuznets, Lois R. "Henry James and the Storyteller: The Development of a Central Consciousness in Realistic Fiction for Children." In *The Voice of the Narrator in Children's Literature*. Ed. Charlotte F. Otten and Gary D. Schmidt. New York: Greenwood, 1989. 187–98.

La Barre, Weston. *Shadow of Childhood: Neoteny and the Biology of Religion*. Norman: University of Oklahoma Press, 1991.

Lacan, Jacques. *Écrits*. 1966. Trans. Alan Sheridan. New York: W. W. Norton, 1977.

Lee, Harper. *To Kill a Mockingbird*. 1960. New York: Warner, 1988.

Lesnik-Oberstein, Karín. *Children in Culture: Approaches to Childhood*. New York: St. Martin's Press, 1998.

———. *Children's Literature: Criticism and the Fictional Child*. Oxford: Clarendon Press, 1994.

Levander, Caroline F., and Carol J. Singley, eds. *The American Child: A Cultural Studies Reader*. New Brunswick, N.J.: Rutgers University Press, 2003.

Levine, Judith. *Harmful to Minors: The Perils of Protecting Children from Sex*. Minneapolis: University of Minnesota Press, 2002.

Lindquist, Galina. "Spirits and Souls of Business: New Russians, Magic, and the Esthetics of Kitsch." *Journal of Material Culture* 7:3 (2002): 329–43.

Lombardo, Patrizia. "Introduction: The End of Childhood?" *The Critical Quarterly* 39:3 (1997): 1–7.

Loukaitou-Sideris, Anastasia. "Children's Common Grounds: A Study of Intergroup Relations Among Children in Public Settings." *Journal of the American Planning Association* 69:2 (2003): 130–43.

Lowry, Lois. *Gathering Blue*. New York: Dell/Laurel Leaf, 2000.

———. *The Giver*. New York: Bantam Doubleday/Dell, 1993.

———. *Messenger*. Boston: Houghton Mifflin, 2004.

Lurie, Alison. *Don't Tell the Grown-Ups: Subversive Children's Literature*. Boston: Little, Brown, 1990.

———. *Only Children*. New York: Random House, 1979.

Macaulay, David. *Black and White*. Boston: Houghton Mifflin, 1990.

MacDougall, John. "Chaos Co-ordinated." *Astounding Science Fiction* (October 1946): 36–57.

Macleod, David I. *The Age of the Child: Children in America, 1890–1920*. New York: Twayne, 1998.

Mailloux, Steven. "The Rhetorical Use and Abuse of Fiction: Eating Books in Late Nineteenth Century America." In *Revisionary Interventions into the Americanist Canon*. Durham, N.C.: Duke University Press, 1994. 133–57.

Males, Mike. *Framing Youth: Ten Myths About the Next Generation*. Monroe, Maine: Common Courage Press, 1998.

———. *Scapegoat Generation: America's War on Adolescents*. Monroe, Maine: Common Courage Press, 1996.

Mantlo, Bill. *Power Pack and Cloak & Dagger: Shelter from the Storm*. Marvel Entertainment Group, 1989.

Marquis, Claudia. "The Power of Speech: Life in *The Secret Garden*." AUMLA: *Journal of the Australasian Universities Language and Literature Association* 68 (1987): 163–87.

Martin, Wallace. *Recent Theories of Narrative.* Ithaca, N.Y.: Cornell University Press, 1986.

McGillis, Roderick. "The Delights of Impossibility: No Children, No Books, Only Theory." *Children's Literature Association Quarterly* 23:4 (1998–99): 202–8.

Mechling, Jay. "Children's Folklore." *Folk Groups and Folklore Genres.* Ed. Elliott Oring. Logan: Utah State University Press, 1981. 91–120.

Meek, Margaret. "The Constructedness of Children." *Signal* 76 (1995): 5–19.

Melville, Herman. *Moby-Dick.* 1851. New York: Macmillan, 1985.

Milne, A. A. *Winnie-the-Pooh.* 1926. New York: Puffin, 1992.

Montessori, Maria. *Education and Peace.* Trans. Helen R. Lane. Chicago: Regnery, 1972.

Morris, Tim. *You're Only Young Twice.* Chicago: University of Illinois Press, 2000.

Morrison, Toni. *Beloved.* 1987. New York: Plume, 1998.

———. *The Bluest Eye.* 1970. New York: Plume, 1994.

———. Interview with A. S. Byatt. *Writers in Conversation* 71. Northbrook, Ill: ICA Video, 1989.

Morss, John R. *The Biologising of Childhood: Developmental Psychology and the Darwinian Myth.* Hillsdale, N.J.: Lawrence Erlbaum Associates, 1990.

———. *Growing Critical: Alternatives to Developmental Psychology.* London: Routledge, 1996.

Muehrcke, Phillip, and Juliana Muehrcke. "Maps in Literature." *The Geographical Review* 64:3 (1974): 317–38.

Munsch, Robert. *Love You Forever.* Illus. Sheila McGraw. Willowdale, ON: Firefly Books, 1986.

Nabokov, Vladimir. *The Annotated Lolita.* 1955. New York: Vintage, 1991.

Nafisi, Azar. *Reading Lolita in Tehran: A Memoir in Books.* New York: Random House, 2003.

Nash, Christopher. *World-Games: The Tradition of Anti-Realist Revolt.* New York: Methuen, 1987.

Natov, Roni. *The Poetics of Childhood.* New York: Routledge, 2003.

Negt, Oskar, and Alexander Kluge. *Public Sphere and Experience.* Minneapolis: University of Minnesota Press, 1993.

Nelson, William. *William Golding's* Lord of the Flies: *A Source Book.* New York: Odyssey Press, 1963.

Nicolaisen, W. F. H. "Maps of Fiction: The Cartography of the Landscape of the Mind." *Onamastica Canadiana* 72:2 (1990): 57–68.

Nodelman, Perry. *Words About Pictures: The Narrative Art of Children's Picture Books.* Athens: University of Georgia Press, 1988.

O'Dell, Scott. *Island of the Blue Dolphins.* 1960. New York: Yearling, 1987.

Oldsey, Bernard S., and Stanley Weintraub. *The Art of William Golding.* New York: Harcourt, Brace, and World, 1965.

Opie, Iona and Peter. *The Lore and Language of Schoolchildren.* 1959. New York: New York Review of Books, 2001.

Padgett, Lewis [Henry Kuttner and C. L. Moore]. "Mimsy Were the Borogoves." 1943. In *Composing: Writing as a Self-Creating Process.* Ed. William E. Coles, Jr. Rochelle Park, N.J.: Hayden, 1974. 64–93.

Peck, George W. *Peck's Bad Boy and His Pa.* 1883. New York: Dover, 1958.

Petrik, Paula. "The Youngest Fourth Estate: The Novelty Toy Printing Press and Adolescence, 1870–1886." In *Small Worlds: Children and Adolescents in America, 1850–1950.* Ed. Elliot West and Paula Petrik. Lawrence: University of Kansas Press, 1992. 125–42.

Pifer, Ellen. *Demon or Doll: Images of the Child in Contemporary Writing and Culture.* Charlottesville: University Press of Virginia, 2000.

Pike, Judy. "A Map of the Wonder City of Oz." *The Baum Bugle: A Journal of Oz* 16:1 (1972): 5–10.

Porter, Eleanor H. *Pollyanna.* 1913. New York: Yearling, 1986.

Postman, Neil. *The Disappearance of Childhood.* New York: Random House, 1982, 1994.

Rabkin, Eric S. "Infant Joys: The Pleasures of Disempowerment in Fantasy and Science Fiction." *Nursery Realms: Children in the Worlds of Science Fiction, Fantasy, and Horror.* Ed. Gary Westfahl and George Slusser. Athens: University of Georgia Press, 1999. 3–19.

Rathmann, Peggy. *Officer Buckle and Gloria.* New York: Putnam, 1995.

Relph, E. *Place and Placelessness.* Research in Planning and Design series. London: Pion Ltd., 1976.

Rohmann, Eric. *My Friend Rabbit.* Brookfield, Conn.: Roaring Brook, 2002.

Romanes, George John. *Mental Evolution in Man: Origin of Human Faculty.* 1888. New York: Arno Press, 1975.

Rose, Jacqueline. *The Case of Peter Pan, or the Impossibility of Children's Fiction.* 1984. Philadelphia: University of Pennsylvania Press, 1993.

Rowling, J. K. *Harry Potter and the Goblet of Fire.* New York: Scholastic, 2000.

———. *Harry Potter and the Sorcerer's Stone.* New York: Scholastic, 1997.

Rudnytsky, Peter L. "'Mother, Do You Have a Wiwimaker, Too?' Freud's Representation of Female Sexuality in the Case of Little Hans." In *Psychoanalyses/Feminisms.* Ed. Peter L. Rudnytsky and Andrew M. Gordon. Albany: State University of New York Press, 2000. 39–53.

Rushdie, Salman. *The Wizard of Oz.* London: British Film Institute, 1992.

Scobie, Alex. "Comics and Folkliterature." *Fabula: Journal of Folktale Studies* 21:1–2 (1980): 70–81.

Seiter, Ellen E. "Survival Tale and Feminist Parable." In *Children's Novels and the Movies.* Ed. Douglas Street. New York: Frederick Ungar, 1983.

Sendak, Maurice. *Where the Wild Things Are.* 1963. New York: HarperCollins, 1991.

Sheets-Johnstone, Maxine. *The Roots of Power: Animate Form and Gendered Bodies.* Chicago: Open Court, 1994.

Shine, Muriel G. *The Fictional Children of Henry James.* Chapel Hill: University of North Carolina Press, 1968.

Siegel, Alexander W. "Methodological and Metatheoretical Issues in the Development of Cognitive Mapping of Large-Scale Environments." In *Mind Child Architecture.* Ed. John C. Baird and Anthony E. Lutkus. 1979. Hanover, N.H.: University Press of New England, 1982. 23–47.

Simonson, Louise, and June Brigman. "The Kid Who Fell to Earth." *Power Pack* 1:16 (November 1985).

———. "Man and Dragon Man." *Power Pack* 1:7 (February 1985).

———. "Power Play." *Power Pack* 1:1 (August 1984).

———. "Rescue." *Power Pack* 1:4 (November 1984).

————. "Sea Hunt." *Power Pack* 1:10 (May 1985).

————. "Secrets." *Power Pack* 1:6 (January 1985).

Smith, Henry Nash. *Virgin Land: The American West as Symbol and Myth.* Cambridge, Mass.: Harvard University Press, 1950.

Spivak, Gayatri Chakravorty. "Can the Subaltern Speak?" *Marxism and the Interpretation of Culture.* Ed. Cary Nelson and Lawrence Grosberg. Chicago: University of Illinois Press, 1988. 271–311.

————. "The Problem of Cultural Self-Representation" (interview with Walter Adamson). In *The Postcolonial Critic: Interviews, Strategies, Dialogues: Gayatri Chakravorty Spivak.* Ed. Sarah Harasym. New York: Routledge, 1990. 50–58.

Stahl, J. D. "Satire and the Evolution of Perspective in Children's Literature: Mark Twain, E. B. White, and Louise Fitzhugh." *Children's Literature Association Quarterly* 15:3 (1990): 119–22.

Stainton Rogers, Rex, and Wendy Stainton Rogers. "Word Children." *Children in Culture: Approaches to Childhood.* Ed. Karín Lesnik-Oberstein. New York: St. Martin's Press, 1998. 178–203.

Steedman, Carolyn. *Strange Dislocations: Childhood and the Idea of Human Interiority, 1780–1930.* Cambridge, Mass.: Harvard University Press, 1995.

Steinbeck, John. *The Red Pony.* 1945. New York: Penguin, 1965.

Stewart, Susan. *Nonsense: Aspects of Intertextuality in Folklore and Literature.* Baltimore, Md.: Johns Hopkins University Press, 1979.

Stowe, Harriet Beecher. *Uncle Tom's Cabin.* 1852. New York: Penguin, 1988.

Sturgeon, Theodore. "Baby Is Three." In *More Than Human.* New York: Ballantine, 1953. 63–118.

Sulloway, Frank J. *Freud, Biologist of the Mind.* New York: Basic Books, 1979.

Tatar, Maria. "Is Anybody Out There Listening? Fairy Tales and the Voice of the Child." In *Infant Tongues: The Voice of the Child in Literature.* Detroit, Mich.: Wayne State University Press, 1994. 275–83.

Travers, P. L. *Mary Poppins.* 1934. Bantam, 1981.

Trites, Roberta Seelinger. "Manifold Narratives: Metafiction and Ideology in Picture Books." *Children's Literature in Education* 25 (1994): 225–42.

————. *Disturbing the Universe: Power and Repression in Adolescent Literature.* Iowa City: University of Iowa Press, 2000.

Twain, Mark. *Adventures of Huckleberry Finn.* 1885. New York: Dover, 1994.

Urwin, Cathy. "Power Relations and the Emergence of Language." *Changing the Subject: Psychology, Social Regulation, and Subjectivity.* 1984. Ed. Julian Henriques, Wendy Hollway, Cathy Urwin, Couze Venn, and Valerie Walkerdine. New York: Routledge, 1998. 264–322.

Van Allsburg, Chris. *Jumanji.* Boston: Houghton Mifflin, 1981.

————. *The Polar Express.* Boston: Houghton Mifflin, 1985.

Vernon, John. *The Garden and the Map: Schizophrenia in Twentieth-Century Literature and Culture.* Urbana: University of Illinois Press, 1973.

Vygotsky, Lev. *Thought and Language.* 1934. Trans. and introduction by Alex Kozulin. Cambridge, Mass.: MIT Press, 1996.

Wall, Barbara. *The Narrator's Voice: The Dilemma of Children's Fiction.* New York: St. Martin's Press, 1991.

Wallace, Jo-Ann. "Technologies of 'the Child': Towards a Theory of the Child-

Subject." *Textual Practice* 9:2 (1995): 285–302.

Watson, Victor. "By Children, About Children, For Children." In *Where Texts and Children Meet*. Ed. Eve Bearne and Victor Watson. New York: Routledge, 2000.

Westfahl, Gary. Introduction to *Nursery Realms: Children in the Worlds of Science Fiction, Fantasy, and Horror*. Ed. Gary Westfahl and George Slusser. Athens: University of Georgia Press, 1999. ix–xiii.

Wharton, Edith. *The Children*. 1928. New York: Scribner, 1997.

White, E. B. *The Annotated Charlotte's Web*. 1952. Ed. Peter F. Neumeyer. New York: HarperCollins, 1994.

Wiesner, David. *The Three Pigs*. New York: Clarion Books, 2001.

———. *Tuesday*. New York: Clarion Books, 1991.

Wilder, Laura Ingalls. *Little House in the Big Woods*. 1932. Illus. Garth Williams. New York: HarperCollins, 1971.

Wilkie, Christine. "Digging Up *The Secret Garden:* Noble Innocents or Little Savages?" *Children's Literature in Education* 28:2 (1997): 73–83.

Williams, William Carlos. *White Mule*. 1937. New York: New Directions, 1967.

Wolf, Virginia. "The Linear Image: The Road and the River in the Juvenile Novel." *Proceedings of the Thirteenth Annual Conference of The Children's Literature Association*. University of Missouri, Kansas City (May 16–18, 1986), 41–47.

———. "The Magic Circle of Laura Ingalls Wilder." *Children's Literature Association Quarterly* 9:4 (1984–85): 168–70.

Wood, Denis, with John Fels. *The Power of Maps*. New York: Guilford Press, 1992.

Wright, John K. "*Terrae Incognitae:* The Place of the Imagination in Geography." *Annals of the Association of American Geographers* 37:1 (1947): 1–15.

X-2: X-Men United. Dir. Bryan Singer. 20th Century Fox, 2003.

Zelizer, Viviana A. *Pricing the Priceless Child: The Changing Social Value of Children*. New York: Basic Books, 1985.

Zipes, Jack. *Fairy Tales and the Art of Subversion: The Classical Genre for Children and the Process of Civilization*. New York: Routledge, 1983.

Zornado, Joseph L. *Inventing the Child: Culture, Ideology, and the Story of Childhood*. New York: Garland, 2001.

index

Page numbers in italics refer to figures.

(Coveney), 10

Porter, Eleanor, 136–38. See also *Pollyanna*

positivism, 93

postcolonial studies, 11, 111

Postman, Neil, 3, 93–94, 96–97, 112, 114. See also *The Disappearance of Childhood*

postmodernism, 38, 39, 44, 58, 156

post-structuralism, 5, 30, 32, 79, 82, 117, 124, 156n13

"The Power of Speech: Life in the Secret Garden" (Marquis), 123

The Power of Maps (Wood), 60, 155n7

Power Pack (Simonson and Brigman), 110, 143–44, 148–50, *149*

"Power Relations and the Emergence of Language" (Urwin), 117

Pricing the Priceless Child: The Changing Social Value of Children (Zelizer), 145, 146

The Principle of Hope (Bloch), 124

"The Problem of Cultural Self-Representation" (Spivak), 16, 114

Prout, Alan, 11–12, 86–87, 91. See also *Constructing and Reconstructing Childhood;* James, Allison

psychological novel, 29, 31

psychological realism, 44, 49

Public Sphere and Experience (Negt and Kluge), 26

questions (evasive/subversive), viii, 20, 26–27, 125, 128, 154n9

Rabelais and His World (Bakhtin), 139

Rabkin, Eric, 103–4, 140. *See also* "Infant Joys: The Pleasures of Disempowerment in Fantasy and Science Fiction"

Ragged Dick (Alger), 129

Rathmann, Peggy, 77. See also *Officer Buckle and Gloria*

rationalism, 2, 3, 25, 27, 66, 71, 72, 73–74, 76, 77, 79, 81, 82, 86, 87, 91–93, 95, 96, 99, 117, 126, 127, 138–40, 142, 153n5, 155n10

"Read All Over: Postmodern Resolution in Macaulay's *Black and White*" (Kaplan), 78

Reading Freud: Explorations and Entertainments (Gay), 86

realism, 22, 31–32, 37–38, 39, 42–44, 73–74, 79, 156n12

recapitulation, 25, 85, 87, 88, 90, 101, 102, 107, 109, 111, 155–56n 6 and 8

Recent Theories of Narrative (Martin), 29–30

The Red Pony (Steinbeck), 55

relativism, 3, 5, 6, 15–16, 32, 43, 58, 78, 79, 85, 139–40

Relph, E., 59. See also *Place and Placelessness*

representation, 4–5, 17, 21, 23, 30, 31, 32, 37–39, 42–44, 73, 78

Resistance to Theory (de Man), 2

reterritorialization, 28, 54, 57, 60, 61, 63, 65, 71, 79, 80, 140–41

rhetorical self-fashioning, 97

"The Rhetorical Use and Abuse of Fiction: Eating Books in Late Nineteenth Century America" (Mailloux), 97–98

Ritter, Gretchen, 154–55n5. *See also* "Silver Slippers and a Golden Cap"

Rohmann, Eric, 77. See also *My Friend Rabbit*

Romanes, George, 85. See also *Mental Evolution in Man*

romanticism, 18, 25, 26, 42, 51, 54, 80, 81, 93, 94, 96, 98, 100, 101, 102, 107, 108, 109, 111, 114, 129, 147, 151, 156n13

The Roots of Power: Animate Form and Gendered (Sheets-Johnston), 117, 119

Rose, Jacqueline, 9–11, 12, 16, 21. See also *The Case of Peter Pan, or the Impossibility of Children's Fiction*

Ross, Tony, *135. See also* Camp, Lindsay; *Why?*

Rousseau, Jean Jacques, 52, 80, 90, 95, 97

Rowling, J. K., 7. See also *Harry Potter and the Sorcerer's Stone*

Rudnytsky, Peter L., 154n8. *See also*